MW01196727

Taíno Indian Myth and Practice

RIPLEY P. BULLEN SERIES

UNIVERSITY PRESS OF FLORIDA

Florida A&M University, Tallahassee
Florida Atlantic University, Boca Raton
Florida Gulf Coast University, Ft. Myers
Florida International University, Miami
Florida State University, Tallahassee
University of Central Florida, Orlando
University of Florida, Gainesville
University of North Florida, Jacksonville
University of South Florida, Tampa
University of West Florida, Pensacola

Taíno Indian Myth and Practice

The Arrival of the Stranger King

William F. Keegan

FOREWORD BY JERALD T. MILANICH

University Press of Florida
Gainesville/Tallahassee/Tampa/Boca Raton
Pensacola/Orlando/Miami/Jacksonville/Ft. Myers

12 11 10 09 08 07   6 5 4 3 2 1

Library of Congress Cataloging-in-Publication Data
Keegan, William F.
    Taíno Indian myth and practice : the arrival of the stranger king /
William F. Keegan ; foreword by Jerald T. Milanich.
        p. cm.
Includes bibliographical references and index.
ISBN-13: 978-0-8130-3038-8 (alk. paper)
        1. Taino Indians—Antiquities. 2. Taino mythology. 3. Indians—First
contact with Europeans. 4. Hispaniola—Antiquities. 5. Caonabo, Cacique,
d. 1496. 6. Taino Indians—Kings and rulers—Biography. 7. Caciques
(Indian leaders)—Hispaniola—Biography. I. Title.
F1619.2.T3K44   2006
972.91'01—dc22   2006028480

The University Press of Florida is the scholarly publishing agency for the
State University System of Florida, comprising Florida A&M University,
Florida Atlantic University, Florida Gulf Coast University, Florida Inter-
national University, Florida State University, University of Central Florida,
University of Florida, University of North Florida, University of South
Florida, and University of West Florida.

University Press of Florida
15 Northwest 15th Street
Gainesville, FL 32611-2079
http://www.upf.com

For Shaun

Contents

Figures

Tables

Foreword

This is not your father's history of the Taíno Indians, the people who were living in the Bahamas and the Caribbean region when Europeans (beginning with Christopher Columbus in 1492) invaded their lands. It is a pot-stirrer of a book, a book that everyone with an interest in Bahamian and Caribbean archaeology and ethnohistory and in the relationships between mythology and social behavior will want to read and reread.

William F. Keegan, the author of *Taíno Indian Myth and Practice: The Arrival of the Stranger King*, enjoys a reputation as an anthropological theoretician and a thinker who is not afraid to employ new tactics and approaches in his quest to understand the past better. In this volume Keegan, my colleague at the Florida Museum of Natural History, turns his considerable talents to a subject he knows well: the archaeology and history of the Taínos. In the late fifteenth and early sixteenth centuries the Lucayos (Bahamas) and Hispaniola (modern Haiti and the Dominican Republic) were part of the realm of the Taínos. That same region also was the arena in which Europeans and the people of the Americas first came into contact and conflict with one another.

In this unique volume, Keegan shows how and why those interactions between Amerindians and Europeans were in part structured by the beliefs and behaviors of the Taínos, including the legend of the "stranger king," as well as the Spaniards' beliefs and behaviors.

Keegan first lays out the unique theoretical perspective through which he is going to interpret the significance of the legend. He argues that the stranger king was an actual person, the famous cacique (chief) Caonabó. Readers then are taken on an extraordinary journey, which teaches us how and why the legend of the stranger king came into being. Keegan presents data indicating that cacique Caonabó was indeed a stranger, a king who came to Hispaniola from the Lucayos to the north. He also shows not only how the myth of Caonabó is reflective of Taíno social organization but why such a myth found prevalence among the Taínos.

As noted above, our journey also takes us to 1492 and beyond to see how the idea of a stranger king helped to shape the contact situation between the Taínos and Christopher Columbus when he arrived on the north coast of Hispaniola.

To make things even more interesting, Keegan interprets his own presence as an archaeologist working in the Bahamas within the context of the stranger king, an anomalous foreigner who comes from elsewhere to become a part of a new community. That status in part structured his own interactions with the modern residents of the community in which he worked. Here are boxes within boxes, though, as the author notes, this is a story with no real middle but with an end.

This is an exciting, provocative book, one I loved reading. Keegan is not afraid to cast off old, confining epistemologies and strike out in new directions. Not everyone will agree with him, but all of us have been given more to think about.

Jerald T. Milanich
Series Editor

Preface

Prehistorians typically deal with a nameless and faceless past. Although we struggle to bring the past to life, we often do so without knowing the people about whom we are writing. It is therefore exciting to investigate the life and times of an individual whose life bridged the gap between oral and written histories—a person who lived on the cusp. Many of the oral traditions were repeated long after the introduction of writing, and they continued to serve as both a social and a moral compass. In the present case our subject is Caonabó, who was arguably the most important cacique (ruler or chief) in Hispaniola when the Spanish invasion occurred.

Over the past 25 years my colleagues, students, volunteers, and I have worked in the places where the first pages of written history were recorded in the Americas. From the central Bahamas to the Turks and Caicos Islands to the Baie de l'Acul and the north coast of Haiti, we have sought to illuminate the Taíno cultures that were so rapidly extinguished by the Spanish. The present narrative begins with the events of the early contact period. These events were recorded by Europeans, however, often after the fact, and by people who never visited the Americas, who had political and polemical motives and medieval European frames of reference. We need to keep these potential pitfalls in mind when assembling the (hi)story.

In writing this story it is impossible to keep the historian out of history. There is no such thing as a clean narrative. The past is created by the people, events, and themes that the author chooses to represent the past. Writing, like art, involves exclusion as much as it involves inclusion. As a result, the present work, like all histories, will inform the reader as much about the author as it does about the past. This narrative attempts to weave the written past together with the archaeological record, both of which are filtered through me. From my perspective: how was *myth*—the oral histories of past ages used to create the structural foundations of a society—expressed in *practice*—the reproduction of these structural foundations through the individual acts of those who define social life through their daily participation. I realize that my definitions for myth and practice may not correspond exactly to the way in which these terms have been defined by others. Yet my main concern is how beliefs structure, legitimize, and facilitate the negotiation of, and participation in, social groups.

In this regard, the Spanish legend of Caonabó raises interesting questions. How was he viewed by the Taínos and the Spanish? How did his personage reflect mythical categories that in turn structured the practice reproduced in the sociopolitical organization of the peoples who lived in Hispaniola? I do not want to devote a great deal of effort to contextualizing this study. I recognize that we must be wary of overgeneralizing; in fact this work specifically seeks the *conjoncture* (short-term cycle) between *événement* (event) and *longue durée* (extended past) (Braudel 1997). Thus "Taíno," as an ethnic or culture designation, does not adequately represent the diversity of societies living in Hispaniola at the turn of the sixteenth century (see Curet 2003; Hulme 1993). Neither can the focus on one individual be used to define the structure of a complex system. I will not belabor these well-rehearsed points.

The bottom line, the threads that interlace the narrative, can be stated as three propositions: (1) for the native peoples of Hispaniola ("Taínos"), the cacique known as Caonabó was imbued with mythical characteristics; (2) for the Spanish, this same individual was a real person, a "Lucayan" who came from the Bahama archipelago; and (3) for the archaeologist, this individual can be shown to have come from a particular archaeological site in the Bahama archipelago. Thus we will confront the construction of the past in which one individual embodied practice through myth. What interests me, in general, is what does this teach us about writing the past? More specifically, what can the integration of these very different perspectives tell us about beliefs and reality in fifteenth-century Hispaniolan society and U.S. society today?

Acknowledgments

After 25 years of working in the West Indies I have far too many people and institutions to recognize for their contributions. I expect that some who might expect to see their names here have been left out, so I apologize at the outset. First, I wish to thank the peoples of the Commonwealth of the Bahamas, the Turks and Caicos Islands, and the Republic of Haiti for their generous hospitality during fieldwork. In this regard, I appreciate the assistance of Gail Saunders (Bahamas) and M. Jean Yves Blot (director of the Bureau National d'Ethnologie) for providing permission to conduct my research.

Funding for this research came from the American Philosophical Society, the National Geographic Society, the Wenner-Gren Foundation for Anthropological Research, the Nova Albion Foundation, the Center for Field Research (Earthwatch), the Caribbean Research Foundation, the University of Florida, the Florida Museum of Natural History, and numerous private contributions. I would especially like to thank Bill and Ginny Cowles, the late Grethe Seim, and Reed and Barbara Toomey. Individuals who contributed both time and energy to the various projects include Jean Borchardt, Sylvia Chappell, Michael Dion, Bob Gezon, Peter O'B. Harris, Robert Hoffman, Frank Keegan, Dennis Kendrick, Ralph and Mary Lou Pax, Bill Rogers, Geoff Senior, and Warren Stortreon. Special thanks to Chuck Hesse for helping to make all of this possible.

This work has benefited greatly from the contributions of numerous individuals who at the time were graduate students: Aline Gubrium, Sharyn O'Day, Sherri Littman, Sofia Marquet, Lee Ann Newsom, Lee Roth, Pete Sinelli, Anne Stokes, and Corbett Torrence. Dick Franz, Elise LeCompte, Sylvia Scudder, Dave Steadman, and Elizabeth Wing, colleagues at the Florida Museum of Natural History, also made important contributions. I owe the greatest debt to Betsy Carlson, who somehow managed to keep my research on track for almost 10 years.

Many other people deserve to be recognized. Glen Freimuth directed excavations by the Caribbean Research Foundation in 1982. Brian Riggs has been a constant source of help and information regarding the archaeology of the Turks and Caicos. The Hall family—Emanuel, Constance, Robert, Evan, and Doreen—provided invaluable assistance in Bambarra, as did Carlin Forbes, Headley and Avis Forbes, Marcus and Ianthe Forbes, Simon and Gertie

Forbes, Danny Forbes, and the others who adopted me and accepted me as a "Bambarra man." Jean-Claude and Kathy Dicquemar of Cormier Plage made incredible contributions to the fieldwork in Haiti. The work there would not have been possible without them and without the help of my good friend and colleague John de Bry. Finally, my own family made numerous sacrifices and contributions to the research. They all worked with me on Grand Turk and Jamaica. Lorie has tolerated my long absences and even cheerfully excavated when the need arose. Dan helped out in Haiti, Lindsay worked hard on Middle Caicos, and Caroline managed the snack train in Jamaica.

Finally, I would like to thank Dave Steadman, former chairman of the Department of Natural History, and Doug Jones, director of the Florida Museum of Natural History, for their support and encouragement. Kathy Deagan read and commented on sections of the book related to her research interests, as did Betsy Carlson, Antonio Curet, Sylvia Chappell, Michael Dion, Peter O'B. Harris, and Bob Preucel.

The University Press of Florida has, as always, been a pleasure to work with. John Byram, editor-in-chief, Michele Fiyak-Burkley, project editor, and Jerry Milanich, editor of the Ripley P. Bullen Series, provided invaluable assistance in getting the book to press.

There is still one name that I have not mentioned: Shaun Dorsey Sullivan. This book is dedicated to him.

1

Culture and Chaos, Myth and Practice

Some version of the tale of the "stranger king" is told in virtually every culture in the world. It is the story of an immigrant king who deposes the former ruler and marries his daughter. Although the versions differ with regard to details, the basic story line is as follows: "The heroic son-in-law from a foreign land demonstrates his divine gifts, wins the daughter, and inherits half or more of the kingdom. Before it was a fairy tale, it was a theory of society" (Sahlins 1985: 82). Accounts of the stranger king have been retold numerous times in anthropological works (Frazer 1911–1915; Hocart 1969, 1970). Marshall Sahlins (1985: chapter 3) devoted an extended essay to such beliefs, with an emphasis on those from Fiji and Hawaii. Sahlins provided the groundwork for the study of anthropological history in this study. He demonstrated how belief in a stranger king not only justified king/subject relations but also structured the reactions of native peoples during initial contacts with Europeans.

I have commented on similarities between Sahlins's account of Hawaiian interactions with Captain James Cook and Taíno interactions with Christopher Columbus (Keegan 1992). Columbus's activities brought him headlong into the Taíno myth of Caníbales (mythical Caribs) and the Spanish myth of cannibals. Just as Cook's expedition to Hawaii led to his association with the god Lono, the Taínos identified Columbus as a Caníbale. To complete the circle, the Taíno cacique—and Columbus's main protagonist—Caonabó was identified as a Caníbale (Spanish for Carib) by Gonzalo Fernández de Oviedo y Valdés, one of the principal Spanish chroniclers (chapter 2).

Although the story of the stranger king has been discussed many times, it is worth one more outing. First, anthropological history fits well with emerging themes regarding the role of culture. Sahlins (1985) clearly illustrated how all aspects of a society converge at the point of social reproduction. Beliefs play a central role in coordinating often disparate goals and objectives of both individual agents and more general structures defined by economy, polity, demography, and sociology. In this regard, Patrick Kirch (2000) has done a fine job of translating anthropological history (a là Sahlins) into an archaeological context. My first objective in this book is to situate the theme of anthropological history in a different context by outlining what I see as an emerging theory of *culture*. My portrait of the theory may not match that of others, but I propose it as one means of integrating divergent approaches in anthropology and archaeology.

Second, if mythology, beliefs, worldviews, or whatever else we want to call them are truly a theory of society, then these must be given primary attention in efforts to re-create the past. Instead of treating myths as *ad hoc* justifications for anthropologically constructed categories, we need to reverse the causal arrow and view myths as structuring social reproduction. Thus my second objective is to show how myth structured initial contacts between the Taínos and the Spanish and how myth and practice provided identities to the main characters.

A somewhat tangential example is worth mentioning. One of the major un-resolved issues in Caribbean archaeology is the identity of the Island Caribs. It is often repeated that the Island Caribs claimed that they came from South America and that in their encounters with Arawakan groups in the islands they ate the men and married the women (Rouse 1948). This story can be recognized immediately as a version of the story of the stranger king. Yet in this case the lack of a formal social hierarchy in Island Carib society seems to have allowed every man to be a "king." In other words, it is not one male leader who fulfills the role, but all Island Carib men who participated in eating the Arawak men and marrying the Arawak women.

The purpose of the story was to define the origins of the people who told it. The story justified the Island Carib invasion of an already occupied territory and proclaimed that they were fierce. It also justified their resistance to the Europeans who would supplant them and sent the message that they would violate customary human behavior by eating their enemies. Because there is no clear evidence for cannibalism among the Island Caribs, this story can be viewed as just that: a story. To the Spanish, Caribs were the "fierce people."

Third, if myths play a central role in reproducing society, then we should expect physical representation of the social theory that they describe. It is possible to claim that the Taíno stranger king is nothing more than a story. It is worth testing this conclusion, however, and seeing whether or not ethno-historic and archaeological correlates support the actualization of the story. In the present case I argue that Caonabó, the stranger king, really did come to Hispaniola from a foreign land. Moreover, not only his history but also Taíno myths and the structure of Taíno society in general were codetermined.

Finally, and in its own way, archaeological practice reproduces the myth of a stranger king. Although our subjects are dead, we approach them with our own beliefs about who they were and who we are. We invade their sites—which, at least in this case, are in exotic locations—and set ourselves to the tasks of Dr. Frankenstein. We follow the precepts of our beliefs: we make topographic maps, reconstruct the environment, define community plans, classify material remains, and try to breathe life into the past. Thus my fourth objective is to include the archaeologists in my story.

This is not a book with a beginning and middle, although it does have an end. I often feel that theory gets in the way; yet it is essential to understanding the mindset of the author, especially because no anthropologists share the same conception of culture. Therefore I begin with my view of culture, how it got there, and where I see it going.

Culture and Chaos

Marvin Harris once told me that in his opinion archaeologists were the last of the cultural anthropologists. This comment, which I heard him repeat on later occasions, was always something of a source of pride. Yet I also found his comment ironic. On the one hand I could see his point: because there were no longer any pristine cultures untainted by Western culture, the only way to study such cultures was through archaeological methods. Moreover, Harris felt a certain kinship with archaeologists, because many of the "New Archaeologists" enthusiastically adopted his cultural materialism. This outlook remained relatively strong in archaeology even in the mid-1980s. It may be tempting to date the New Archaeology to Lewis Binford's articles published in the 1960s (see Binford 1972). Frank Hole's editorial in *American Antiquity* (1978), however, shows that the battle between old and new was anything but over by that time.

What is ironic is that the New Archaeology largely abandoned the notion of culture. In fact, the concept of culture was the great divide between the old and the new. Whereas traditional archaeologists viewed culture as shared norms and beliefs, the New Archaeologists recast culture as an extrasomatic adaptive system (compare Rouse 1972; Binford 1972; Thomas 1979). Moreover, A. L. Kroeber and Clyde Kluckhohn (1952) had already identified over 200 discrete definitions of "culture." Clearly what was needed was an operational definition, a behavioral definition whose correlates could be observed in the archaeological record rather than simply inferred. Thus we might not be able to say what people thought, but we could certainly describe how they behaved. It was in this frame of reference that processual archaeology developed.

Postprocessual archaeology emerged in response to the apparent fossilization of processual archaeology. While "North American archaeology . . . remained stubbornly ecological, evolutionary, and positivist," postprocessualists embraced diversity (Hodder 1991: 39). There was a renewed interest in culture, this time as meaningfully and materially constituted; and issues such as gender, power, ideology, text, discourse, rhetoric and writing, structure and agency, and history were pursued. Knowledge was recognized as the product of social forces rather than intellectual judgment (Bell 1994), and symbolic, structural, Marxist, contextual, and interpretive frameworks for studying the past were promoted (see, for example, Earle and Preucel 1987). The anarchy (*sensu* Bell 1994) that such diversity promoted was appalling. It promised archaeology without the safety net fastened to normative or adaptive anchors. What would prevent the discipline from falling into the abyss of relativism, from which no certain knowledge could be forthcoming?

My point is that the concept of culture was largely abandoned by American archaeologists in the 1970s (Flannery 1982). Even though approaches more receptive to the notions of culture have emerged, the concept itself remains buried. The new emphasis on social processes is more focused on how individuals navigate and negotiate their statuses and roles in a cultural context, rather than taking an interest in what constitutes culture. Moreover, it is my contention that postmodern archaeology has taken a "linguistic turn" down a blind alley. I offer the name "cultural archaeology" as an alternative turn, an about-face, a new philosophical foundation, and a framework for pursuing the topic so eloquently described by Sir Edward Burnett Tylor (1871: 1):

> Culture or Civilization, taken in its wide ethnographic sense, is that complex whole which includes knowledge, belief, art, morals, law, custom, and any other capabilities and habits acquired by man as a member of society. The condition of culture among the various societies of mankind, in so far as it is capable of being investigated on general principles, is a subject apt for the study of laws of human thought and action.

As an undergraduate I had my first field school with the real Connecticut archaeologist and his skeptical graduate student (SGS) (see Flannery 1976). The behavioral model promoted by the SGS seemed to offer real hope for distinguishing the goals and structures of culture above and beyond the simple transformation of material remains through time. The approach created a methodological individual (remember that history is about people), however, and the notion of robots blindly following cultural, and especially ecological, imperatives soon turned sour. The door was opened for something new, and postprocessual archaeology walked in.

The main emphasis in the critique of the New Archaeology concerned its philosophical foundations. The postprocessual critique focused on what were identified as processual archaeology's positivist roots and an adherence to inference as the means for proving propositions, especially those proposi-

Table 1.1. Hindu Cattle Complex

Attribute	Behavioral	Mental
EMIC	"no calves are starved to death"	"all calves have a right to life"
ETIC	"male calves are starved to death"	"let male calves starve when feed is scarce"

Source: Harris 1979: 38.

tions that served as general formulations. In this regard, Michael Shanks and Christopher Tilley's (1987) question of how many cases are necessary before a proposition is considered proven is apt. Shanks and Tilley, however, failed to recognize (or acknowledge) that at least some processual archaeologists had already abandoned inferential logic and had adopted Karl Popper's (1962) refutationist logic (Bell 1994). According to the refutationists, nothing can be proven, only disproven. The number of cases supporting a proposition does not matter. Still, the refutationist approach suffers from serious epistemological problems as well. There is a real danger of proposing only trivial refutations, like those silly archaeological laws lampooned by Kent Flannery (1982). Moreover, if no proposition is ever proven, then how can we be confident of the accuracy of the surviving, unrefuted propositions? Are we merely waiting for someone to find the black swan that refutes our proposition that all swans are white?

The issue of what we accept as true is not trivial, and it has occupied the minds of philosophers for centuries. Some have attempted to circumvent the issue by restricting the focus of our investigations. Returning to Marvin Harris, he proposed that culture could be divided into four compartments. *Emic* and *etic* compartments recognize that different explanations derive from what is basically a contrast between insider and outsider views, while *mental* and *behavioral* fields contrast how people think with how they behave. For Harris, all that was open to scientific scrutiny was the etic and behavioral box. It is not surprising that such a restricted view of culture would attract staunch critics, especially when this reductionist view of culture processes was promoted as the primary means for explaining cultural phenomena. Clearly, a central goal of anthropology has always been to study culture in its totality.

If our desire is to study culture in its totality, then we must reject Harris's reductionism. Moreover, if we also reject positivism as our guiding logic, and recognize that refutationist logic is only a partial corrective, then what paradigm is available to structure our inquiries and what criteria can be applied to guide us in choosing between competing theories and explanations? Currently the major trend has been a linguistic turn that has moved beyond the structuralist dialectic to embrace hermeneutic and other postmodern approaches.

Critiques of these approaches claim that the only outcome is relativism. Relativism is criticized as a condition in which every explanation is equally valid and therefore no progress can be gained in improving our understanding of the world. It would appear that archaeology has painted itself into a corner.

It is my contention that we have reached this point because of the path we have followed. Rather than promoting "post" philosophies we need to return to the original formulation and select a different course (Latour 1993). Philosophical relativism was the predetermined outcome of a philosophy based on dialectical oppositions. If we begin by believing that every issue can be reduced to dialectical oppositions, then one view must be valid and the other invalid. This was a problem with early applications of the scientific method, in which competing hypotheses were proposed: when one was disproven, the alternative was accepted as proven. Yet there is no logical reason for the alternative to be correct either. Once this simplistic logic was recognized (scientizing), then no alternative was any more valid than any other. Moreover, even refuted hypotheses were often resurrected by claiming that the common methodological assumption—"all else being equal"—had been violated in the experiment.

The methodological dialectic may be a basic feature of human problem solving. It forms the basis for much of decision-making theory and provides the structural logic of computers and efforts to develop artificial intelligence. Everything is reduced to yes/no, on/off, 0/1. While such a reduced model of cognitive function may help to account for instantaneous decision-making, it does not accurately reflect culture in its broader scope.

In contrast it is worth considering philosophical developments in physics. In this regard chaos and complexity theories have developed as frameworks for simultaneously investigating multiple dimensions. I find it unfortunate that the word "chaos" came to be associated with this theory. The term gives the impression that outcomes are random, undirected, and unknowable. Yet nothing in our known world is truly random (Peterson 1998). For example, many archaeologists today conduct stratified random sampling in which a table of random numbers is used to determine sampling units. These "random numbers" are generated by mathematical formulas, however, and are thus not random at all.

Two seemingly simple examples are worth considering. First, we know that clouds exist, and the chemical composition and parameters in which different types of clouds will form have been determined. Yet it is impossible to predict the shape and composition of any particular cloud at any given time and any given location. Furthermore, consider a cloud as an observed phenomenon. The same cloud will have different visual attributes depending upon the position of the observer. A second example that is less ephemeral is the dendritic channels cut by rivers through deltas. Again, these channels are clear and obvious to any observer, but we cannot predict what the specific pattern of channels will look like at any given time. In sum, even though we can write mathematical equations that specify the formation of clouds or river-channel fractals, it is impossible to predict specific cloud formations or river channels.

An excellent example of how we can recognize processes yet not predict their outcome is presented in Ivars Peterson's book *The Jungles of Randomness* (1998). Peterson uses the old carnival ride Tilt-a-Whirl to describe the effects of chaos. The ride is composed of a number of cars attached to an oval track that rises and falls along its course. The cars are attached in such a way that they spin, and in more recent versions the rider can actually control the spin by mechanically turning a wheel. Peterson notes that this ride has remained popular because—although the structure is fixed and static—each ride produces a dynamic new experience. A fixed structure can provide an infinite number of dynamic experiences due to a fundamental premise of chaos theory: outcomes are strongly dependent on initial conditions. Depending on where the car is located on the track, the weight of the individuals in the car, and other initial conditions, each ride will be unique. Here we see a lesson for anthropologists. While someone without a formal education can be taught to maintain and repair the mechanical structure of the ride, an anthropologist with a Ph.D. likely would describe every ride as a unique experience.

My point here is twofold. First, the members of a culture respond to multiple variables in n-dimensions on an instantaneous basis, producing a potentially infinite number of outcomes at each instant. Yet their behavior and decision-making can be described in terms of basic structures. The fact that anthropologists have found regularities in human behavior proves the existence of such basic structures.

Structuralist and dialectical approaches have reached similar conclusions. Yet a basic premise of chaos theory is that issues cannot always be stated as dyads (Lévi-Strauss 1963) or as dialectical oppositions (Marquardt 1992). Nevertheless, chaos theory recognizes that there are "deep structures" that underlie human behavior. In other words, we cannot explain culture based solely on superficial appearances. But there is also the danger of identifying so many variables that no meaningful answer is forthcoming (as in linear-programming models). The issue is one of scale.

For example, optimal foraging theory provides a rigid structure for describing food-getting behavior, yet the complexity of the food quest as an instantaneous process will lead to outcomes that do not exactly match the predictions based on the models. This does not mean that people are not us-ing such cognitive models as a guide, but rather that behaviors based on in-stantaneous responses are difficult to predict with precision. In the same vein, social organization may be based on structures that can be expressed with mathematical rigor (Hage and Harary 1983, 1996), but the nonlinear expres-sion of such "rules" will appear to violate these underlying structures. In fact it is dynamic responses to changing variables that provide evolutionary rigor. If the members of a culture adopted static rules, then their survival would be doomed in an ever-changing world.

The lesson of the Tilt-a-Whirl is that seemingly random outcomes can have an underlying structure, that outcomes are strongly influenced by initial con-ditions, and that the interplay of numerous variables will undoubtedly make pattern recognition and general solutions difficult to discern. Nevertheless, basic structures do exist even if we must seek evidence for them in clouds of meaning and practice.

The Anthropology of Archaeology

Returning to the apparent embrace of postmodern approaches, these ap-proaches can be defused by accepting Bruno Latour's assertion that "we have never been modern" (Latour 1993). By this he means that we have never ad-hered to a hard and fast dichotomy between subject and object. Thus the postmodern critique was an attack on a straw man. Rather than look at what scientists say they do, sociologists, stimulated by the writings of Thomas Kuhn (1970), began to examine the ways in which scientists actually operate. Their approach has achieved a degree of formality under the headings "science stud-ies" and "science and technology studies" (STS). Rather than starting from general philosophical principles, science studies began by observing how sci-entists actually conduct their research. It is worth noting that they describe their work as the "anthropology of science." Perhaps not surprisingly, they found that scientists do not adhere to strict subject-object or core-periphery models of the so-called scientific method.

The reaction of mainstream scientists to their findings was predictable. It has been explosive to the point that the debate between scientists and those who study them has been called the "Science Wars" (Ashman and Baringer 2001; Segerstråle 2000). Scientists claim that practitioners of science studies or STS are attempting to tar them with a postmodernist brush, and they fear that the outcome will result in a descent into relativism. The STS scholars counter that they are simply describing how scientists do science and thus deny these criticisms.

Table 1.2. Comparing the Two Cultures of Biological Ecology

Attribute	Analytical	Integrative
Philosophy	Narrow and targeted, disproof by experiment, and parsimony as the rule	Broad and exploratory, multiple lines of converging evidence, and requisite simplicity to the goal
Perceived organization	Biotic interactions, fixed environment, and single scale	Biophysical interactions, self-organization, multiple scales with cross-scale interactions
Causation	Single and separable	Multiple and only partially separable
Hypotheses	Single hypotheses and null rejection of false hypotheses	Multiple, competing hypotheses with separation among competing hypotheses
Uncertainty	Eliminates uncertainty	Incorporates uncertainty
Statistics	Standard statistics and experimental concern with Type I errors	Nonstandard statistics and concern with Type II errors
Evaluation goal	Peer assessment to reach ultimate, unanimous agreement	Peer assessment with judgment reaching a partial consensus
The danger	Exactly the right answer for the wrong question	Exactly the right question but a useless answer

Source: Holling 1998.

The study of how archaeologists do anthropology can be equally illuminating. For in fact the practice of archaeology has changed little in the past 50 years. New issues certainly have been addressed as the scope of investigations has widened, but the raw materials of archaeology have remained much the same. Archaeologists still rely on excavations (either directly or through the study of museum collections) and still focus on chronology, reconstructing lifeways, and defining cultural processes (Thomas 1979). Many of the methods have remained unchanged, and those that have changed are largely responses to improvements in technology. Years after the New Archaeology supposedly overthrew traditional approaches, field studies and laboratory analyses remain largely the same. This has also occurred with the postprocessual revolution. The methods are basically the same, even if many of the issues have changed (compare Hodder 2000).

The bottom line is that archaeology has continued to operate according to the model of two cultures. Although some have been critical of natural science approaches in archaeology (Hodder 1999), on closer inspection natural science practice is not so different from archaeological practice. The notion of two cultures, first proposed by C. P. Snow (1959) and recently amplified by C. S. Holling (1998), recognizes a division of science between analytical and integrative streams. The first stream is reductionist—the science of parts that attempts "to narrow uncertainty to a point where acceptance of an argument among scientific peers is essentially unanimous" (Holling 1998). The other stream is integrative and uncertain and shares with the social sciences a historical perspective. It is the bridge between analytical science, policy, and politics.

Although I abhor dichotomies and their frequent resolution in triads, there is some truth to the notion that science tends to operate in business-as-usual methodologies that are displaced by periodic theoretical maelstroms. I would argue, however, that this dichotomy reflects the operation of Western thought processes rather than the underlying structure of scientific investigations. Just as chaotic systems have an underlying structure, so too does science.

In his recent book *Pandora's Hope* Bruno Latour develops a different, more chaotic model of how science operates that he calls "circulating reference" (Latour 1999: 99). In this model he identifies five types of activities that must be described in order to understand the operation of a scientific discipline: (1) instruments (mobilization of the world), (2) colleagues (autonomization), (3) public representation, (4) allies (alliances), and (5) links and knots (subject of study). Using a vascular metaphor, the first four are like veins and arteries through which scientific facts circulate. Even though they are numbered sequentially, the numbering is for convenience and is not directional.

Mobilization is "all of the means by which nonhumans [objects] are progressively loaded into discourse" (Latour 1999: 99). This process may involve the use of instruments, equipment, field observations, and so forth. In sum, they are any activity by which the world is converted into arguments. These arguments must be directed at someone, and the history of scientific institutions and autonomization has developed through the rise of disciplines with criteria of evaluation and relevance. It is worth noting that conflict of disciplines need not impede the development of science but may instead be a driving force. Continuing with the loops, nothing is possible without alliances with rich and well-endowed groups, which are usually situated outside of the peer group but which provide funding for research efforts. In this regard scientists must place their discipline in a context sufficiently large and secure to ensure survival. Finally, public representation is a crucial element that is part and parcel of the fabric of facts.

As the "objects" of study, scientists may not recognize these loops, these activities, as forming an integral part of what they do. In fact, some would deny that the public sets the agenda, that funding determines what projects will be pursued, that peers are important, or even that science is discourse. Yet these issues are exactly those described by Ian Hodder (2000) with reference to "reflexive archaeology" at Çatalhöyük. Latour's model of circulating reference illustrates how these loops draw science out of its core. This form of representation explodes the model of science as an internal core separate from, but surrounded by, a corona of social contexts (Latour 1999: 92). Scientific facts circulate through the contextual periphery and thus contribute to the definition of the core.

We turn now to the core itself. The heart of the model is called "links and knots," to "avoid the historical baggage that comes with the phrase 'conceptual content'" (Latour 1999: 99). There certainly are concepts, but science is not something contained: it is the container. According to Latour (1999: 108), science is not—as science warriors would have it—an "Idea floating in Heaven freed from the pollution of this base world"; science is more like a "heart beating at the center of a rich system of blood vessels."

Although this far too brief review has not done justice to Latour's model, I hope that the preceding sketch will suffice as an adequate argument to use as a frame for conceptualizing how science circulates within disciplinary and social contexts. At the same time that the core is being constructed by the periphery, the periphery is likewise constructed through reference to the core.

In order to apply Latour's model to archaeology we must again explode the core. By this I mean that just as a Mandelbrot set is produced through magnifications and replications that could conceivably go on to infinity (that is, it is theoretically possible to fit an infinite volume in a finite space), archaeology must find a way to move simultaneously between levels and scales of meaning. Moreover, by following the orbits of circulating reference we can explode the core of hermeneutic understanding. In doing so, we confront the realization that the concept of a hermeneutic spiral, even a hermeneutic double helix, is far too simplistic. What we are faced with is a cloud of meaning, in which meaning is defined by specific points of reference, a particular starting point, and particular initial conditions. We must acknowledge the harmonic reality of hermeneutic chaos. One of the reasons why Jacques Derrida never made complete sense in his use of deconstruction is that he tried to oversimplify the codetermination of subject and object. He made it a product of language, when in fact language is only one means for expressing practice. Derrida got stuck in a critique of a "modernism" that never really existed, and he did so using a form of expression that could not possibly achieve his goals.

Given the philosophy of his day and the tools that were available to him, Derrida developed a competent critique of modernist philosophy (which as mentioned above is actually a straw man; see Latour 1993). If his horizons had been broader, however, he might have encountered the metaphysical developments that had preceded him in physics. Social scientists promoted physics as the epitome of hard science (more so in the past), but the physics of the twentieth century was far more metaphysical than anything the social sciences have proposed. The use of physics as a model for archaeological practice in the 1970s was strongly criticized and eventually abandoned (see Flannery 1986). Early efforts to imitate the scientific method failed to consider the epistemological roots on which this method was based. Chaos and complexity theories have come to the fore in many disciplines because they provide a new way of looking at the world and not a new form of practice. In this regard, physicists have repeatedly used a "language" that is exceedingly more appropriate for the study of complex structures. While we might suspect that this language is mathematics, and mathematics is certainly crucial for expressing their constructs, the analogy that is used most often is music.

Physicists, especially those who subscribe to superstring theory (Greene 1999), view harmonics as the most compelling form of human expression for capturing the complexity of the universe. Superstring theory defines the basic building blocks of the universe as vibrating strings. Furthermore, where music theory delves into multiple simultaneous expressions, language is forever trapped in a linear grammar. It is time to abandon Ferdinand de Saussure and the linguistic, structuralist, and poststructuralist models and to adopt a theory that allows for simultaneous multidimensional scaling.

Chaos in Culture and Archaeology

Beginning from the proposition that culture is a complex, self-organizing, and chaotic system represented as an n-dimensional hyperspace, the task that presents itself is how a model can meaningfully represent such a system. Here again the model of circulating reference seems appropriate. For simplicity, a set number of dimensions have been represented and are shown as orbits around a material core. A better representation would show the orbits as random paths, as in chaos models of strange attractors (McGlade and van der Leeuw 1997: 18) or in the same way that the paths of electrons in the atomic model are today shown as an electron cloud. Actually, if our interest is in trying to produce an accurate illustration we would need to draw a multidimensional Calabai-Yau shape (Greene 1999: 257). But the issue here is representation and not illustration.

The dimensions that I have selected reflect those aspects that have been recognized as necessary components of a holistic model of culture (Johnson and Earle 1987). Certainly we could apply different labels or select other aspects for representation. These basic dimensions accurately characterize general archaeological practice, however, which is apparent from the table of contents for most books and reports. Such publications typically begin with a chapter on environmental reconstruction and then turn to economy, demography, social organization, political organization, ideology, and so forth. The danger of the model is that it can be viewed as representing every aspect of culture as its own separate orbit or as a linear regression that defines the sequential impact of variables. For this reason I suggest that these orbits be viewed as electron clouds in which there is continuous interaction among every dimension.

The core of the model, the "links and knots" (Latour 1999: 106), represents the basic units of archaeological study. Most archaeological research occurs within this arena and focuses on the recovery, description, and analysis of archaeological remains. It is not necessary to treat these in detail here; they are the subject of numerous books and continued debate. What is important to recognize is that work in this core is not strictly anthropology. The key issue for a cultural archaeology is the transformation of information from this static material field into a dynamic cultural field. It is these processes that Michael Schiffer (1988) has subsumed under the heading "reconstruction theory." Within this frame of reference we also need to consider the perspectives of the observers (Nelson and Kehoe 1990) as expressed in a reflexive methodology (Hodder 1999). The beauty of Latour's model is that it illustrates connections among divergent points of reference. Many of the simple dichotomies in cultural studies thus become points in the orbits rather than extremes of continua. For example, agency and structure become points of reference rather than discrete representations.

"Culture and practical reason" reflects another frame (Sahlins 1976). For example, on the one hand people have the practical necessity of feeding themselves ("diet"), but on the other they tend to do so in a culturally cognized manner and in a social context ("cuisine"). In this regard, studies of human physiology, microeconomic models such as optimal foraging theory, and related ecological studies may describe resource availability, physiological needs, and practical means for satisfying these needs, but they are only a frosted window on the cultural and social contexts of cuisine. In a similar way, an adaptationist perspective on the best solution within known constraints can help to explain why a tool had a particular form and why certain types of raw material were preferred over others; yet it is also necessary to integrate social dynamics with the organization of technology (Cobb 2000). All labor is mobilized and deployed by an organized social plurality. Production, exchange, and consumption can only be understood in a broader social context. My point is that these are not either/or dichotomies. It is not a choice between adaptationist models and models of social reproduction. Nor are they part of a single continuum. These approaches are part and parcel of a continuous cloud of meaning. To ignore either is to miss the boat (see Rainbird 1999).

Finally, all manner of relativism is built into the model. The portrait of a culture that we create will depend on the starting point. Not only is culture strongly dependent on initial conditions, but research is as well. This is especially true when the model is set in motion through the inclusion of a temporal dimension. In this regard, culture can be viewed as a cloud that changes with every passing instant. In practice, archaeologists slice this cloud into discrete units that may be characterized by duration, as in Fernand Braudel's distinctions between *événement, conjoncture,* and *longue durée* (Braudel 1997). It is not a case of one perspective being privileged, but rather that different perspectives are accurate from different points of reference.

Reflected Reality

Even if we knew all of the variables (dimensions) we still could not predict the shape of a cloud. Culture is much the same. Various general theories have been proposed and defended, but none is adequate to answer all of our questions all of the time. There is a real need for a diversity of theoretical approaches. Perhaps someday archaeologists will develop a grand unified theory, but that day is not yet here. In the meantime, there is a lesson to be learned from the New Archaeology. In the absence of a disciplinary paradigm it is incumbent on the investigators specifically to state their questions and to be reflexive about their assumptions and biases.

The discipline has reached a size at which scholarship should prevail over personal whim and fancy. Novel ideas may be slow to catch hold, but as they feed through the loops of circulating reference, colleagues, funding sources, and the public will judge their value. This is much the same as it has always been (Latour 1999). Moreover, we will never have absolute authority as *the* privileged voice of the past; some ideas will prevail no matter what is believed by the discipline as a whole (for example, the contributions of extraterrestrials to past cultures).

One reason for philosophical dissatisfaction is that our subject is not well defined. We want answers to who, when, where, what, how, and why. Yet each of these questions is interdependent, and the solutions involve the interaction of multiple variables. This situation will lead every investigator to propose different answers depending on which variables are emphasized and the scale of analysis in which the investigator is most interested. The time has come to restate our objectives and to recognize that culture is the product of variables operating in *n*-dimensions. Culture is a hyperspace cloud that we try to draw boundaries around. By recognizing *n*-dimensions we acknowledge a stochastic element to cultural processes. A single process does not necessarily produce one outcome or pattern, an investigator may not be able to specify all possible processes and outcomes as multiple-working hypotheses, and our answers are dependent on historical contingencies and scalar effects.

For me, the main issue is not "reading the past" but rather writing the past. The major part of my literary inspiration comes from Truman Capote (1987b). At his death Capote was supposed to be writing a book called *Answered Prayers* (Capote 1987a). The title comes from Saint Teresa de Ávila, who said, "More tears are shed over answered prayers than unanswered ones." In this work, Capote had realized that he was not the innocent bystander in his stories but rather an active participant whose impassioned prose gave life and meaning to the tale. He lamented the fact that he had only developed a partial palette of writing skills and wished that he had devoted more effort to poetry and other means of conveying meaning in a novel. His most famous book, *In Cold Blood* (1966), tells the story of the murder of Herbert Clutter and his family in rural Kansas. The crime struck terror in the hearts of all Americans because it was a seemingly random act of violence. Moreover, while cities have always been regarded as dangerous, even people living on isolated farms in the conservative Midwest were no longer immune to such violence.

The issue of randomness and the active role of the author both struck a cord. Moreover, when Capote visited the set of Richard Brooks's movie adaptation of the book he came to realize that aspects of the book had to be abandoned in a two-hour film ("Ghosts in the Sunlight: The Filming of *In Cold Blood*," in Capote 1987b). Capote (1987b: 623–624) was struck by what he called "reflected reality":

> Reflected reality is the essence of reality, the truer truth. All art is composed of selected detail, either imaginary or, as in *In Cold Blood*, a distillation of reality. As with the book, so with the film—except that I had chosen my details from life, while Brooks had distilled his from my book: reality twice transposed, and all the truer for it.

After reading a collection of Capote's work I began to question how anthropologists structure their writing. After all, our books seek the same goal as Capote did—the nonfiction novel. It was clear that we adhere to certain paradigms that define for us the questions that matter and how we write about such questions (see Terrell 1990). There is also a continuous ferment (foment?), however, in which writing about cultures never seems to measure up to what we are trying to achieve (Marcus and Fischer 1986). Our work always falls short; our palette is always incomplete.

The Structure of the Book

History is all about people. Archaeologists do create general chronologies based on changes in material culture, but the bottom line always is the people who made the objects we recover. Moreover, history is not just about the people who lived in the past; it is also about those who write it. This book is about Caonabó, the most powerful cacique in Hispaniola when the Spanish arrived on the island. It is also about the people who have studied him, for it is in the questions we ask, the methods we use, and the prose we select that this story, this history, is brought to life.

In most of my previous publications I have tried to distance myself from the text. I was the fly on the wall, the omnipresent narrator who wrote the past from a detached and objective perspective. Such objectivity is a farce. It is the product of scientizing archaeology, anthropology, and history, and it needs to be discarded. Indeed, it may be more accurate to write this book as a play.

Setting

Hispaniola and the Turks and Caicos Islands in the late fifteenth century and late twentieth century

Main Characters

Caonabó, Taíno cacique in 1492
Shaun Sullivan, archaeologist from the University of Illinois, Urbana-
    Champaign
Bill Keegan, archaeologist from the Florida Museum of Natural History

Other Characters

Christopher Columbus
Bartolomé de las Casas
Earthwatch Institute Volunteers
Graduate Assistants

Story Line (sound bite)

Archaeologist uncovers evidence for a mythical and historical personage and attempts to write his story.

Singing the Past

The common thread that ties this work together is the story of Caonabó. Thus chapter 2 retells the story of Columbus's first voyage to the Americas and his relationship with the Taíno caciques. The Spanish first told the story, so we need to recognize that it contains misunderstandings as well as the application of Spanish notions of social and political structures. The result was that Taíno mythical beliefs were woven into the fabric of the interactions. It is therefore possible to interpret how Taíno myth structured everyday practice. One of the key elements in the story is that Caonabó was identified as a Lucayan, someone who came from the Bahama archipelago. How could the most powerful chief in all of Hispaniola have been recruited from these relatively insignificant islands to the north? Chapter 3 looks at the archaeological evidence for the regional polity in which Caonabó emerged, a site worthy of a stranger king in the Lucayan Islands. Site MC-6 on Middle Caicos, Turks and Caicos Islands is identified as the most likely candidate for Caonabó's boyhood home.

In chapter 4 I outline a model of Taíno social organization that not only made it possible for a stranger king to come to Hispaniola but, based on matrilineal and avunculocal principles, produced a stranger king at each succession. Chapter 5 is devoted to the initial excavations at site MC-6 on Middle Caicos. It focuses on the work conducted by Shaun Sullivan and considers the role of disciplinary beliefs in structuring archaeological practice. I include this focus on Sullivan and his work because my later work at the site is best described as derivative. My return to Middle Caicos was based on the questions that Sullivan asked, the methods he employed, and the conclusions that he reached. My work at the site in 1999 and 2000 is described in chapter 6.

In chapter 7 I try to bring all of the various ideas together into a coherent portrait of Caonabó and the northern West Indies at the end of the fifteenth century. The goal is to use an individual, and the work of those who studied this individual, to create a historical narrative that informs us of the articulations of Spanish, Taíno, and anthropological cultures. In this regard I use the logic of circulating reference, the chaotic structure of culture, and the articulation of *événement*, *conjoncture*, and *longue durée* to write a story of the past. Finally, a glossary of Taíno words, names, and geographical locations is found at the end of the book.

The Legend of Caonabó

My goal is to create a narrative of the initial encounters between the Spanish and native peoples of Hispaniola with specific reference to Caonabó. My focus is on the principal characters (Columbus, Caonabó, Guacanagarí) and on the Spanish accounts of their actions and deeds. This chapter examines the various layers of narrative that have colored these accounts, considering personal motives and especially modes of expression (for example, mythology and even Catholic numerology). For the most part I have tried to write a straightforward and coherent legend. I have avoided some of the contexts that complicate the story, although these are pursued in later chapters as the legend is fleshed out and contextualized.

In writing this story I have relied extensively on English translations. To be honest, my command of the Spanish language, especially as written in the sixteenth century, leaves much to be desired. I rely on the testimony of scholars, who repeatedly have noted difficulties in interpreting the correct translation for certain actions (Dunn and Kelley 1989; Henige 1991). Even modern native speakers of the language can be confused by the lexicon and grammar of that day (Varela 1984). For example, interpretations of Columbus's first voyage have produced competing reconstructions in which, on given days, Columbus sailed in opposite directions. The relatively simple issue concerns whether Columbus meant that he was sailing *to* or *from* a particular geographical location. Thus if San Salvador was the first landfall then Columbus sailed west and south, but if Grand Turk was the first landfall then he sailed west and north (see Fuson 1987).

There are only a few written accounts of the earliest encounters, recorded by Bartolomé de las Casas, Ferdinand Columbus, Ramón Pané, Gonzalo Fernández de Oviedo y Valdés, and Peter Martyr. Yet in most cases they did not actually witness the actions that they recorded. Their testimonies are at times conflicting. While the story is relatively seamless, it would be possible to give references for every sentence I have written. I have chosen instead to cite only those passages that are contentious and include the opinions of the translator. I owe a debt to Oliver Dunn and James E. Kelley Jr. (1989) for their excellent translation and concordance for the first voyage, to S. Lyman Tyler

(1988) for his extended translation of the account by Las Casas, to Benjamin Keen (1959) for his translation of the book by Ferdinand Columbus, to Sam Wilson (1990) and Carl Sauer (1966) for their erudite accounts of the early contact period, to David Henige (1991) for his study of Columbus's *diario*, and to Antonio Stevens-Arroyo (1988) for his review of mythology as recorded by Ramón Pané. Issues surrounding the use of "eyewitness" accounts and their evolution into ethnohistory are reexamined in later chapters.

What follows is my version of the multidimensional Spanish:Taíno narrative. It is the story of living peoples and mythical beings and the tension between individual characteristics and group representation. Both sides of the dyad brought multiple inferences to the table. In the same way that the native spirits foretold the coming of the Spanish, the Spanish created a human geography based on the real and mythical geographies of the native peoples they encountered. The issue is not finding a single correct translation but sorting impressions as filtered through the medium of written language.

The Spanish Invasion

It is truly amazing that we know anything at all about Christopher Columbus's first voyage across the Atlantic Ocean. It was very unusual to keep a detailed ship's log in 1492. Moreover, Columbus's *diario* is no ordinary ship's log, being far more detailed than a typical log (Henige 1991). In addition to recording sailing conditions, it also records descriptions of the native peoples and landscapes—and with every passing day everything got bigger and better. The people were described as the finest on earth; the harbors were bigger and better than any in Europe, and the land was like Andalusia in the spring (Dunn and Kelley 1989). What would become the "Enterprise of the Indies" began with a public relations campaign. "To the Spanish humanist, Ramón Iglesia, Columbus seemed to be writing the promotion literature of a tourist board which he did with Italian exuberance" (Sauer 1966: 29).

Having sailed through the Bahamas and along the north coast of Cuba, Columbus set out across the Windward Passage for an island whose mountains soon rose to the east. From the beginning he sought gold. It was well known in the "science" of the day that gold was to be found in humid, tropical climates. Columbus was convinced that gold had to be there, and in response to his inquiries the native peoples repeatedly directed him to the south. On he sailed through treacherous waters.

On December 6, 1492, the *Santa María* and *Niña* (Martín Alonso Pinzón had set off 12 days earlier with the *Pinta* and its crew to seek his own fortune) approached an island.[1] The Lucayan and Cuban Taínos aboard his ship called it *bohío* (which glosses as "home" in the Taíno language), which Columbus renamed La Ysla Española (the Spanish Island). The Indian guides expressed great anxiety and trepidation at the prospect of landing there. As Columbus had heard while sailing along the north coast of Cuba, the "Caribs" or "Cannibals" lived in Hispaniola. He understood the Caribs to be consumers of human flesh. Yet the *diario* gives the impression that each new landfall was viewed as threatening to the Lucayans on board, and every unfamiliar island was the home of the Caribs. Thus any descriptions of "Caribs" from the first voyage must be read as garbled hearsay. The peoples of the Windward Islands today called Island Caribs were never encountered. What the Spanish learned of Caribs clearly reflects the mythological beliefs of the Taínos and not a record of living peoples (Keegan 1995a). Unfortunately, most historians have failed to recognize this confusion and thus attribute characteristics to the Island Caribs of the Windward Islands that are unwarranted.

Columbus had great difficulty attracting the native peoples to his ships while sailing along the north coast of Hispaniola. For ten days he observed signal fires along the coast but had no interactions at all with the island's inhabitants. The main villages appeared to have been located in the interior and not on the coast, so he decided to send an expedition upriver to attempt contact. The village that his emissaries visited was on the Trois Rivières near modern Port de Paix, Haiti. After peaceful relations with the inhabitants were established, the floodgates were opened. Stalled by contrary winds, the two ships tacked back and forth in the Tortuga channel until they finally reached the Baie de l'Acul, which Columbus called the Mar de Santo Tomás. During this time the ships were visited by hundreds (and on one day more than a thousand) Taínos, who came in canoes or swam to the ships. The rulers (caciques) of the villages and provinces (cacicazgos) along the north coast competed with each other to make their invitation to Columbus the most appealing. Yet in the end the competition was decided by a careless act.

On Christmas Eve the two ships sailed to the east with a light wind and departed from the Mar de Santo Tomás. In an unusual move, Columbus had sent the ship's boats ahead on the previous day to identify a safe passage into the bay at Cap Haïtien. Around 11:00 p.m. the two ships were a league off the headland that marks the entrance to Cap Haïtien. Columbus named it Punta Santa (today Point Picolé). Confident that the course was well charted, Columbus went to bed. Because the sea was calm and the libations had flowed for the feast of the Nativity, the man at the helm went off to sleep and turned the rudder over to one of the ship's boys. He did so against Columbus's explicit orders.

Shortly past midnight the *Santa María* had its belly ripped open on a coral reef. Awakened by the sound of an explosion that could be heard "a full league off" (about three miles), Columbus quickly assessed the situation and ordered the main mast cut away to lighten the vessel. He also sent Juan de la Cosa, the ship's master, into a boat to cast an anchor astern in order to keep the vessel from being driven farther onto the reef. Instead Cosa fled to the *Niña*. The captain of the *Niña* refused to let Cosa aboard and sent a longboat to aid the admiral. It was too little too late; the *Santa María* was stuck fast.

The wreck of the *Santa María* occurred in the Taíno province of Marien, which was ruled by a cacique named Guacanagarí. Guacanagarí wept openly upon learning of the wreck and sent weeping relations to console Columbus throughout the night. Afraid to risk the *Niña* in salvaging the *Santa María*, Columbus enlisted the assistance of Guacanagarí. His people recovered everything, including planks and nails, and assembled the materials on the beach. So thorough were the Taínos that not a single "agujeta" (lace-end or needle) was misplaced. Thus Guacanagarí became the first Taíno cacique to establish a strong bond with the Spanish. Furthermore, Guacanagarí's life-long friendship with Columbus can be interpreted as an unsuccessful effort on his part to enhance his status in the island's political hierarchy.[2]

Guacanagarí

Columbus took the sinking of the *Santa María* as a sign from God that he should build a fort in this location. Guacanagarí gave him two large houses to use. With the assistance of the cacique's people, the Spaniards reportedly began the construction of a fort, tower, and moat in the village, using the timbers and other materials salvaged from the *Santa María*. Because the *Niña* could not accommodate all of the sailors, about thirty-nine men (there is some debate concerning the actual number) were left at La Navidad with instructions to trade for gold.

When word reached Columbus that the *Pinta* had been spotted in a river at the eastern end of the island, preparations were hastened for their return to Spain. Three days later, on December 30, Columbus and Guacanagarí sealed their friendship with the exchange of gifts. Guacanagarí removed the crown from his head and placed it on Columbus's. In return, Columbus dressed Guacanagarí in a fine red cape, high-laced shoes, a necklace of multicolored agates, and a silver ring. Both men, perhaps unwittingly, had chosen the most important symbols of the other's culture. Columbus's "coronation" meant as much—if not more—to a European as it would have to a Taíno. In return, the gifts of a scarlet cape and red beads (the possessions of a man who until then had been a common sea captain) were perhaps the greatest honor that Columbus could have bestowed. Red was the Taíno color of life, the color of male virility (see Roe 1982 for a discussion of color symbolism in South American mythology). After the exchange Columbus provided a display of the weapons aboard the *Niña* and promised to protect Guacanagarí from his enemies. These enemies, at least as Columbus understood them, were the Caniba or Caníbales.

Columbus departed from La Navidad on January 4. He caught up with the *Pinta* on January 6 near Monte Cristi on the modern border between Haiti and the Dominican Republic. The two ships again were separated during the Atlantic crossing, during which they encountered a violent storm. Columbus was the first to reach Spain and entered the port at Palos on the morning of March 15, 1493. Pinzón and the *Pinta* arrived later the same day. It is said that Pinzón, who was already ill, was so disheartened that Columbus had reached Spain before him that he lost the will to live and let his illness consume him.

The story of Columbus's first voyage is steeped in myth and hyperbole (see Wilford 1991). Spanish sailors have been disparaged for plotting a mutiny during the voyage, although there is no evidence for this other than Columbus's word. It has recently become clear that it was the skill and bravery of Spanish sailors that led to the successful return of two ships to Europe. Pinzón and the *Pinta* reached Europe first and arrived in the harbor at Lisbon on March 5. By some strange twist of politics the Portuguese king allowed Columbus and Pinzón to return to Spain.

When Columbus returned to La Navidad on November 28, 1493, he learned that all of the Christians were dead and that the fort had been burned to the ground. According to Dr. Diego Álvarez Chanca (a physician who left invaluable accounts of the events of the second voyage), they had already seen dead bodies on the beach. Their identity was unknown, but they had the appearance of Spaniards. Columbus was told that soon after he returned to Spain the Spaniards fell to fighting among themselves. Some went off into the country to seek their fortune, but King Caonabó murdered those who remained there under the command of Diego de Arana. History records that the Spaniards were killed because they abused the local people; they raped, looted, pillaged, and abused the hospitality of their hosts. If such local violations led to their deaths, however, then the local leader should have ordered the killing. Guacanagarí claimed that he was innocent, that he was a friend of Columbus, and that he himself had been wounded in battle defending the Spaniards. Columbus apparently believed him and did not blame him for the destruction of La Navidad.

Instead, Caonabó—the primary cacique for this region and the ruler to whom Guacanagarí owed fealty—was blamed. As proof, Columbus's son Ferdinand wrote that when Caonabó was later captured he admitted to killing twenty of the men at La Navidad (Keen 1959). Would another leader have acted differently? Whatever abuses the Spanish may have committed, Caonabó could not allow a second-level cacique like Guacanagarí to harbor a well-armed garrison of Europeans in his village. His own survival would have been threatened if he had done so.

Faced with the destruction of La Navidad, Columbus moved his base 115 km to the east and established the first European colony in the Americas at a place he named La Isabela in honor of his queen. Before he set out on his next voyage of exploration (this time to southern Cuba and Jamaica), he stopped to visit Guacanagarí on April 25, 1494. The cacique, upon learning of the admiral's arrival, feared his wrath. This fear dated back to Columbus's return to La Navidad in 1493. During Columbus's passage through the Leeward Islands he had taken on board a number of Indian women in Guadeloupe that he called "Caribees." They are described as Igneri (Island Arawak) women who were captives of the Caribs. When the ships reached what remained of La Navidad, Guacanagarí helped these captives to escape. To make matters worse, he kept one of the freed captives as a wife. Believing that Columbus had returned to seek retribution for his heinous act, Guacanagarí went into hiding. Columbus appears to have harbored no animosity over the loss of the "Caribee" captives, but he was in too much of a rush to wait for the return of his old friend.

In March 1495 Columbus and Guacanagarí found that they again needed each other. The Taínos in the Vega Real (the central part of the island) were in open rebellion. Columbus marched into the interior to quiet the rebellion, accompanied by his brother Bartholomew, 200 "Christians," 20 horses, and 20 dogs. Guacanagarí and his warriors also marched at the admiral's side. Revenge was the reason for the unrest. Guacanagarí was hated by the other caciques for cooperating with the Spanish. They flaunted this hatred by killing one of his wives and stealing another—capital offenses in Taíno society (note that this was why Guacanagarí had gone into hiding the previous year when Columbus came to visit him). The account of the campaign in the Vega Real contains the last words written about Guacanagarí.

Guacanagarí is an interesting character who had history thrust upon him following the sinking of the *Santa María*. He was apparently a middle-level cacique who saw the opportunity to improve his station in life and tried to do

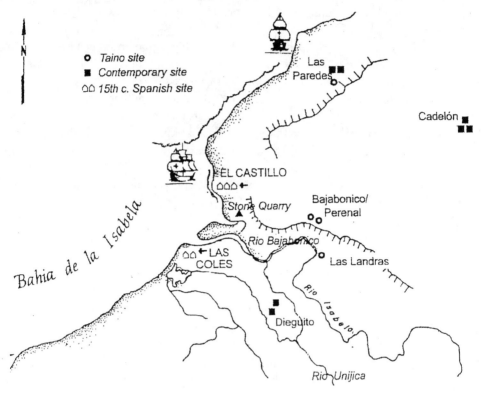

2.1. Map of La Isabela (courtesy of Kathleen Deagan).

so. Where others came to view the Spaniards as their enemy, he came forward and embraced Columbus as a friend. Had circumstances been different he might have achieved the political success that King Kamehameha I achieved in Hawaii with the aid of European weapons (Sahlins 1985).

Colonization Begins at La Isabela

Samuel Eliot Morison (1942) called it the Grand Fleet: 17 ships, 1,200–1,500 men, horses, pigs, mules, cattle, chickens, sheep, goats, dogs, cats, rats as stowaways, wheat seed, grapevine cuttings, chickpeas, melons, olives, fruit stones, onions, lettuce, radishes, and sugarcane from the Canary Islands (Deagan and Cruxent 2002: 6–7). They departed from Spain on September 25, 1493. Their objective was to establish the first full-fledged European colony in the New World. To achieve this end they carried everything needed to reproduce an Iberian homeland in what Columbus had described as an earthly paradise: "I believe that in the world there are no better people or a better land" (Dunn and Kelley 1989: 281).

Departing from the ruins at La Navidad, Columbus sailed east in search of an appropriate location to establish his colony. After 28 days of sailing against the prevailing trade winds Columbus selected a small peninsula at the top of a bluff to the north of the Río Bajabonica (Figure 2.1). No Taínos were living on the site when Columbus landed and began to build the town that he named for his queen. Several native villages were nearby, however, and Columbus decried the steady stream of villagers who came day and night to trade local products for European objects. I use the term "objects" rather than "goods" because the villagers often accepted broken goods and things of no use that the Spanish would have otherwise discarded. The value of these objects derived from having been transported across the sea (from "heaven") and not from their potential use.

The sight of so many ships, men, barnyard animals, and all of the other things needed to establish an Iberian outpost must have both amazed and frightened the native peoples. At the end of the first voyage the few Spaniards who were left behind had been dispatched quickly. Now it was clear that these strange (mythical) beings had returned to stay. This time they brought with them European diseases, a gift that the Taínos could not refuse. Most of the men that Columbus brought with him soon fell ill, and almost half of them died. They were affected by the long period of confinement in closed quarters aboard ship combined with the difficulties of acclimatization to a tropical climate and gastrointestinal problems. Some of these men recovered, but others carried more deadly pathogens that soon spread to the native population.

It is not certain in which cacicazgo the colony was established (Deagan and Cruxent 2002), but at the end of the second voyage there was no mention of caciques competing to greet the Spanish. The two major polities in the area were Magdalena (Macorix) and Magua. Guatiguaná ruled the Macorix from a village on the Río Yaquí that was 10–12 leagues from the Spanish settlement at Santiago. The second was ruled by Guarionex, who was identified as a Taíno, whose village was near the Spanish settlement at Concepción de la Vega. As Kathleen Deagan and José María Cruxent (2002) point out, La Isabela may have been in a borderland, with both Taíno and Macorix settlements nearby. This border location could explain why the Spanish settlement was not immediately challenged by a cacique.

La Isabela was close to the territory of the Macorix de Arriba, whose name means "foreign tongue" in the Taíno language. This location would explain why Friar Ramón Pané reported that the information he collected about religious beliefs was related to him in the Macorix language. After making his initial report, Columbus then asked Pané "to go and live with another leading cacique, named Guarionex, the lord of many people, since the language of these folk was understood throughout the land." Pané countered: "Lord [Christopher Columbus], how is it that Your Lordship wishes that I go live with Guarionex without knowing any language other than that of Macorix?" (Stevens-Arroyo 1988: 76). Clearly, Macorix and Taíno were mutually unintelligible languages. The Taíno language apparently was used as the *lingua franca* on the island. Most of Columbus's dealings over the next several years were with Guarionex, so it would seem that La Isabela was indeed located near his cacicazgo and that it was of greater importance to the Spanish than was Magdalena (Macorix).

The importance of these Taíno villages was magnified by the insatiable Spanish need for food. Shortly after La Isabela was established, Columbus sent Alonso de Hojeda into the interior to search for gold. When Hojeda returned with tales of more gold than anyone could imagine, a larger expedition was organized. This grand entrada left La Isabela in March 1494. Columbus led the entrada, accompanied by 20 horsemen and nearly 400 men on foot (virtually every man well enough to march). The 20 horses that had survived the voyage proved especially devastating in hostile encounters with the Taínos. The Taínos believe that horse and rider were one beast, like the mythical centaur, and fled at their approach.

Deagan and Cruxent (2002: 7) describe the spectacle of troops marching in file with banners flying to the sound of drumbeats and trumpets. The entrada marched for about 160 km, but it is not clear that it accomplished much. It may have succeeded in its goal of intimidating the native peoples, but the notion that a few hundred Spaniards were viewed as much of a threat at that time is questionable.

One outcome was the construction of a packed earth and wood fort in the gold-producing region known as the Cibao. This fort was called Santo Tomás (named for doubting Thomas in the New Testament—for those who had to see the gold deposits with their own eyes) and was manned by a contingent of 50 men (Deagan and Cruxent 2002: 8). Yet when Columbus returned to La Isabela his worst fears had been realized. Another epidemic had killed most of those who remained behind, and fire had destroyed almost two-thirds of the wood and thatch houses in which the men were living.

Faced with high mortality, diminished supplies, and growing unrest at La Isabela, Columbus had his back to the sea. Twelve of the ships had been sent back to Spain to resupply the colony, and there was no means for escape. To make matters worse, Pedro Margarite, the captain at Fort Santo Tomás, sent word to Columbus that Caonabó was preparing to attack the fort. Immediately an expeditionary force of 470 men under the command of Alonso de Hojeda was sent to pacify the Vega Real, to accustom the native peoples to subjugation, and to accustom the Spaniards to native foods (Deagan and Cruxent 2002: 9). With imported rations in short supply the most important of these directives was the requirement that they feed themselves by taking advantage of Taíno hospitality. Hojeda also was expected to reinforce the fort and to remain there as governor.

Whether imminent attack on the fort was real or imagined, no attack was forthcoming; but sending Hojeda back to the Vega Real was the equivalent of loosing a bull in a china shop. Upon crossing the Río del Oro (Río Mao) Hojeda was told that five Taínos had taken clothing from Spaniards that they had helped to cross the river. Hojeda sent the local cacique, his brother, and one of his nephews as prisoners to La Isabela. In addition, he had the ears cut off another of the cacique's relatives in the public plaza. When the prisoners arrived at La Isabela, Columbus ordered that all of them be decapitated in public. The cacique of a nearby town arrived soon after to plead for their release, with the promise that no further harm would come to the Spanish or their belongings. Only then did Columbus revoke the sentence.

While that was going on at La Isabela, a large group of Taínos attacked five Spaniards. A horseman was able to free them and inflict severe wounds on the attackers, and the Spaniards all returned safely to La Isabela. Clearly, relations with the Taínos quickly had turned ugly. As Las Casas pointed out, rather than seek their goals through peaceful means the Spanish assumed that the way to achieve their goals was through fear and intimidation (Tyler 1988: 140).

Columbus soon grew weary of facing continuous problems of such great magnitude. He was never cut out to be an administrator. He was a man of great plans—an explorer who longed to get away. Thus he set out to explore Cuba and Jamaica at the end of April 1494, using the pretense of continuing exploration at the command of the sovereigns. He departed during a period of unrest and turmoil and left Diego Columbus in charge of the colony.

Caonabó

Columbus may have been lucky in choosing the location that he did for La Isabela.[3] If he indeed settled on the political boundary between two competing cacicazgos in which two different languages were spoken, then it is possible that neither cacique would have had the authority or been very anxious to enter what might be called a demilitarized zone. Perhaps each of the caciques whose buffer Columbus breached waited for the other to react. As a result, they lost any military advantage that they had when the Spanish first arrived.

In relatively short order La Isabela was built, a fort was established in the interior, and the Spaniards began extracting tribute from the native population.

In contrast, the reaction of Caonabó to foreigners in his territory in 1493 was immediate and swift. His military action against the Spaniards at La Navidad attests to his status. Guacanagarí's village was more than 80 km as the crow flies (more than 90 km by foot) from Caonabó's village (Wilson 1990). Despite this distance, from a political perspective Caonabó could not let a subordinate chief harbor a garrison of well-armed Spaniards. These were not the actions of a lower-level cacique; indeed Las Casas and Oviedo both identified Caonabó as one of the five principal caciques on the island.

On his return to Hispaniola in 1494, Columbus was distracted by the need to establish a beachhead on the island; thus Caonabó was ignored for a while. With the establishment of Fort Santo Tomás, however, Caonabó and his brothers were again identified as the main threat to the Spanish enterprise.

Caonabó, the paramount cacique (*matunherí*) for the Maguana cacicazgo, was described as "a man well up in years, experienced and of the most piercing wit and much knowledge" (Keen 1959). He was strong, authoritative, and brave. His main settlement was located on the west side of the Cordillera Central, where the Spanish town of San Juan de Maguana was established after he was deposed (Figure 2.2). This town, which still exists today, is the site of the largest Taíno earthwork in all of the West Indies. It is today called Corales de los Indios and measures more than 125,000 square meters (Wilson 1990: 24–26). The next largest earthwork on Hispaniola is Chacuey (35,721 square meters), and the third is Casa de la Reina (10,164 square meters). Caonabó held wider powers as well through his alliance with Behecchio, the principal cacique of the Xaragua cacicazgo to the west. The alliance was sealed by Caonabó's marriage to Anacaona, the sister of Behecchio. Between them Behecchio, Caonabó, and Anacaona held sway over almost half of Hispaniola.

In reading the accounts of the chroniclers it is hard to see why Caonabó was considered such a threat. Indeed Sauer (1966: 85) concluded that Caonabó was not a menace. Furthermore, his cacicazgo reportedly had little gold, and there is no indication that he made any offensive moves against the Spanish after ridding himself of the pestilence at La Navidad. Perhaps his power and fame came from a reputation based on past deeds. It is possible that the Taínos who were being abused by the Spanish referred to their big and powerful brother (Caonabó) who would eventually come to their rescue. Or perhaps the perceived threat derived from Columbus's personal anger over the destruction of La Navidad. The motives are difficult to sort out.

There are three versions of what happened to Caonabó (see Tyler 1988: 162–165). Columbus's son Ferdinand reported that Caonabó was one of the

2.2. Location of principal towns in Hispaniola.

first caciques captured when his father waged war against the Indians in the Vega Real. This account does not fit the timing of the attack on the Vega Real, however: Guarionex was the only cacique mentioned by name in that attack, which probably occurred after Caonabó had been captured. In the second version, Peter Martyr reported that Columbus sent Alonso de Hojeda to ask Caonabó to come to La Isabela to see him. Caonabó agreed but brought with him an army. In this account Hojeda managed to capture Caonabó en route and bring him to La Isabela without his army.

Bartolomé de las Casas disputed both of these accounts. With regard to the second he says: "What we used to say at the time was that Caonabó replied to Hojeda: 'Let the Admiral come here and bring me the bell of turey that speaks, for I do not have to go there'" (quoted and translated in Tyler 1988: 165). Because Caonabó had made no effort to meet with Columbus prior to this time, the air of superiority reflected in the Las Casas account seems to be the most credible.[4] Las Casas also believed that the seriousness and authority of Caonabó would have led him to challenge the Spaniards. From my perspective, this challenge amounts to one stranger king telling the new stranger who wants to be king that he needs to come to him. In other words, the interlopers may have impressed Caonabó, but he was not going to give up his home-court advantage; nor was he going to sully himself by behaving below his status as *matunherí*.

A key passage in that account is the reference to *turey*. First, the "bell of turey" is a specific reference to the bell in the church at La Isabela. The Taínos considered its peal to be the voice of the spirits, because the people came to the church when it called. *Turey* is a Taíno word that refers to an object as coming "from heaven," which also means anything that came from over the horizon. Thus any object or person that came from a foreign land could be classified as *turey*. Perhaps because of their obsession with gold, the Spanish emphasized that *turey* was used as the name for very rare objects that were made of a gold-copper alloy (called *guanín*). The Taínos were not familiar with the process of smelting gold (all of the locally produced gold objects were cold hammered), so these objects must have originated in mainland South America. In this regard, Arie Boomert (1987) provides an excellent account of protohistoric exchange between the islands and the mainland.

When Columbus first arrived in the West Indies, he interpreted the Taínos as saying "come and greet the men who come from heaven, bring them something to eat and drink." Columbus's concept of heaven and the Taíno concept of heaven were not exactly the same, but they did overlap enough to cause confusion. We also need to recognize that the Taínos apparently used one word to refer to what Western cultures would distinguish as distinct levels of representation. For instance, the Taíno term *cemí* was apparently used in reference to a pantheon of major deities, lesser gods who played more immediate roles in their lives, and the objects crafted of wood, bone, shell, cotton, and stone with which they represented these spirits and deities. As José Oliver (2005: 255) notes: "*cemís* were active agents in the changing fortunes of the political landscape of the Taíno." Westerners would never confuse the statues and other representations with the true and inaccessible God Almighty. The Taínos were idolaters. Moreover, *cemí* is a conceptual quality that does not need to be transformed into an object (Oliver 2005: 246).

The third account of Caonabó's capture reads like a legend. Concerned with the threat that Caonabó posed to Fort Santo Tomás, Hojeda and nine horsemen went to visit him as emissaries of Columbus. When Caonabó heard they were coming, he was especially pleased. He had been told that they were bringing a gift of *turey* and was fascinated by stories of the bell in the church at La Isabela, which the Taínos described as *turey* that speaks (this part of the story is related to the second story of his capture).

When Hojeda arrived, he told Caonabó that he was bringing a gift of *turey* from Biscay (the location of the main ironworks in Spain), that it came from heaven, that it had a secret power, and that the kings of Castile wore it as a great jewel during their *arietos*, the Taíno word for ceremonial songs and dances (Tyler 1988: 163). Hojeda then suggested that Caonabó go to the river to bathe and relax, as was their custom, and that he would then present his gift. Having no reason to fear a few Spaniards in his own village, Caonabó one day decided to claim the gift and went off to the river with a few retainers. While he was at the river (about 2 km from the village), Hojeda tricked him into going off alone together. He presented Caonabó with the highly polished silver-colored handcuffs and manacles that he had brought. Hojeda instructed Caonabó in how they were worn and placed the cacique on his horse. With Caonabó as his captive, Hojeda and his men, with swords drawn, made haste to return to La Isabela. The trap was set and successfully sprung.

Roman Catholic numerology may be relevant here. The number nine is the result of three times three and thus represents even greater holiness than does the number three (for example, various trinities). Moreover, according to St. Augustine the number ten (in this case nine horsemen plus Hojeda) signifies perfection, as evidenced by the ten commandments and numerous other historical references (such as the ten shores of Egypt, ten ropes of the tent of the tabernacle, the height of cherubs in the temple, and the ten horns of the apocalyptic beast). Ten is the round and perfect number that forms the base of our decimal system and is the universal number of Pythagoreans. Thus the number of individuals involved in the capture of Caonabó reflects perfection, while the addition of his number to the group (Hojeda plus nine horsemen plus Caonabó) reflects the number of desanctification (eleven) and imperfection according to St. Teresa (the number of Christ's apostles following the suicide of Judas Iscariot; see Keegan 1992).

It is reported that Columbus decided to send Caonabó to Castile along with as many slaves as the ships would hold, although some dispute whether he was ever sent to Spain. The official report is that the ships sank and Caonabó was lost at sea. It was further reported that Caonabó's brothers were determined to seek retribution by waging a cruel war against the Spaniards that would drive them from their lands. Yet there are no records of any substantial military successes by the Taínos of Hispaniola, so it appears that the brothers failed to achieve their reported objective. Within a decade the native population was decimated by warfare, cruelty, enslavement, and disease.

Disease is mentioned last because it was the least of their problems. It has been argued that the Spanish were innocent bystanders as European diseases killed the native peoples of the Americas (Deagan and Cruxent 2002). In other words, the Spaniards may have been sick, but they were not culpable. Prior to 1517, however, when the first smallpox pandemic spread across the Americas, disease was only a peripheral factor. The colonists' failure to respect human life along with their failure to heed their monarch's insistence that the Indians be treated as their vassals resulted in a tremendous human tragedy.

It is possible to identify two conceptual stages in the conquest. In the first stage the agricultural resources of the Taínos were viewed as inexhaustible.

Yet by 1494 there already was widespread famine on the island (Wilson 1990). A similar situation occurred during the conquest of Puerto Rico (Anderson-Córdova 2005: 343). In the second stage human resources were viewed as inexhaustible. Even if people could not be sent to Spain as slaves, they could at least be put to work on encomiendas. By 1505, however, the Taíno population of Hispaniola and neighboring islands had declined to the point where enslaved Africans were brought to the island as laborers.

After Caonabó

Following the capture of Caonabó in the fall of 1494, the next cacique to fall victim to the Spanish was Guarionex. He was described as "a peaceable and prudent man, knowing the effectiveness of their horses in battle, and considering that the very capable cacique Caonabó had not been able to contend against them successfully, refused to engage in war" (Tyler 1988: 189). Yet his subjects had grown weary of demands for food, tribute, and whatever else the Spanish desired, and they impressed upon Guarionex the need to strike back. The plan was to attack the nearby Spanish garrison at Concepción. Unfortunately for the Taínos, Bartholomew Columbus got word of their plans. In a preemptive strike at midnight, Columbus's vastly outnumbered forces captured the 14 caciques (including their supreme leader, Guarionex) who were in charge of the 15,000 men that the Taínos had assembled for the battle.

Bartholomew Columbus later released the caciques, and Guarionex went into exile. The Spanish had broken the Taínos' will. They had attacked at night, a time when only the spirits were about. There was no further organized resistance to the Spanish invasion on the island of Hispaniola. Moreover, the coming of the Spanish and the fate of the native peoples had been foretold. The Taínos' principal deity had told his people that they faced a foreign invasion that would bring death and ruin.

Caonabó's wife, Anacaona, was the sister of Behecchio, the cacique of Xaragua. The Spanish considered Xaragua to be the most cultured of all of the Taíno cacicazgos (Wilson 1990). The main settlement was located near the modern city of Port-au-Prince, and Xaragua incorporated most of western Haiti, with the possible exception of the Guacayarima peninsula in the southwest. The success of Xaragua may in part be due to its insulated location on the western side of the island and the alliance with the powerful cacique Caonabó to the east, who was known for his ferocity and provided the front line in dealing with rival caciques. Following the capture of Caonabó by the Spanish, Behecchio's army moved into the area of the Río Nieba in the Magua cacicazgo

(Wilson 1990). This move suggests that he was trying to shore up local support and defenses for his southeastern border.

When Bartholomew Columbus went to Xaragua to demand tribute in 1495, Behecchio replied that there was no gold in his territory; thus he could not give anything of value to the Spanish. Columbus then demanded cotton, fibers, and cassava bread instead, and Behecchio agreed to provide these items. The cacicazgo of Xaragua apparently met its tribute obligations for several years. Moreover, Anacaona maintained a residence closer to the coast, where she had a storehouse of high-status goods. Female craftspersons living on the island of La Gonâve reportedly produced these goods, which included *duhos* (wooden stools used by the caciques), dishes, basins, and other containers of highly polished black wood (Sauer 1966: 60) as well as a thousand cotton items. She gave Bartholomew Columbus 14 wooden *duhos* and seems to have been in control of the distribution of the major status items in the province. In other words, while her brother was able to establish a tributary relationship involving the payment of agricultural items, it was Anacaona who controlled the high-status goods. The importance of females in Taíno society is attested in these gifts.

When Behecchio died (between 1496 and 1502), Anacaona took over as the ruler of Xaragua. Her rule was short-lived. She was brutally murdered by Nicolás de Ovando in 1503 shortly after he became the Spanish governor of the island. It is reported that 84 of her subordinate caciques were either hanged or herded into the royal house and burned to death. Anacaona received a more humane sentence and was hanged.[5] Diego Velásquez was given credit for the massacre and was rewarded with the governorship of the western part of Hispaniola. He later led the brutal conquest of Cuba, in which Bartolomé de las Casas participated. Las Casas was so appalled by the inhumanity of the conquest that he dedicated his life to being the "Defender of the Indians." Although the story is by this point greatly truncated, Ovando succeeded in destroying all remaining vestiges of Taíno autonomy by 1504. The entire island finally was firmly under Spanish control. In their successful control of the native peoples, however, they had decimated the population and lacked a reliable source of local labor. In lieu of Taíno laborers the Spanish turned to the import of enslaved Africans.

Of Cannibals and Kings

The premise of this book is that Caonabó was both a real person and a stranger king. Those who have taken a literal reading of the chronicles view him as a man of Lucayan birth who managed to become (or was recruited to be) a cacique in Hispaniola (for example, Lovén 1935). It is possible that reference to Caonabó as a king who came from across the waters is entirely allegorical. As discussed in chapter 1, many societies have myths of kings arriving from distant lands. The notion of a stranger king is common in Polynesian mythology, and the Maya were said to be awaiting the return of Quetzalcoatl from the east across the sea when Hernán Cortés arrived on the Mexican coast. Some have said that this foreign status allows the king to impose his will on his subjects (to subjugate or literally make them objects) because he is not one of them: he is different and often divine (Sahlins 1985). Furthermore, the notion of a stranger king carries a good deal of metaphysical baggage with regard to the notion of place.

A bit of etymology is warranted here. The first definition of "stranger" in English is "one who is neither friend nor acquaintance." This definition focuses on personal relations. The first translation of the Spanish equivalent, *extranjero*, is "foreigner," which focuses on space. In contrast, the Spanish word *desconocido* refers to someone unknown in a personal sense. The English word "stranger" comes from the Old French *estrangier*, which translates as "foreigner."

The first problem in sorting out the story is that the Taínos and Spanish did not communicate well, especially during their first encounters. Columbus himself wrote: "Also, I do not understand the language, and the people of these islands do not understand me, nor do I or anyone else I have on board understand them. As for the Indians I am carrying on board, I often take one thing from them to mean the opposite" (Dunn and Kelley 1989: 183). Therefore it is imperative that we do not take the Spanish chroniclers at their word. Spanish accounts must be sifted through multiple filters to identify the factors that conditioned what they wrote. In addition to personal motives (such as Columbus promoting his "discoveries") and political agendas (for example, Las Casas defending the native peoples), there are questions concerning what was observed and by whom, how European attitudes and beliefs were imposed on these observations, and what information was communicated to the Spanish by the native peoples. In this regard I turn to the issue of Taíno beliefs. Were the Spanish merely told of mythological justifications for the position of this king and therefore simply misunderstood and accepted the stories as real? This is a complicated issue. The facts are few, but those that are recorded are worth considering.

One fact is clear. The Spanish chroniclers viewed Caonabó as a foreigner. Oviedo claimed that Caonabó was a Carib (Lovén 1935: 57). Las Casas disagreed and instead identified the Lucayan Islands as Caonabó's homeland. In both cases, Caonabó came from a foreign land (1958: 212).

Putting the objections of Las Casas aside for the moment, it is worth considering Oviedo's association of Caonabó with Caribs. One possibility is that this is simply a case of displacement. For example, in a similar report Oviedo stated that Archaic peoples lived on the Guacayarima peninsula of southwest Haiti. The Archaic period began around 4000 BC, when a new migration of peoples from South America who practiced a flaked- and ground-stone technology but supposedly lacked pottery and agriculture are thought to have entered the islands (but see chapter 3). Conventional wisdom holds that they were displaced by the Ceramic Age peoples (who entered the islands after 500 BC) and were pushed into marginal locations where they survived until European contact (see Keegan 1994). Based on the accounts by Oviedo and Las Casas, it was initially concluded that Archaic peoples were living on the Guacayarima peninsula of Haiti and in western Cuba (Guanahatabey or Guanahacabibe province) in the late fifteenth century (Lovén 1935). Archaeological evidence, however, has since shown that Ceramic Age peoples occupied the Guacayarima peninsula (Rouse 1992) and that Oviedo's account is inaccurate. In fact Las Casas reported that Oviedo was wrong. What could be the source of this error? One possibility is that Oviedo, who had not yet visited the Americas, simply misunderstood where the Archaic peoples were living and confused the names "Guacayarima" and "Guanahatabey" (Keegan 1989a).

Whatever the source of confusion, we are faced with a situation in which archaeology contradicts ethnohistory. It would be easy simply to disregard the ethnohistoric account as reflecting a misinterpretation of the available evidence. Yet a historical anthropology should look for meaning in all of its sources. Might Oviedo really have meant something in identifying Caonabó as a "Carib" even if his use of the term does not match our current understanding of the peoples who are now described by this name? More importantly, what meaning(s) did the name "Carib" have at the end of the fifteenth century?

The term "Carib" is derived from Columbus's *diario*, the so-called daily log of the first voyage. Thus the process of assigning meaning to the term necessarily begins with the deconstruction of the *diario*. The document that has survived is a holographic manuscript written by Bartolomé de las Casas (the most complete version is Dunn and Kelley 1989). Ten passages in the *diario* mention "Caribes," "Caniba," "Canima," and/or "Cannibales." All of these passages are abstractions made by Las Casas, so it is possible that the original text was altered (see Henige 1991 for an excellent review of who wrote the *diario*). It is apparent throughout the text that Las Casa did not substantially modify the original content. The following quotation from the entry of November 4 is an excellent example: "He [Columbus] understood also that, far from there, there were one-eyed men, and others, with snouts of dogs, who ate men, and that as soon as one was taken they cut his throat and drank his blood and cut off his genitals" (Dunn and Kelley 1989: 132).

The retention of such seemingly farfetched observations (which subsequent explorations would have challenged) by Las Casas suggests his substantial conformity to the original text. Moreover, where Las Casas did amend the text he usually did so in margin notes (Fuson 1987). Accompanying the words quoted above is a notation in the left margin: "todo esto devian de dezir dlos caribes" (all this must be said of the Caribes). This note and quotation are the first reference in the *diario* to the consumption of human flesh. Both indicate that, even though Las Casas knew these beings by the name "Caribes," they had not yet been named that by Columbus. Three weeks would pass before Columbus in his entry of November 22 introduced the names "Caniba" and "Cannibales"; not until December 26, when he reached the Taíno province of Caribata in the Baie de l'Acul on the north coast of Hispaniola, did the name "Caribe" appear.

A careful reading of those passages indicates that the word "Carib" is actually an amalgam of four distinct concepts: (1) Caribes, understood by the Spanish to be real people when in fact they were creatures who existed only in Taíno mythology; (2) Caniba (Canima), the name Columbus used to denote the people or subjects of the Kubla Khan ("gra Can"), whom he believed to be the ruler of Cathay (China); (3) Cannibales, a synonym for Caribes used by the Taínos to describe the mythological beings who consumed human flesh,[6] which was corrupted by the Spanish to mean living people who were anthropophagous;[7] and (4) Carib and Island Carib, which are modern anthropological constructs based on Spanish accounts, used as names for indigenous cultural groups in lowland South America and the West Indies.

Whether the Caribes are properly assigned to the realm of Taíno mythology can be determined in two ways: by the interplay of actors from different cultures and by the Spanish record of the physical and behavioral characteristics that the Taínos attributed to the Caribes. The first is important because only one of the cultures (the Spanish) recorded the events; the second is important because it suggests certain ideational categories of the Taínos.

With regard to the interaction of cultures, no native peoples living in the Americas looked anything like the Spanish. Had Caribes truly been known to the Taínos they would not have confused them with the Spanish. Yet they did so. The *diario* records (Dunn and Kelley 1989: 167):

And when they saw that he [Columbus] was taking this route [toward the land of the Caribe], he says that they could not talk, because the cannibals eat them, and that they are people very well armed. The Admiral says that well he believes there is something in what they say, but that since they were armed they must be people of intelligence; and he believed that they must have captured some of them and because they did not return to their own lands they would say that they ate them. They believed the same thing about the Christians and about the Admiral when some Indians first saw them.

These words speak to the interplay of different cultural categories. To the native peoples, Columbus and his men possessed the physical characteristics of Caribes, especially in their clothing, their armament, and the taking of captives who never returned. This mythic association of the Spanish and Caribes by the Taínos reappears in a prophecy recorded by Fray Ramón Pané, who reported that the principal god Yucahuguamá (often shortened as Yocahu) told of the coming of a clothed people who would destroy the Taínos:

> And they say that this cacique had affirmed that he had spoken with Giocauuaghama [Yocahuguamá in Las Casas] who had told him that whoever remained alive after his death should enjoy the rule over them only a short time, because they would see in their country a people clothed which was to rule them and to slay them and that they would die of hunger. At first they thought these would be the Cannibales; but reflecting that they only plundered and fled they believed that it must be another people that the cemi spoke of. Wherefore they now believe that it was the Admiral and the people he brought with him. (Bourne 1906: 334)

At first the Taínos thought that the prophecy foretold the coming of the "cannibals," but the Taínos later decided that the prophecy foretold the coming of the admiral and his men (Arrom 1974; Bourne 1906; see below). It is therefore likely that the Taínos knew of these Caribes only through their mythology.

In addition to these ethnological incongruencies, the corporeal basis for Caribes can be dismissed on the basis of two categories of evidence that demonstrate that they existed only in Taíno mythology. The first is the physical appearance and behavior of the Caribes and their associates. The second is the Taíno practice of associating *cemíes* (spirits) with islands, caves, and other geographical locations. In other words, the Taíno cosmos, as in all other cultures, had topographical associations.

The three earliest references to Caribe anthropophagy all contain the same basic description: "one-eyed men, and others, with snouts of dogs, who ate men" (Dunn and Kelley 1989: 132). Other investigators have assumed that Columbus was simply making an accounting of strange beings, a practice then common in European depictions of Asia (Milbrath 1989). But unlike Cyclops, Amazons, and dogfaces, in whom the Spanish lost interest when they failed to materialize (Myers 1984), the Cannibals proved useful in justifying the enslavement of the indigenous people (Davis and Goodwin 1990). The attributes of having one-eye, having the face of a dog, and eating human flesh cannot be separated. They are all components of a mythical entity, as evidenced in the syntax of Columbus's report: "He [Columbus] says that after they [Taíno captives] saw him take the route to this land [Hispaniola] they could not speak fearing that they would have them to eat; and he could not take away their fear. And they say that they have but one eye and the face of a dog" (Dunn and Kelley 1989: 177).

The association of eating human flesh and jaguars/dogs is present in the cosmography and corporeal art of South America and the West Indies. In the South American lowlands, whence the Taínos originated, this mythology centers on jaguars. In his study of corporeal art in pre-Columbian Puerto Rico, Peter Roe (1991) has argued that the dog came to represent the jaguar through a process of "mythic substitution" because of the absence of jaguars from the islands. Jaguars did make it to the islands, but only in the form of jaguar-tooth pendants, like the one found at the Pearls site on Grenada.

A direct mythical connection to dogs occurs through the cemí Opiyel-gobirán, the Guardian of the Dead. Friar Pané recorded that this cemí "comes out of the house at night and enters the forests. They go there to seek him and bring him back to the house. They bind him with cords, but he returns to the forests" (Stevens-Arroyo 1988: 234). Here the theme of capture and escape (close and remote) is replayed with a significant distinction between the cultural and supernatural realms in an allegory of both death and migration. This cemí always escapes and returns to the forests, but humans are captured and never return. Juan José Arrom (1974) identified a particular wooden statue recovered from the Turks and Caicos Islands as representing Opiyelgobirán. While this may be correct, in my opinion the stone amulets that depict a square-faced deity with legs drawn up (bound) and whose arms are not represented are the perfect image of a dog spirit (Figure 2.3). These cemíes were made to be worn around the neck, reflecting a symbolic effort to control the world of the dead.

The one-eyed man lacks a conspicuous presence in Taíno mythology. Louis Allaire (1981) has suggested that the one-eye motif may have some relation to the eye-like structure that occurs on the heads of lizards (saurian pineal). If Caribes are associated with Opiyelgobirán, then the cemí known as Corocote merits consideration. Corocote is the twin of Opiyelgobirán. He is associated with amorous sexual escapades (synonymous with anthropophagy) and with the mythical island of Guanín (Roe 1982: 239). In turn, guanín is one of the native Caribbean names for gold and is associated with the rain-

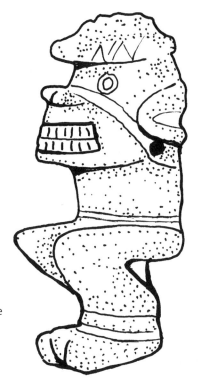

2.3. Pendant depicting the dog spirit, Opiyelgobirán, from the Caicos Islands (12 cm tall and 5 cm wide; National Museum of the American Indian, Smithsonian Institution #03.2200).

bow in the particular form of half-circles interfaced to form a complete circle (Vega 1980). One particularly interesting example of the interfaced rainbows is an ornament made from a human cranium (see Figure 7.1). Although this representation, which gives the appearance of an eye, has been described as a belt ornament, it could just as easily have been worn adorned with feathers on the forehead. Sven Lovén (1935: 506) reports that the cacique's crown was a headband with a gold centerpiece. Moreover, structuralist analysis interprets the rainbow theme as representing the bridge between the binary opposition close:remote (Stevens-Arroyo 1988: 191–193). The rather complicated linking of Opiyelgobirán, Corocote, and Caribes is forged through a layering of contexts that follows the pattern of better-known cosmologies. It is no accident that one-eyed men, dogfaces, and eating human flesh are conjoined.

In the Lévi-Straussian model proposed by Antonio Stevens-Arroyo (1988), Taíno cemíism is divided into twelve principal spirits according to dyadic oppositions. The primary oppositions are male/female, culture/without culture, and close/remote. In Stevens-Arroyo's terminology, this last dyad composes the "Spirits of Fruitfulness" and the "Spirits of Inversion." The first are *cemíes*

Table 2.1. The Taíno Pantheon Based on Ramón Pané

Gender and generation	Order of fruitfulness	Order of inversion
Masculine	Yucahu(guamá)	Maquetaurie Guayaba
	Lord of the yuca	Lord of the dead
Twins	Baibrama	Opiyelguobirán
	Guardian of workers	Guardian of the dead
	Baraguabael	Corocote
	Guardian of nature	Guardian of sexual delights
Feminine	Attabeira	Guabancex
	Earth and serpent mother	Driver of wind and water; hurricane
Twins	Márohu	Guataúba
	Announces the sun	Announces stormy weather; thunder
	Boinayel	Coatrisquie
	Announces the fertilizing rain	Carrier of flood waters

Source: Stevens-Arroyo 1988: 239.

whose activities help the Taínos, and the second are those who do not follow cultural rules: "The Spirits of Inversion, as I have named them, correspond to what Jung would call the unconscious in human psychology. They are intuitive and irrepressible emotional forces that supplant reason, yet provide a feeling in tune with the numinous. They cannot be denied, yet neither can they be anticipated. They come and go as they will . . ." (Stevens-Arroyo 1988: 240).

The distinction between fruitful and destructive spirits is not so clear-cut. Even the spirits of fruitfulness could cause negative results if they were not kept in balance. For example, rain had to come at the right times and in the right amounts. If the spirits were not properly served, an unbalance could occur, to the detriment of the people and their crops.

Two of the cemíes associated with Caribes compose the Masculine Order of Inversion. Moreover, the flesh-eating Caribes quite obviously possess the characteristics of this mythical order: they remove people from their villages (they do not return to life) and therefore consume human flesh. Stevens-Arroyo (1988: 14) interprets this mythic cannibalism as reference to "territorial rights in the process of tribal fissure and the prohibition against return migration rather than to anthropophagy." In other words, the mythology originally grew out of the migratory lifestyle that characterized the peoples who colonized the West Indies (but see below with regard to myth in relation to the justification for a stranger king). This interpretation fits the repetitive theme concerning movement between cultural and supernatural (noncultural) realms (close:remote) found in descriptions of the Caribes.

Finally, the Caribes were ubiquitous. Columbus encountered them in the Bahamas, Cuba, and Hispaniola on his first voyage and continued to speak of

Caribes on later voyages. Caribes were uniformly feared and were always to be found to the east—the direction of open ocean, in which the mythical islands were located. The absence of Caribes from Pané's list of Taíno *cemíes* accounts for their absence from Stevens-Arroyo's table. The question becomes: why did Pané leave Caribes off his list of *cemíes*?

Three possible reasons come to mind. First, and most likely, because the Spanish believed that Caribes and Caníbales were living peoples, Pané would not have attributed references to them as descriptions of the spirit world. Second, given the nature of the data, the research methods, and the short time spent collecting the information, Friar Pané probably failed to complete his list ("Las Casas also says that Ramon was . . . a simple-minded man so that what he reported was sometimes confused and of little substance" [Bourne 1906:314]). Finally, he may have limited his list to the twelve principal *cemíes* because of the importance of the number twelve in his own religion.

In a related incident, all evidence points to the conclusion that Columbus actually made his first landfall (sighting of a light on the horizon before midnight) on October 11 (based on this sighting he claimed the prize of 10,000 *maravedís* offered by the king and queen), yet the date of discovery has been fixed as October 12, the day he went ashore. As a nautical term, "landfall" refers to the sighting of land and not the act of standing on it (Fuson 1987). Moreover, the entry in the *diario* began on October 11 and continued through the day of October 12 without reference to the change in date (all other days were noted specifically in the text; Dunn and Kelley 1989). As mentioned previously, in Catholic numerology the number eleven is associated with desanctification. Columbus was a very religious man, as reflected in his *Libro de las Profecias* (West and Kling 1991). In addition, in his later years he adopted the signature "xpo ferens" (the Christbearer) to signify his belief that he was an instrument of God. Clearly Columbus's interpretations and writings were biased not only by his personal experiences in Europe but also by his beliefs. Whatever the reason for the omission of Caribes in Pané's account, it was only through the deconstruction and structuralist analysis of Columbus's *diario* that Caribes reemerged as a category of spirits.

Perhaps the most telling association of the Caribes with mythology came as Columbus prepared to leave Hispaniola. As noted above, the Taínos viewed Columbus's direction of travel to the east as appropriate for Caribes returning to their home. Columbus was told that to the east were the islands of Matininó, Carib, and Guanín, which contained much gold and copper (Dunn and Kelley 1989: 331, 337, 339, 343). The *diario* entry for January 16 (Dunn and Kelley 1989: 343) reads:

The Indians told him [Columbus] that on that route he would find the island of Matininó, which, he says, was inhabited by women without men. . . . But he says that it was certain that there were such women, and that at a certain time of year men came to them from the said island of Carib, which he says was ten or 12 leagues from them; and that if they gave birth to a boy they sent him to the men's island and if to a girl they let her stay with them.

As Columbus departed from the West Indies on his return to Spain, he believed that the Caribes occupied their own island: Carib Island.

One reason why other investigators have failed to appreciate the mythological significance of this quotation is that they have read it literally. They believed that the Spanish record is an accurate account of Taíno reality. Yet Taíno reality (all reality) is structured by myth. We could spend a lifetime looking for Carib Island, Matininó, or Atlantis, for that matter. Although Morison (1942) and others have identified Matininó with the island of Martinique because the names sound similar, Arrom (1975) has shown that Matininó means literally "without fathers" and that no such island ever existed. By extension it can be concluded that Carib Island existed only in a mythic cosmos.

The charting of the Taínos' mythical geography has only recently begun. Stevens-Arroyo (1988: 159) reports that two "islands" were the focus of mythological events: Matininó, which represents women alone; and Guanín, which represents sexual union. Matininó and Guanín appear to be focal islands, due to their presence in those parts of the mythology that the Spanish recorded, but other islands are also noted. For instance, Coaybay and an island alongside it called Soraya are associated with "the house and the home of the dead" (Stevens-Arroyo 1988: 230). Although not mentioned in the mythology recorded by Ramón Pané, Carib Island is mentioned by Columbus and is predicted by structuralist logic. Carib Island provides the male opposition to Matininó (female) in an insular sexual dyad and completes the triad with Matininó and Guanín (sexual union) (Lévi-Strauss 1963; Roe 1982: fig. 10).

The path of deconstructing the codetermined concepts of "Carib" in Taíno and in Spanish referents has proven somewhat tortuous, so the conclusions reached (given the caveats and justifications above) need to be summarized. First, "Caribe" (and its derivative "Caníbales") is a Taíno word.

Second, Columbus arrived in the Americas looking for the Caniba, literally "the people of the *gra Can*." Columbus came to believe that the Caniba (Canima) were the same as the Caribe and that they were enemies of the Taínos (actually, they were enemies in the sense that death is the enemy/opposite of all living beings). Columbus did not believe that the Caniba ate human flesh. This is worth repeating because it is so important. Columbus recognized that the Taínos thought he was a Cannibal, and he stated specifically that he did not believe that the Caníbales ate human flesh.

Third, Columbus and his men were initially identified as Caribes/Caníbales because they were traveling to the east; they wore clothing, bore arms, and carried off Taínos from their villages.

Fourth, the Taínos believed in mythical beings called Caribes who were associated with the world of the dead. Caribes were typically described as having one eye, having the face of a dog, and eating human flesh. These characteristics match those attributed to the spirits of the dead, Opiyelgobirán and Corocote. These are what Stevens-Arroyo (1988) has called Spirits of Inversion, because they are the antithesis of Taíno culture. Other spirits shared these characteristics, which is in keeping with the redundancy and repetition observed in Native American cosmologies (Roe 1982).

Fifth, Caribes and Caníbales were spirits who had the capacity to cross between the natural and supernatural worlds. Taíno caciques were also able to cross between these realms.

We must also recognize that the Taínos believed in mythical places. These included a land inhabited only by women (Matininó) and a land with much gold (Guanín, also the land of sexual union). These "islands" are cosmographic and not geographic. In addition, structuralist logic would predict a belief in a male land that would complete the female:sexual union:male triad. This role is filled by Carib Island, which was reported by Columbus but missed by later anthropologists (Matininó:Guanín:Carib). Whatever the Spanish really believed, they found it expedient to describe indigenous peoples as anthropophagous to justify their enslavement (Davis and Goodwin 1990). Finally, modern investigators have contributed to the confusion surrounding the native peoples of the West Indies at the time of European contact by their failure to distinguish between myth and reality.

Today most investigators recognize the Island Caribs as a fierce people who invaded the Lesser Antilles just prior to European contact (Rouse 1992). The modifier "Island" is used to distinguish them from Carib peoples living on the mainland. In the seventeenth century the Island Caribs told the French that when they colonized the islands they ate the Island Arawak men who were already living there and took their women as wives. Their claim of eating humans led to their erroneous association with the Caníbales reported by Columbus. Moreover, Columbus's reported discovery of a society that regularly consumed human flesh moved cannibalism to the fore of Western thought. There it has remained, at least since the publication of the essays of Michel de Montaigne (1967) in 1580. As Neil Whitehead (1984) noted, it was the "European pre-occupation with this subject, still evident today, rather than its over-all sociological significance for Carib peoples that necessitates such a detailed treatment of the topic" (81).

It is also reported that the Island Caribs were raiding Puerto Rico from a base on St. Croix when Europeans arrived, yet most Caribbean archaeologists have dismissed this notion (Allaire 1996). In the late fifteenth century the Island Caribs were living in the Lesser Antilles from Guadeloupe south. Allaire believes that the Taínos of the Greater Antilles knew of these people, which must be the case if smelted gold was being obtained from South America (Boomert 1987). If the Taínos knew of the Island Caribs, then they could not possibly have confused the Island Caribs with the Spanish. The Taíno notion of Caribes and the living peoples of the Windward Islands represent completely different categories of meaning.

The Golden House

Oviedo's association of Caonabó with Caribs is of interest because it gives the cacique the characteristics of being mythical (divine) and fierce, which ties directly into the Taíno belief system. Columbus reported that the Taínos were docile and could easily be enslaved (Dunn and Kelley 1989). This myth of the "peaceful Arawaks" has been maintained to the present (Michener 1988). In contrast, Caonabó was considered fierce and was a foreigner. In this regard he embodied the notion of Carib more than the prevailing notion of Taíno.

Other aspects of Caonabó reinforce his mythical status. His name, for example, has been translated as "golden house" or "golden most," yet the chroniclers suggest that Maguana province did not contain a lot of gold (Sauer 1966). Despite a reference to a place called Niti at which gold was procured in Maguana province, the focus of Spanish gold extraction was outside of Caonabó's territory, in the Cibao. Moreover, the name of Caonabós principal wife, Anacaona, has been translated as "golden flower." Arrom (1980) offers a slightly different translation. While he agrees that *caona* can be translated as gold, he notes that *ana* is not the Arawakan word for flower. He concludes that a more accurate translation of her name is "center of heavenly wealth." This translation transforms her association with a physical object (gold) to a more mystical association with *turey* and *guanín*.

Why all this emphasis on gold when the Taínos reportedly had little interest in this mineral? Although gold was not of value in itself, gold that came from somewhere else was valued. In the Taíno worldview this gold or *guanín* came from the sky (*turey*). Here we see the contrast between the Spanish greed for an object of value and a Taíno belief in the significance of exotic things. It reflects two separate meanings associated with the same material.

So Caonabó and Anacaona were "heavenly." The list of synonyms for heavenly must also include *guanín*, *turey*, Carib (for a male), and Matininó (for a female). Columbus himself was addressed with terms for heavenly and Carib, a situation that again reinforces the meaning of something or someone exotic or foreign. Need I further emphasize the importance of the concept of foreign objects and foreign persons?

In the Taíno worldview, caciques were the intermediaries between the sacred and secular; they carried with them a status that we might associate with the divine. Some caciques were carried on litters, and their people followed orders under threat of death. Such absolute authority and the ability to pass between the cultural and supernatural realms suggest that justifications for their status must be contained in Taíno mythology.

One point of articulation again concerns the use of numbers. Four was the perfect number according to the Taínos. This number appears in the repeated mention of Caonabó "and his three brothers." Brothers are never mentioned elsewhere, and in Taíno mythology one of the main antagonisms is between brothers-in-law. We would expect brothers-in-law to be important where matrilocal residence is practiced, because the male moves to the village of his wife. But why emphasize brothers? And why is the only other reference to brothers found in the context of one of two variants of the Taíno origin myth?

One version of the origin myth introduces Deminán (the only one named) and his three twin brothers. The brothers went to the house of the main god Yaya to get food. As they saw him returning, they accidentally dropped the gourd in which the bones of Yaya's son (Yayael) were stored. When the gourd was dropped, the seas were created and the bones of Yayael were transformed into fishes. In this way the people obtained the most important meat source in their diet, but the flood drove Deminán and his three brothers from their primordial home. Moreover, Deminán was tardy in coming to the house and only arrived after Yaya had returned. When he asked Yaya for food (cassava, the Taínos' staple crop), his request was denied. He had to steal cassava for the people. Deminán is the culture hero of this origin myth. It was he, as a man, who obtained the gifts of culture from the gods (Stevens-Arroyo 1988: 111).

Is it a coincidence that the myth tells the story of one named individual who has three unnamed brothers who support him? Stevens-Arroyo (1988) suggests that only Deminán was named because he was specially blessed; he was *caracaracol*, which glosses as "scabby one." This reference is used to denote the rough skin characteristic of someone with syphilis. It was four such scabby ones (identical *caracaracoles*) who captured the eels without genitals that the woodpecker opened into women. *Caracol* is also the name of a crescent-shaped gold ornament that was worn in the nose or the ears. It has been interpreted as equivalent to *turey* and was the most precious possession of the Island Caribs (Rouse 1948: 553).

The *conjoncture* of golden house (or golden most), golden flower, golden ornament, and three unnamed brothers may be a random coincidence. Given his exalted status, however, Caonabó may have been associated personally with the Taíno origin myth. In many cultures it is common to trace the lineage of leaders to the gods or revered ancestors. Peter Siegel (1997) has discussed the role of ancestor worship among the pre-Taíno Saladoid peoples. He associates this worship with a concept of *axis mundi*, in which a central line joins the natural, cultural, and supernatural worlds and provides a bond between the living and the dead. Siegel suggests that the central plaza in which the dead were buried was the *axis mundi* for Saladoid peoples. Yet in Taíno times the central plaza was no longer a cemetery: it was the location of the cacique's house. Thus the cacique appropriated the *axis mundi*, and his *bohío* (house) can be viewed as representing the cave from which the chosen people emerged.

As Stevens-Arroyo (1988: 152–153) points out, "it must be stressed that the richness of symbolism provided in the simple narration recorded by Pané is an integral part of the Taíno religious heritage." Thus the blurring of reality and myth is a natural process. It only seems incommensurate when compared to Western notions of an omnipotent yet separate God. The connection between Caonabó and the mythical ancestors can be pursued in the other version of the Taíno origin myth. In this case, the exalted status of Caonabó may be in part because the caves from which human life emerged were located within his province.

In this Taíno origin myth a section of Hispaniola called Cauta contained two caves: Cacibajagua, which is translated as "Cave of the Jagua," and Amayaúna, which is translated as the "Cave without Importance." After many struggles with the sun, the first people emerged from Cacibajagua. The account of these struggles chastises human failings but also recognizes the importance of Deminán Caracaracol as the mythical ancestor who freed the men from the cave, took gifts of culture from the gods, and helped to create women. Caonabó's cacicazgo, located on the south side of the Cibao mountain range in central Hispaniola, is the logical location for the mythical caves. Moreover, as Stevens-Arroyo (1988) has noted, Taíno mythology is resplendent with the dialectic of close and remote. Caonabó himself reflects this duality in his position as stranger king. His proposed status as the guardian of Cacibajagua would again punctuate the dyad close:remote.

One final reading of Taíno mythology seems remarkably close to ethnohistoric reports concerning Caonabó. The first version of the origin myth relates the story of the chief god Yaya (who had no name), his wife (who had five names), and their son, Yayael. Yayael tried to overthrow his father and was banished. When the son returned after four months, the father killed him, placed his bones in a gourd, and stored them in the rafters of the house. His wife, who was desperate to see her son, later took down the gourd. When she accidentally dropped the gourd, the great sea and all the fishes burst forth.

We can read a number of things into this story. First, as I have argued elsewhere (and argue again in chapter 4), in a matrilineal society the son does not inherit his position from the father. Thus it was wrong of Yayael to attempt to try to assume his father's position, while at the same time it was natural for his mother to try to see his remains (Yayael was a member of his mother's clan). The issue of banishment may also relate to the practice of the son moving away (matrilocal residence) to establish a new household (or found a new settlement on the larger scale). This pattern would fit the practice for a matrilineal conical clan in which brothers from the same mother were the progenitors of new colonies. In this regard Caonabó seems to break the rules. He was a foreigner, a Lucayan, who returned to Hispaniola to assume the mantle of power. Could he have done so if he were not his father's wife's brother's son? Moreover, his three brothers are also mentioned in the chronicles. Brothers are a problem in all societies because they are potential competitors for inheritance. Here again is the jumbling of close and remote. Do the lessons of Taíno mythology describe how people are supposed to behave or how they are not supposed to behave? The challenge is to try to decipher this indigenous theory of culture.

Yet when attempting to deconstruct a text it is possible to devolve into what I have called hermeneutic chaos. It is not simply a matter of following an ever downward spiral but rather an effort to deal with simultaneous meanings. The two origin myths could be rewritten: In the beginning god (Yaya) created fish, and men (Deminán and his brothers) were drawn to eat these fish even though they were the transformed body of god's son (Yayael). Compare this to Catholicism, in which the transubstantiation of the body and blood of Christ (God's son) is the basis for the sacrament of the Eucharist. Moreover, Christ's 12 apostles were called "fishers of men." Did Ramón Pané create a Taíno (Macorix) belief system based on the most cherished truths of Catholicism? Once again, Sahlins provides a parallel with the Fijian phrase that translates as "fish-

Table 2.2. Summary of the Mythical Qualities Attributed to Caonabó

His name is translated as "golden house" or "golden most"
His principal wife's name is translated as "golden flower"
Gold is associated with the mythical island of Guanín

Oviedo described him as a Carib (Caribe), which were mythical beings to the Taínos
Las Casas described him as a Lucayo, a foreigner
Foreign gold (*guanín*) was the most precious object of the Taínos (*turey*)

He had three unnamed brothers, as did the culture hero Deminán
He was the guardian of the sacred caves from which human life emerged

---

ers of fish, fishers of men" (see Hocart 1952: 120–121). They are "fishers of turtle for ceremonial occupation, but fishers of men when the chief has need for human sacrifices" (Sahlins 1985: 100).

Conclusions

We cannot discount the role that myths played in coloring what the Spanish wrote about Caonabó and the Taínos. Mythology, fables, parables, and other "just so" stories are never straightforward. These (in this case oral) traditions reproduce the Taínos' separate reality by turning it on its head, sidewise, and in other dimensions. What an outsider might interpret as a prescription, a member of the culture would easily recognize as sarcasm and proscription (see Roe 1982). For this reason I have tried to summarize the "facts."

The Spanish certainly misinterpreted the stories that they were told by the Taínos. They also imposed their own concepts of nature and culture on the stories that they wrote—tales that are now our histories and/or ethnohistories. Furthermore, their reports were written to present themselves in the best light. Such self-interest produced conflicting results. Columbus's *diario* was written with exuberance at finding gold and the best and finest people, harbors, and lands in world. As counterpoint, the writings of Bartolomé de las Casas derided the Spanish treatment of the Taínos and extolled the virtues of the native peoples.

To impose myself on this analysis once again, Caonabó fascinates me because he was identified as a Lucayan. First, there is a personal empowerment in that Caribbean archaeologists for years have viewed the Bahamas (Lucayan Islands) as peripheral to Caribbean archaeology. In other words, "you don't do Caribbean archaeology if you work in the Bahamas." Yet *my* islands produced the most powerful cacique in all of the West Indies! Second, Caonabó's history seems to fit perfectly with the organization of an avunculocal chiefdom

(Keegan and Maclachlan 1989). Thus, to my mind, the strictures of the Taíno sociopolitical system allowed for the possibility of a foreigner who assumed a position of supreme status. In fact, if we are correct in concluding that succession passed from a mother's brother to his nephew, then every cacique would be a stranger king (next chapter). None of the other alternatives would allow for this. Finally, there are very few large and complicated sites in the Bahamas that are worthy candidates for the homeland of this stranger king.

Postscript

Because we are dealing with men of action (actions of men?), it is worth taking a final look at what happened to Christopher Columbus. By 1499 the Spanish rulers had grown weary of Columbus. They initially had failed to realize how valuable the Americas could be and had granted him far too many concessions. Moreover, he was a terrible administrator, he made excessive claims of impending wealth that he never delivered, he was always in need of additional support, and he was repeatedly denounced by those who had abandoned his colony and returned to Spain. As a last resort, the king and queen sent Francisco de Bobadilla to inspect the colony and report on its status.

Bobadilla sailed from Spain in late June 1500 with plenary powers and with a commission to remove Columbus from his position as governor (Sauer 1966: 102). When he arrived in the harbor at Santo Domingo, his first sight was of Spaniards hanging from gallows on either side of the Río Ozama. Five Spaniards had been hung the previous week, and five others were awaiting execution. Infuriated, Bobadilla stormed into the city of Santo Domingo only to find that Columbus was away in the interior, chasing Spaniards who refused to submit to his rule. Bobadilla immediately took control of the colony and had Columbus and his brothers Diego and Bartholomew shackled and imprisoned when they returned. They were sent to Spain on the first available ship to stand trial. When Columbus reached Spain, the monarchs released him; but the Hispaniola colony was never again his to govern. After completing his duties, Bobadilla set out to return to Spain but died when his ship sank in the hurricane of July 1502.

Christopher Columbus was allowed one final expedition. In 1502–1504 he sailed with four ships to the coast of Central America. Two ships were lost due to shipworms on the Río Belén in Panama.[8] Columbus sailed his remaining two ships to Jamaica. The ships were leaking so badly that he ran them aground on the north coast. Columbus and his crews lived on these ships in St. Ann's Bay for over a year. The story goes that he built a canoe and sent Diego Méndez as a representative to the governor of Hispaniola, seeking assistance.

Méndez found Governor Ovando in Xaragua, where he witnessed the execution of Anacaona and her subordinate caciques. Ovando supposedly replied that the rescue operation would be expensive and that he wanted to be paid for such services in advance.

Whatever really transpired, Columbus did manage to get back to Spain in November 1504. He arrived only days before his main supporter, Queen Isabel, died. It is possible that by this time Columbus was insane. His account of the final voyage suggests a man who had taken leave of his senses (Sauer 1966). Columbus would remain in Spain, where he died penniless in 1506. That was the end of the Admiral of the Ocean Sea. Was it irony, pathos, fate, or justice that led Columbus and the Taínos to the same end?

Actually, Columbus did have one more expedition—or should I say exposition: the Columbian Exposition in Chicago in 1893–1894. At this time he was resurrected as a tragic hero and mythical ancestor of the United States of America just in time for the 400th anniversary of his first voyage (Irving 1828; Wilford 1991). He was promoted as embodying the American Dream: a man who stood by his convictions, worked hard, and forever changed the world.

Caonabó's Homeland

The narrative in chapter 2 presented my characterization of initial encounters between the Spanish and the native peoples of Hispaniola. The main goals of the chapter were to establish the importance of Caonabó as a historical and mythical figure and to examine the basic layering of contexts that were combined to create his story. It should be clear not only that the story contains an accounting of actual deeds by living persons but that these persons were imbued with qualities that I have chosen to describe as mythical. In other words, we are not simply dealing with ethnographic "facts": we are dealing with meanings created by the Taínos, by Columbus, by the chroniclers, and by me.

The main premise, assumption if you will, is that Caonabó was one of the most powerful chiefs on the island. Ample evidence indicates that at least some of the personal characteristics attributed to Caonabó reflect an effort to establish his divinity among the Taínos and his role as the principal protagonist for the Spanish. In this regard, Caonabó was a mythical (legendary) figure. I call this myth because modern Western culture does not recognize divinity as a human characteristic, although the Taínos apparently did. Moreover, in my opinion, the Spanish used this notion of divinity to inflate their deeds in capturing and deposing this Taíno demigod. In other words, the Spanish not only conquered the native societies but had to overcome a supernatural being to do so.

Second, the story of Caonabó's capture was so important it was retold by the three principal Spanish chroniclers of the day (and in three different versions). This event must have been viewed as the defining moment of the conquest. Thus we would expect that all of the tools in the chronicler's palette were used to create a compelling story. I have noted the use of Roman Catholic modes of expression, especially with regard to numerology. We can question the degree to which numbers were imposed on the story, but the numbers of individuals involved in the capture may reflect the superiority of Catholic beliefs, in which the perfect number is ten (Hojeda and his horsemen), over Taíno numerology, in which four is the perfect number (Caonabó and his three brothers).

Finally, the symbolic significance that the Taínos attached to gold (*guanín* or *turey*) was very different from the primarily economic meaning that the Spanish attached to gold. In sum, accounts of Caonabó and his capture conflated local and European belief systems and economic goals.

The main conclusion of the narrative is that Caonabó was a real and very powerful individual. Although he was imbued with mythical qualities, a broader view of his life can be inferred. As Las Casas wrote:

> Este [Caonabó], fue valerosisimo y enforzado señor, y de mucha gravedad y autoridad, y segun entendimos a los principos a esta isla [Española] vinimos era de nacion Lucayo, natural de las islas de los Lucayos, que se pasó dellas acá, y por ser varon en las guerras y en la paz señalado, llegó a ser rey de aquella provincia [Maguana] y por todos muy estimado.

Was he correct? Did Caonabó come from the Lucayan Islands?

In order to address those questions we need to examine additional layers of meaning and context. The goal here is to place Caonabó in spatial and historical relief and to identify the places where he lived. The main premise is that an individual who achieved the power and status attributed to Caonabó did not come from an ordinary village in the Lucayan Islands. This is a huge assumption. Yet all narratives are based on such assumptions, and in the end it is the reader who must judge whether the weight of the evidence bears out such underlying beliefs.

The archaeology of the earliest encounters between the Spanish and the Taínos has been well established during the past two decades. Excavations on the island that Columbus renamed La Amiga in the Mar de Santo Tomás (Baie de l'Acul, Haiti) have indicated the need to revise the culture history for the area and to recognize that what is called Taíno is the product of multiple interacting groups with distinct cultural attributes. In addition, excavations have been undertaken at the places identified as Columbus's first settlements of La Navidad (1492) and La Isabela (1493) (Deagan 1987, 1989, 2004; Deagan and Cruxent 2002). These excavations provide material evidence for the evaluation of early interactions between the Spanish and the Taínos. For instance, the chroniclers reported that the Spanish town of San Juan de Maguana was established in the village of Caonabó. Finally, archaeological surveys to identify Lucayan settlement patterns have investigated all the major islands in the Bahama archipelago (Keegan 1992). Information from all these sources is used to identify Caonabó's position in the regional political hierarchy and to identify the Lucayan settlement at which he may have spent his youth.

Frame of Reference: Time-Space Systematics

Before turning to specific localities we need to establish a broader frame of reference. For more than 60 years archaeologists have labored to place the material remains recovered from prehistoric sites in spatial and historical boxes. Who lived where and when did they live there? In order to evaluate the arguments that follow, the reader needs a basic introduction to the culture history and familiarity with terms that are specific to the region.

For the most part, these historical and spatial boxes (time-space systematics) were created by classifying pottery decorations and other aspects of material culture according to their degree of similarity and difference. The basic assumption has been that similar modes of form and decoration denote similar norms, which in turn denote the peoples and cultures that produced them (Rouse 1972). In short, our cloud of culture can be defined according to similarities and differences in material remains. Everywhere we encounter assemblages of diagnostic "modes" (for example, fine-line incised decoration) we are observing a particular culture. I do not intend to justify or contradict this method for defining cultures but simply wish to point out the basic premise of the time-space model as it has been applied in the West Indies.

The dominant culture-historical framework is based on the theoretical orientation of Irving Rouse (1939). Rouse (1992) developed a system of classification that has provided the basic framework for the region. He uses a three-tiered taxonomy in which increasing larger spatial units were grouped together based on similarities observed in the material remains (Curet 2004). The smallest units are called "styles," which are based on the range of characteristics ("modes") observed in a very localized area. In this regard they contain the widest range of diversity. For example, there was a widespread use of fine-line incised decorations on pottery vessels in Haiti, Cuba, and Jamaica. Anyone working with site assemblages from these areas will immediately recognize differences in form and execution, which can be interpreted as reflecting differences in the norms of representation in these areas. At least five distinct styles employing fine-lined incision have been identified: Meillac (Haiti), Finca (southwestern Haiti), Bani (Cuba), White Marl (Jamaica), and Montego Bay (western Jamaica). These styles are named for the archaeological site at which they were first described.

Because those styles share a common decorative technique (fine-line incision), although they differ somewhat in execution, they have been grouped into a more encompassing category called a "subseries." Subseries are named for one of the styles with the addition of -*an* as a suffix. In the present example, all five of those styles are classified as members of the Meillacan subseries.

3.1. Ostionan pottery from Haiti (Florida Museum of Natural History collections).

3.2. Meillacan pottery from Haiti (Florida Museum of Natural History collections).

Finally, the broadest category is the "series." Series are named for a particular style but are distinguished by the use of *-oid* as a suffix. The Meillacan Ostionoid series is an example of the broadest level of classification. At this level the diverse styles in different sites on different islands are classified as conforming to an overarching normative framework or historical tradition. In practice such traditions are equivalent to what archaeologists once called "culture."

Recently, the concept of series has been associated with notions of historical continuity. Series represent an evolutionary trajectory in which new "modes" are viewed as having been added to an existing template or tradition. As a result, subseries may share very few similarities. For example, the initial appearance of Ostionoid pottery is classified on the basis of the Ostiones style of the Ostionan subseries.[1] Ostionan subseries pottery looks nothing like Meillacan subseries pottery, although both subseries are lumped into the Ostionoid series. Ostionan pottery is characterized by red-paste and red-painted vessels with no use of incision and little appliqué, while Meillacan pottery in many areas has a black paste and complicated incised and appliqué decorations but almost no use of red paint. If we were to look at these subseries (Figures 3.1 and 3.2), the indisputable conclusion would be that they represent entirely different cultures. Why would anyone classify such different subseries as members of the same series?

To answer that question we need to make a very brief tour of Caribbean culture history to provide a basic background to the Ceramic Age in the region and to provide the reader with the basic tools needed to evaluate the arguments that follow. But first, I offer the answer to the question of classification. Rouse (1992) views all of the Ceramic Age as developing along a single trajectory. Thus there must be a single line of development, despite the dramatic differences between the Meillacan and Ostionan subseries. Rouse has maintained the belief that all of the late Ceramic Age in the Greater Antilles was an indigenous, local development. Once the first propagule of Ceramic Age peoples arrived in the islands, there was no further migration of peoples from South America (or other locations) that could have affected the evolution of ceramic styles. In contrast, other archaeologists have identified every change in pottery style as representing the migration of new peoples and cultures (for example, Chanlatte Baik 2003; Rainey 1941; Veloz Maggiolo 1991). This is the classic example of why the either/or dialect does not work (see the discussion below).

Following Rouse (1992), a bare-bones outline of Caribbean culture history can be written as follows (details are added later in this chapter). About 5000 BC peoples employing a flaked-stone-blade technology migrated from Belize

3.3. Chican pottery from Hispaniola (Florida Museum of Natural History collections).

to Cuba and then onto Hispaniola (Lithic Age) (Wilson et al. 1998). About 3000 BC a second wave of migrants from South America entered the islands and introduced the use of a ground-stone technology (Archaic Age) (compare Callaghan 2003). The Archaic culture occupied the northern Lesser Antilles and spread west into Cuba, although likely interactions with the indigenous Lithic Age peoples are not well defined. More details could be added (Keegan 1994), but the essential information is that people practicing flaked-stone and ground-stone technologies were living in the islands when the next wave of immigrants arrived.

The Ceramic Age begins with the introduction of pottery making and horticulture from the Orinoco River basin of northeastern Venezuela (compare Keegan 2006b). These people reached Puerto Rico by 400 BC, although they did not occupy the islands to the north and west until about 1,000 years later. The earliest immigrants manufactured Saladoid series ceramics, named for the Saladero site on the Orinoco River. Two subseries have been defined: the Cedrosan Saladoid, which includes a wide variety of vessel shapes decorated with painted, incised, and modeled decorations; and the Huecan Saladoid, which lacks painting. The meanings of the Cedrosan and Huecan Saladoid have been hotly contested but are beyond the objectives of this book (see Chanlatte Baik 1981, 2003; Hofman and Hoogland 1995; Rouse 1992).

The key issue for current purposes is the origin of the culture that we call Taíno. Conventional wisdom holds that a new Ostionan Ostionoid series developed in Puerto Rico around AD 600 and spread north and west into the remainder of the islands. The Ostionan migrants then gave rise to Meillacan Ostionan peoples in central Hispaniola about AD 650, and these people spread west and north into Cuba, Jamaica, and the Bahama archipelago. The Ostionan Ostionoid were also the progenitors of the Chican Ostionoid, which developed in the southeastern Dominican Republic around AD 800. Chican motifs spread west across Hispaniola into eastern Cuba and south and east as far as Saba (Curet 1992a; Hofman 1993). The distribution of Chican Ostionoid pottery (Figure 3.3) is viewed as reflecting the distribution of the ethnohistoric Taínos. According to this scheme, the ethnohistoric Taínos are viewed as the outcome of cultural evolution in Puerto Rico untainted by outside influences (Rouse 1992).

In essence, Caribbean culture history is a narrative. It is the story of how "peoples and cultures" colonized the islands and how their material culture (mostly pottery decorations) changed through time (see Rouse 1992).[2] It is crucial that we examine the assumptions on which this classification system was based. Does the distribution of Chican Ostionoid pottery accurately represent the distribution of Taíno culture? Was Ostionan Ostionoid pottery the foundation on which all subsequent pottery styles developed? Was Puerto Rico the hearth and home of Taíno culture? In sum, who were the "Taínos" that the Spanish chroniclers described? As these questions indicate, the handwriting is on the wall. What follows is a different view of Caribbean culture history that challenges the most basic and cherished beliefs. It is a view that moves Puerto Rico from center stage to the periphery.

Rouse (1992) set his baseline in Puerto Rico. I argue that the baseline needs to be moved to Hispaniola. Moreover, the ethnohistory of Hispaniola should no longer be applied uncritically to the archaeology of Puerto Rico, Cuba, and other areas simply because Chican Ostionoid pottery is present (Curet 1996; Curet and Oliver 1998; Oliver 1998; Siegel 1997). For example, Antonio Curet (2003: 19) recently noted that Puerto Rican societies had a distinct political organization: "Hispaniolan and Puerto Rican polities used significantly different ideological foundations, a reflection of differences in the nature of the political structure and organizations." He continued: "Judging from the striking differences mentioned, they likely developed from distinct types of ancestral societies, and/or through different and divergent historical processes" (Curet 2003: 20). If the organizations of these societies were different and distinct, then there is no reason to expect that the archaeology and ethnohistory of these different groups will be the same. The current work focuses on the archaeology of those areas for which we have written accounts; yet these written accounts are not tantamount to ethno-facts (Maclachlan and Keegan 1990).

Hispaniola

First Encounters

Hispaniola is today split between the Republic of Haiti (western one-third) and the Dominican Republic (eastern two-thirds). Sailing from Cuba, Columbus arrived at the western end of Haiti near the modern settlement of Môle Saint-Nicolas. Moving onto the north coast, his expedition encountered several problems. First, the channel between Tortuga and the main island proved to be difficult to navigate. A strong current runs to the west, and the strong trade winds seem to be amplified in the channel. Columbus's ships progressed very slowly as they tacked back and forth against these twin natural forces. I can attest to the difficulty of this passage. We made a trip from Cap Haïtien to Môle Saint-Nicolas in a motorboat. It took less than five hours to reach Môle, but our return trip took over eight hours to cover the 110 km. In addition to the problem of trade winds and currents, there are often high seas in the channel even in the absence of storms.

Columbus reported that the main villages in the area were located upriver and were not on the coast. The first village that his men visited was along the Trois Rivières near modern Port de Paix. It was described as having 1,000 houses and 3,000 men. If the Spanish were counting only heads of households, this would translate to a population of more than 15,000! Once peaceful relations had been established, Columbus's two ships were visited by hundreds of Taínos who came in canoes or swam to the ships—on one day more than a thousand (Dunn and Kelley 1989). Even given Columbus's penchant for exaggeration, this area must have had a very large population.

La Amiga (Île à Rat)

On December 20 Columbus entered the Baie de l'Acul, Haiti. He named the outer harbor Mar de Santo Tomás and described it as large enough to hold all the ships in the world (Dunn and Kelley 1989: 275). In this sea he also observed a small sandy island that he renamed La Amiga ("girlfriend"). There is no report of people living on the island, but sailors aboard the *Niña* reported that "rhubarb" was seen growing on the island. Several days later, after the sinking of the *Santa María*, Columbus sent a longboat to this cay from Guacanagarí's village to collect some of this plant. As Dunn and Kelley (1989: 275n1) note, however, this is not the same plant that we call rhubarb but rather an Asian plant that was used for medicinal purposes.

Today La Amiga is called Île à Rat, although the original French name may have been Île Ara (Macaw Island). The archaeological site on Île à Rat occupies all of this tiny island or cay (less than 1 square acre), which guards the mouth of the Baie de l'Acul (Keegan 2001). Located 2 km from the main island, it is composed of calcareous sand with humic enrichment. The surrounding marine environments include extensive coral reefs, bare sand, and seagrass shoals. The inner part of the bay is a large lagoon with a constricted opening. It is a major nursery area for marine fishes, and the entire region is today heavily fished from nearby coastal villages. This huge shallow bay continues to support thousands of people in the surrounding countryside, despite severe resource depletion after 7,000 years of use and abuse.

Because the island is so small it is possible that it was used only as a fishing camp. Based on our findings, however, it appears that there were permanent habitations on the island. The excavations that we completed were made in a midden deposit near the center of the island. The deposit, over 70 cm deep, contained a high percentage of decorated pottery, some bowl fragments with burned food remains on their interiors, and a substantial number of griddle sherds that would have been used to bake cassava bread. In addition, the remains of meals were apparent in the quantity of small mollusks and fish bones that we recovered. These deposits contain the full range of materials expected for a long-term settlement and do not look like the product of repeated short-term occupations. We would expect far less decorated pottery and less evidence for meal preparation if this were simply a fishing camp (Grouard et al. n.d.; Keegan et al. n.d.). Further investigations are needed to define activities on the island more fully.

The island is the ideal location for a small settlement. It is located amid abundant marine resources, it affords a vantage of the entire bay, and it is breezier and less mosquito infested than the main island. One possible impediment to permanent settlement is finding a source of potable water. It is possible that the island supports a small freshwater lens, probably just behind the beach. But even if water was not readily available on the island, a freshwater spring on the eastern point of the entrance to the inner lagoon of the Baie de l'Acul is only a short boat ride away. From Île à Rat a local chief could monitor trade and resource extraction along a substantial length of coastline.

One factor in the occupation of the island concerns the procurement of marine resources. A steady supply of fish and shellfish was needed for the large villages that were upriver and away from the coast. The need for marine protein seems to have been especially pressing, because it is reported that only a five-day to eight-day supply of food was on hand (Sauer 1966). Given the absence of significant populations of terrestrial fauna, specialized fishermen living on the coast would have been crucial to the survival of inland settlements on Hispaniola. In a related case, some of the coastal villages in southern Cuba, where the land was poor, are reported to have specialized in fishing (Lovén 1935: 504). As discussed below, fresh and preserved meats likely were imported from the southern Bahamas (Turks and Caicos Islands). Yet the sea can be unpredictable. Days can pass when fishing is nonproductive or even impossible. Meats had to be preserved, and the Taínos accomplished this by smoking and salting fish. Moreover, test excavations revealed that the entire island is literally carpeted with juvenile conch shells. There are far more *Strombus gigas* shells than we would expect in a settlement of this size. In addition, most of the fish bones in the site are the head parts of small fishes, which may reflect the processing of fishes prior to their export to villages on the main island (Grouard et al. n.d.).

Despite its small size, Île à Rat was probably a spiritually charged place. In this regard it is telling that the Taíno origin myth begins with the creation of the sea and fishes. As noted earlier, in the beginning god (Yaya) created fishes, and people were drawn to eat these fishes even though they were the transformed bones of god's son (Yayael). Fishes represent the beginning of time. This mythic association correlates with the importance of fish in Taíno subsistence. In other words, fish were not only good to think about: they were good to eat. The spirits had to be propitiated. The discovery of a shell tube for inhaling *cohoba* (a narcotic snuff) on the island is evidence for ritual activities associated with communication with the supernatural realm.

The notion of small islands or cays as spiritually charged places has not previously been espoused for the West Indies. Yet small offshore cays apparently were of special significance to the Taínos and Lucayans. Archaeological sites have been found on virtually every tiny cay in the Bahamas, and those that have been excavated show substantial evidence for ritual activities. For example, a shell inlay carved to represent teeth may originally have been part of a wooden statue left on Pelican Cay, Middle Caicos (described below). Furthermore, the sites on small cays in the Bahamas contain far more decorated potsherds from vessels imported from the Greater Antilles (as denoted by their noncarbonate tempers) than do sites on the main islands. These small islands may have been viewed as the back of a turtle poised in the heart of the most productive fishing grounds.

The pottery, faunal remains, and other materials in the site suggest that there were long-term residents on Île à Rat. It is likely that a few families lived here as representatives of a cacique who lived in a village on the main island. In many island societies the ruler controls access to all of the productive resources in their territory (see Kirch 2000). Long-term residents on Île à Rat could have supervised fishing in the area, collected "taxes," and provided hospitality and respite for fishermen caught in a sudden storm. Columbus's report that rhubarb was growing on the island suggests that there were gardens, although the island is not large enough to provide sufficient horticultural produce to feed a large group. Moreover, pottery, stone, and possibly water all had to be procured from the main island. Exchange, then, was the lifeblood of the settlement. In other words, while the cacique was dependent on the vigilance of his representatives on the island and on the marine foods that were transferred to the main island, the people who were living on Île à Rat were dependent on resources obtained from the main island.

Several scenarios could be proposed to account for the individuals who may have lived on the island. The Taíno worldview would suggest that a proper cultural balance required the presence of men, women, and children. These dimensions of age and gender were essential complements, and such complementarities should have been reproduced on this spiritually charged island. With regard to gender, it was men who cleared the fields and women who tended the gardens; and it was women who made the nets and men who used them to capture fishes (Las Casas reports that Lucayan women made the fishing nets; see Lovén 1935). Such an engendered economy requires the participation of both sexes. Furthermore, children represent continuity in a society and embody additional balance through their membership in the lineage of one parent and eventual bond through marriage in an affinal lineage. More mundane functions would be the contributions of children to the gleaning of small fishes, mollusks, echinoids, and crustaceans from tide pools and the shallows, childcare for younger siblings, and the process of learning the proper roles and activities expected of adult members of the society.

Returning to the archaeological evidence, the island has two distinct cultural components that are separated by a stratum of sterile sand. One or more storm events probably deposited this sand, because the few potsherds recovered from this stratum have an abraded, water-worn appearance. There is very little mixing of the cultural components. The pottery in the lower strata is predominantly Meillacan (dated to between AD 900 and 1300 on the island), although there is also Ostionan subseries pottery intermingled at the lowest levels. It is worth noting that archaeological surveys conducted along the coast revealed small Meillacan sites on virtually every sand beach in the Baie. These small sites reflect a more dispersed population distribution at this time and more direct access to the sea. For some reason these low-lying coastal beaches were abandoned by the end of the Meillacan period. The absence of Chican sherds on these sites suggests that they were abandoned before the beginning of the Chican period (dated to between AD 1300 and 1500 on the island). It is possible is that rising sea level made these locations unsuited for habitation (see Scudder 2001). Or it may reflect their inundation by storms and the reorganization of Taíno communities into larger settlements oriented toward the interior.

Fishing practices also changed. Stone and pottery net sinkers (*potalas*) are common in the Chican deposits on Île à Rat (Figure 3.4) but are absent from the Meillacan strata. Furthermore, virtually identical stone net sinkers were found at the contact period sites of En Bas Saline and La Isabela in Hispaniola (Deagan, personal communication, 2005; Deagan and Cruxent 2002: fig. 2.8) and also are reported from Puerto Rico and Cuba (Martínez Arango 1997). Despite the absence of such net weights in Meillacan strata, the presence of a shell net gauge indicates that Meillacan peoples also were using nets (Figure 3.5). Because nets can be used in various ways, the differences between these strata probably reflect a shift in technology. During Meillacan times stationary seine nets may have been used. The grapefruit-sized stone balls found in the deposit may have been the weights for such nets. In contrast, the small, thin, and flat net weights found in the Chican deposit would have been ideal for cast nets. The flat surface of these stones would promote their aerodynamic movement when cast, and their thin profile would facilitate the full weight of the stone dropping and closing the net after contact with the surface of the water. Although Richard Price (1966) has reported that cast nets were not used in the Americas prior to European contact, the remains of small, bait-sized, schooling fishes in pre-Columbian deposits suggest that some means for netting these fishes must have been used. Cast nets are today the preferred method for capturing such fishes.

Finally, there also were changes in the way in which meals were cooked. Meillacan pottery is characterized by in-turned, casuela and boat-shaped vessels. In contrast, Chican vessels were larger and flared outward from the shoulder. Vessels with a restricted opening are better suited for the transport of liquids and limit contamination from dust and dirt. These features were incorporated in Chican vessels, which are constricted at the shoulder; but their outward-flaring rim would provide greater access to the contents and facilitate their manipulation during cooking (Espenshade 2000). Thus the foods cooked during Meillacan times may have emphasized a more liquid process such as boiling fish, while the more open Chican vessels would have been well suited for pepper pot and thicker stews, which may have required periodic stirring to prevent the contents from burning.

3.4. Stone net sinkers from Île à Rat (photo by Betsy Carlson).

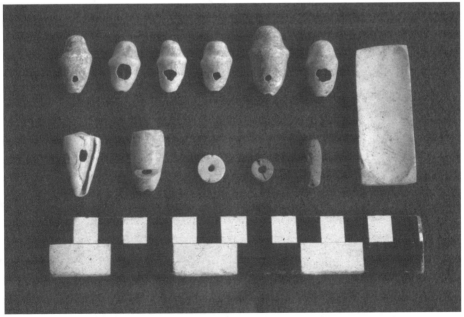

3.5. Shell net gauge (*far right*) and other shell fishing implements (photo by Betsy Carlson).

In sum, Île à Rat presents the reflected reality of Taíno culture. The island is tiny, yet its catchment provided an abundance of marine resources that far exceeded the productive capacity of the larger, inland settlements in terms of protein. Moreover, the island was strategically located and spiritually charged. Thus we would expect the engendered economy to be reproduced on the island. Finally, there is evidence for changes in subsistence strategies and food preparation, and the ceramics indicate the need to revise the current ceramic chronology.

Île à Rat and the Regional Ceramic Chronology

The site on Île à Rat is of special significance to archaeologists because the pottery there indicates that we need to revise the ceramic chronology for the islands west of Puerto Rico. As expected, there is a clear break between the Meillacan and Chican occupations on the island. The Meillacan deposit is below the Chican deposit, with a sterile layer of sand separating the two. A different situation occurs in the lowest strata, where Meillacan and Ostionan sherds are found together. This mixing of styles could be explained as part of an evolutionary sequence during which Meillacan motifs gradually replaced Ostionan decorations. This does not seem to be the case, however, because the Meillacan and Ostionan sherds have completely different pastes (Cordell 1998). Thus Île à Rat provides our first indication that these styles were contemporaneous. If pottery styles reflect broader cultural differences, then two different cultures were living in this area. Evidence from elsewhere on Hispaniola and in the Turks and Caicos Islands reinforces this conclusion. To appreciate the full ramifications of this situation it will be necessary to take a broader view of time-space systematics.

We know that Saladoid pottery is present in archaeological sites on Puerto Rico by 400 BC, and it is possible that Saladoid pottery also moved across the Mona Passage to the eastern Dominican Republic at an early date. Because Cedrosan Saladoid motifs are for the most part absent, however, Rouse (1986) proposed that there was a frontier on the Mona Passage that was not breached until 1,000 years later during the Ostionan Ostionoid wave of expansion (circa AD 600). According to this framework, the Ceramic Age peoples in all of the Greater Antilles are the descendants of Ostionan Ostionoid peoples from Puerto Rico.

In contrast, research by Marcio Veloz Maggiolo and Elpidio Ortega indicates that pottery was being made in the eastern Dominican Republic by 350 BC. This Punta Cana style is composed of motifs that are characteristic of both Meillac and Boca Chica styles (Veloz Maggiolo and Ortega 1996; compare Rouse 1941). In these styles painting was largely abandoned in favor of modeled, incised, and appliqué decorations. Whether pottery making diffused across the Mona Passage to Archaic peoples already living there or whether Ceramic Age peoples from Puerto Rico migrated to the Dominican Republic is not yet clear. In any case, an interesting juxtaposition emerges. In eastern Puerto Rico and Vieques Island some social groups abandoned painting in favor of zoned-incised-crosshatch designs (Rodríguez 1989). This Huecoide or Huecan Saladoid phenomenon has generated substantial debate, especially with regard to whether it reflects a separate migration from South America (for example, Chanlatte Baik 1981; Hofman and Hoogland 1995; Rodríguez Ramos 1999). We now see a similar and somewhat earlier abandonment of painting in favor of incised and appliqué motifs in the eastern Dominican Republic. Moreover, Meillacan designs, which are more developed in western Hispaniola, Cuba, and Jamaica, also show a preference for the zoned-incised-crosshatch decorations that are the most common Huecan motif. In contrast, the primary style in western Puerto Rico (Ostionan) maintained the use of red paint to the exclusion of incised and modeled designs.

In the traditional version of the ceramic chronology, the Ceramic Age in Cuba began with the arrival of Ostionoid colonists from the east (Rouse 1992). Yet recent investigations have revealed an ever-increasing number of sites at which pottery is found in association with an Archaic stone-tool kit (Dacal Moure and Rivero de la Calle 1984; Jouravleva 2002). In the eastern Dominican Republic the El Caimito, Guayabal, and Punta Cana sites have pottery associated with Archaic tools dating back to at least 350 BC. Because these sites are close to Puerto Rico, however, where pottery making was introduced by about 400 BC, the presence of pottery in these sites has been interpreted as the result of diffusion across the Mona Passage and not as a separate and unique phenomenon.

The situation in Cuba is less easy to explain. Radiocarbon dates from the Jorajuría and Playita sites in Matanzas, if correct, indicate that pottery was present as a component of Archaic assemblages by 2160 BC (Jouravleva 2002). Furthermore, there are other dates that also precede the arrival of Ostionan colonists (circa AD 700). In the vicinity of Guantanamo Bay, for example, Jorge Ulloa Hung and Roberto Valcárcel Rojas (2002) have identified sites with pottery that are radiocarbon dated to AD 250 and 350. Most of the pottery in these sites is simple and plain, lacking any diagnostic characteristics. Nevertheless, pottery making arrived much earlier in Cuba and Hispaniola than has been admitted (compare Rouse 1992). It is not yet clear whether this technology was dispersed from Puerto Rico at an early date, whether it arrived from other regions such as Florida or Central America, or whether it reflects an independent invention.

This conjunction of an Archaic lithic technology with ceramics has been variously termed "apropiadores ceramistas" (Ulloa Hung and Valcárcel Rojas 1997), "ceramica temprano" (Ulloa Hung and Valcárcel Rojas 2002), and "protoagricola" (Dacal Moure and Rivero de la Calle 1984; Pablo Godo 1997). It has become the major focus of Cuban archaeologists, because its interpretation currently defies traditional Marxist categories of cultural evolution (Keegan and Rodríguez Ramos 2005). It also defies traditional Caribbean taxonomic dogma (for example, Rouse 1992). In sum, beginning as early as 2000 BC, peoples who used a flaked-stone technology began to use pottery, albeit as a minor component of their toolkit. The reasons for adopting pottery are not yet evident, but the presence of pottery points to changes in pre-Columbian Cuban societies that merit further investigation.

Whatever the original source, it is possible that Meillacan style pottery can be pushed back in time by more than 800 years (to 350 BC). If this is the case, then it is not the outgrowth of the Ostionoid series, which developed in Puerto Rico after AD 600 (see Rouse 1992 and Siegel 1992). In this regard, the Meillac style would more accurately be described as a derivative of the Punta Cana style (Veloz Maggiolo and Ortega 1996). The identification of a separate origin for at least the Meillacan subseries is also supported by the association of Meillacan design motifs with decorations observed on the stone bowls produced by Archaic peoples (Rouse 1992). Petrographic analysis of pottery samples from the north coast of Hispaniola by Ann Cordell (1998) showed that Meillacan pottery has a distinctive paste and thus reflects a different tradition from Ostionan and Chican subseries pottery from the same area. In other words, although Ostionan and Chican subseries share certain paste characteristics, Meillacan subseries pottery reflects entirely different methods of making and decorating pottery. In the old days these differences would have been sufficient to define a distinct ceramic tradition (see Rouse 1939, 1941, 1992).

Conventional wisdom views the development of Taíno Culture as commencing about AD 1000 with the Ostionan Ostionoid pottery series. In addition to changes in the pottery, the emergence of Taíno Culture in Puerto Rico was marked by a shift from personal objects of significance to the development of ball courts and communal architecture along with changes in house form and burial practices (Curet 1992b, 1996; Curet and Oliver 1998; Roe 1995b; Rouse 1992). These developments began with the terminal Saladoid development of an Ostionan pottery subseries that is viewed as having been exported from Puerto Rico to neighboring islands. As argued here, however, the notion that Taíno Culture is captured in the evolution of pottery series from Cedrosan Saladoid to Ostionan Ostionoid to Meillacan Ostionoid to Chican Ostionoid is not accurate. In addition, it is not clear whether all of the changes detected in Puerto Rico were transmitted to Hispaniola. For example, the chroniclers described large houses in Hispaniola and Cuba, while archaeologists in Puerto Rico find evidence for smaller, nuclear-family-sized structures during the later prehistory (Curet 1992b). Thus the archaeology of Puerto Rico may not provide a good model for the archaeology of Hispaniola (Curet 2003).

The use of pottery to trace population movements and the wholesale diffusion of culture needs to be reconsidered. The early dates for pottery in Hispaniola and Cuba in association with Archaic toolkits indicate that Ostionan Culture was not transmitted *in toto* to these islands. Two alternative scenarios can be proposed. First, pottery making may have diffused at a very early date from Puerto Rico to Hispaniola and Cuba (circa 350 BC), where it was adopted by Archaic peoples who were already living there. Second, pottery making may have had an independent origin in Cuba and may have diffused to Hispaniola prior to the arrival of Ceramic Age peoples from South America. In both cases, the use of pottery was independent of the Ceramic Age peoples of Puerto Rico, and the cultural baggage associated with those peoples should not be attributed to the peoples of Hispaniola and Cuba.

For some unknown reason the pottery made to the west of Puerto Rico was decorated primarily with modeled and incised designs and lacked the painted motifs that occur in Cedrosan Saladoid and Ostionan Ostionoid wares. In some ways the lack of painting across the Mona Passage mirrors the abandonment of painting across the Vieques Passage. While the Huecan peoples of Vieques apparently retained ties to other Saladoid peoples in the Lesser Antilles (Hofman and Hoogland 1995), as reflected in the elaborate stone and shell personal adornments they made, the peoples of Hispaniola seem to have struck out on their own. This new conclusion proposes that Meillacan and Chican motifs developed and were elaborated for centuries before a second wave of Ostionan peoples struck out from Puerto Rico.

There is solid evidence to accept a separate Ostionan expansion beginning after AD 500. This wave of Ostionan peoples rapidly dispersed through the northern islands. They can be distinguished by their practice of decorating their pots with red paint. By AD 700 there were Ostionan ("redware") sites in the Dominican Republic, Haiti, Jamaica, the Turks and Caicos, and the Bahamas. While Ostionan peoples in Jamaica and the Bahamas may reflect the happenstance landing on islands that earlier peoples had not reached, the evidence put forth for Hispaniola (Veloz Maggiolo 1991) documents the presence of peoples using ceramics there in the first centuries BC. Furthermore, Cuban archaeologists no longer recognize an Ostionan colonization of their island (Ulloa Hung, personal communication, 2005), despite early and well-established traditions of pottery making. For these islands the Ostionan colonists from Puerto Rico were relative latecomers. It is not simply the expansion of Ceramic Age peoples into lands inhabited by Archaic Age peoples. The Ostionan expansion must have involved confrontation, hybridization, and multidimensional interactions of peoples and cultures from different times, places, and backgrounds. These new data are important because they indicate that Hispaniola and Cuba already supported distinct and diverse cultures prior to the date attributed to the beginning of the Taíno period.

The Meanings of "Taíno"

Throughout this book I have tried to restrict my use of the name "Taíno" to the contact-period peoples of Hispaniola and the Turks and Caicos Islands, because this was the area in which the initial Spanish observations were made. I do so because there was enormous cultural diversity throughout the islands (Curet 2003). Although the Spanish asserted that all of the people on Puerto Rico, Hispaniola, Cuba, and the Bahamas shared one culture, I tend to side with Peter Hulme (1993), who suggested that we speak of "Taíno" with a lower-case *t* when all of the peoples of the Greater Antilles and Bahamas are labeled with the same term. Nevertheless, if we recognize that culture is chaotic, and its configuration is always changing, then "Taíno" is just a name that needs to be more specifically defined in each use.

In the previous section I have discussed the simultaneous presence of multiple pottery styles on Hispaniola. In fact, at around AD 800 all of the pottery subseries employed by Rouse to define historical relations were in use. We need to abandon the notion that all of Taíno Culture evolved from a single Ostionan Ostionoid migration that began after AD 600. When we recognize multiple colonists and multiple local accommodations, the diversity observed, but discounted by the Spanish, comes into clearer focus.

A second dimension of diversity concerns language (Figure 3.6). Las Casas (1951: vol. 1, 18–21) reported that there were at least three different languages spoken on Hispaniola. Taíno was considered the universal or common language, a sort of *lingua franca* or *lingua jural*. It was spoken throughout the island. The second language was Macorix de Arriba, which glosses as "foreign, almost barbaric" (Harris 1994: 8). It was spoken in three provinces of the north cordillera, including the cacicazgo of Mayabonex, who was one of the principal caciques on the island. Finally, there was Macorix de Abajo, which could not be understood by the Macorix de Arriba. Ramón Pané said that these people called themselves the Nuhuirei (Harris 1994). They occupied one small province at the western end of the north cordillera near Monte Cristi and the western part of the Vega Real north of the Río Yaquí in the Domini-

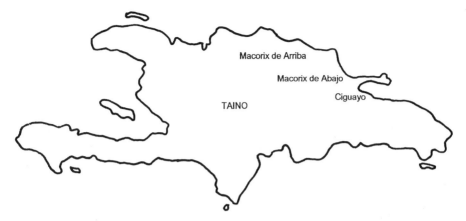

3.6. Map of language groups.

can Republic. The province in which this language was spoken is associated with a people called Ciguayo. Peter Martyr D'Anghiera (1970: 127) called them Ciguaia and said: "The natives are ferocious and warlike, and it is thought they are of the same race as the cannibals. . . ." Part of this description may come from Columbus's first voyage. Columbus had a hostile encounter with the inhabitants of the Samaná peninsula, who, unlike the people he had met previously, attacked him with bows and arrows. He concluded that these must be the Caníbales of whom he had heard earlier in the voyage. Thus the characteristics attributed to the Ciguayo may also be derived from a confusion of myth and reality.

The political geography of Hispaniola in the late fifteenth century provides another means for defining "Taíno." There is considerable debate about how the island was carved up among the named cacicazgos. As Samuel Wilson (1990: 14) notes, the boundaries would have been constantly shifting. Political power can be defined along multiple dimensions, which contributes to the chaotic nature of the boundaries. For example, a cacique might have had different levels of control in a region according to economic, military, or social criteria (Wilson 1990: 111). The boundaries of every cacicazgo are different depending upon which dimension is emphasized. Paramount caciques were not the sovereign kings that the Spanish thought, and their cacicazgos were not the definite territories of feudal lords. The caciques apparently ruled through charisma and entrepreneurship; their rule was based on their abilities to use persuasive rhetoric to convince the Nitaínos (elites), common people, and other leaders to follow them (Wilson 1990: 102; Redmond and Spencer 1994).

Moreover, there must have been population centers and relatively uninhabited borderlands that distinguished these different polities.

The primary information on polities comes from André Morales (Mártir de Anglería 1989) and Bartolomé de las Casas (1951). Morales listed 5 province groups and 53 named provinces but did not provide geographical details. Las Casas listed 5 supreme and 2 independent caciques and 27 provinces that were described in sufficient detail to map. Previous investigators have treated these two reports as contradictory and have thus proposed different maps of the political boundaries (for example, Charlevoix and de Francisco 1977; Rouse 1948; Vega 1980; Wilson 1990). In contrast, Peter O'B. Harris (1994) views the two lists as complementary. He finds considerable conformity between Morales's province groups and Las Casas's list of caciques. Combining these, he proposes eight province groups (three south-north pairs and two matching singles in the northeast and southwest) and overlays these on the Taínos' conception of the island to create a cosmographic map of Hispaniola. It should be noted that Harris used watersheds to draw the boundaries for the cacicazgos on his map. Although these certainly do not reflect the chaos of edge effects (which Harris acknowledges), they do provide a convenient convention for cartographic representation.

The Taínos conceived of Hispaniola as "'a monstrous living beast of female sex,' whose vagina and anus are formed by a marine cave under the western cape of Guacayarima, which means 'place of anus, or filth'" (Mártir de Anglería 1989: 629). Based on this depiction, Harris (1994: 10) "hypothesized that the eight province-groups conform with key body parts of the beast: two eyes, mouth, forelegs, two hind legs, and private parts." For the Taínos, the head was to the east, as reflected in the name "Caizcimú" for southeast Hispaniola. *Cimú* glosses as "front, forehead, first" in the Taíno language (Mártir de Anglería 1989: 354–355). Harris goes on to suggest that the south-north pairs reflect a ranking in which cacicazgos to the south were senior to those in the north, as in right hand/elder brother, left hand/younger brother. He also proposed that the northeast/southwest pair has astronomical significance, related to the position of the sun during the summer and winter solstices.

Once again we see how cosmography structured Taíno Culture. Cacicazgos are not simply political units defined by the anthropological duality of control and management. Power is imbued by corporeal position with regard to the beast, and not simply cacical authority. They are part of a living beast, a monstrous mother-earth, that gives priority to females and uses spatial locations to reinforce political ranking. Moreover, there is again reference to the heavens. The world begins in the east (sunrise) and ends in the west (sunset), especially on the days of the summer and winter solstice. And the mythical islands Matininó, Carib, and Guanín are located to the east.

La Navidad (En Bas Saline)

It is clear from Columbus's *diario* that he entered the bay at Cap Haïtien before the *Santa María* was wrecked. Although numerous expeditions have been launched to find the wreck of the *Santa María*, none has been successful. These failures are often justified by Columbus's statement that all of the ship's timbers were salvaged to build the fort and everything else that could be recovered was brought ashore. In other words, there is nothing left for underwater explorers to find.

With regard to the land site, Columbus wrote to the sovereigns that a fort was built in the village of Guacanagarí, composed of a moat, a tower, and a palisade (Deagan 1989). Columbus departed before the fort was built, however; although he left instructions for those constructions, on the second voyage the only eyewitnesses described a "somewhat fortified" large house (Deagan 2004).

The location of Guacanagarí's village and the first Spanish settlement of La Navidad is the subject of debate. Tracing Columbus's route, Samuel Eliot Morison (1942) concluded that the *Santa María* had sunk just offshore from the Haitian town of Limonade Bord de Mer. In 1976 Dr. William Hodges, a medical missionary with an insatiable avocational interest in archaeology, discovered a large archaeological site about 1 km inland from Limonade Bord de Mer and 10 km east of Cap Haïtien. There are no similar large archaeological sites of the right time period in the area (Deagan 1989).

Between 1983 and 1987 teams from the Florida Museum of Natural History (then Florida State Museum) excavated the site of En Bas Saline, which is named for the Haitian farming community on the site. The excavations were under the direction of Kathleen Deagan (1987, 1988, 2004). Her teams produced a detailed topographic map, did an electromagnetic conductivity survey, made a complete surface collection, and dug 25 cm^2 test units at 10 m intervals across the north-south and east-west axes of the site (Williams 1986). In addition, 93 m^2 of larger-scale excavations were undertaken to investigate particular features identified by the various types of survey (Deagan 1987: 344). During the course of the project they accumulated a large body of circumstantial evidence to support the identification of this village as the town of Guacanagarí and the site of La Navidad. The evidence included the size and configuration of the site, the highly decorated pottery, a well-like structure not reported for other Taíno sites, European objects and animal bones, and traces of an enormous fire. Sixty-two percent of the excavated artifacts are from postcontact deposits (Deagan 1987: 346), and the later deposits show evidence for a Taíno/Spanish "colono-ware" in which Spanish forms were adapted to Taíno manufacturing techniques (Cusick 1989, 1991). Even if this is not the site of La Navidad and the village of Guacanagarí, it was the village of a powerful cacique.

It also is worth noting that Clark Moore, an avocational archaeologist who has worked in Haiti for more than 25 years, has identified a series of Taíno villages along the north coast. He has proposed that these large villages, which are evenly spaced at about 28 km apart, were connected by an aboriginal road (Moore 1998). The road begins in the west at En Bas Saline and runs east to the village sites at Madrasse, Carrier, and Mapou and finally to village sites in the western Dominican Republic. Side roads also connect the inland villages to coastal settlements. Sections of the proposed Taíno road follow documented sections of the Spanish and French colonial roads.

Whether or not En Bas Saline has a direct link to written history, it exemplifies the structure and content of a chiefly village. The site is crucial to the purposes of this study because it is the only large Taíno village in Haiti that has been systematically excavated in recent years.[3] The archaeological materials provide an important point of reference.

En Bas Saline is located along a now dry tributary of the Grande Rivière du Nord. It is on the edge of a mangrove swamp and a saline basin that connect it to the coast. The most visible part of the site is a large C-shaped earthwork that averages 20 m wide and 80 cm tall. The earthwork was purposely constructed and is not the result of accretion or midden accumulation, as indicated by borrow pits along its inner side and a very low density of artifacts in the fill of the earthwork itself. It is wrapped halfway around a central plaza and is open to the south. It measures 350 m from north to south and 270 m from east to west (these measurements are for the whole site including the southern midden, not just the earth ridge itself; Deagan 2004). This layout is typical of other village sites reported for Hispaniola (Rainey 1941; Rainey and Ortíz Aguilú 1983; Veloz Maggiolo 1991).

One surprising result of Deagan's research is that maps produced using electromagnetic conductivity and surface collections revealed a mirror image to the earthwork. In other words, although the ground was level, soil conductivity and the density of materials on the surface revealed a C-shaped distribution on the south side of the plaza as well. Because Deagan was primarily interested in the postcontact occupation of the site, the possible meanings of an oval-shaped village with an earthwork along one side and a buried midden deposit on the other have not been explored.

At the center of the oval is a plaza that is relatively devoid of artifacts. The exception is a mound near the center of the plaza in which the remains of a large oval wattle-and-daub structure at least 15 m in diameter were discovered. This structure had been burned. Deagan found a cinder-like substance associated with the structure that was identified as cristobalite, a phase of quartz formation that occurs at temperatures of around 1400° C (Deagan 1987: 346). The burned structure and cristobalite are evidence for an intense fire in which the wattle-and-daub structure must have acted like a kiln.

In addition, Hodges located a very deep pit that he thought was a well. He excavated part of it in 1977 and found an infant burial, which he removed to his museum in Limbé. Deagan later excavated the rest of the feature, which appeared to have two or three construction episodes that resulted in a pit nearly 2 m deep. Deagan recovered pig and rat bones at the lowest levels of this pit. There was also evidence for the *cohoba* ritual (the use of narcotics to communicate with the supernatural), including a snuffer tube and vomit spatula fragment. In sum, it appears that the "well" at La Navidad was periodically reused and that it finally served as a burial pit (Deagan 2004).

Two other features in the plaza were enormous straight-sided hearth-like trenches that were filled with debris (such as ash, pottery, bones, food remains, and shells). These features are radiocarbon dated to AD 1300 and probably are evidence for the ceremonial feasting described for the Taínos (Lovén 1935: 506). A similar pit feature was found at the Cinnamon Bay site on St. John, U.S. Virgin Islands, which also has been identified as the aftermath of a feast (Wild 2001). Competitive feasting is a characteristic of avunculocal chiefdoms like the Taínos (see chapter 4), and a similar situation is described for Haida and Tlingit potlatches on the Northwest Coast of North America (Rosman and Rubel 1971).

Radiocarbon dates from the deepest stratigraphic units indicate that En Bas Saline was first occupied sometime in the thirteenth century (Deagan 1987: 345). Virtually all of the pottery can be classified as Chican, which is the subseries associated with the Classic Taínos. Less than 1 percent of the assemblage could be classified as Meillacan, and these sherds came from the deepest levels. The radiocarbon dates and pottery styles are consistent with the chronology in Rouse (1992), which has Chican pottery and associated cultural phenomena supplant Meillacan culture on the north coast after AD 1200.

Plant and animal remains in the site provide a final point for comparison. Lee Newsom (1993) analyzed the plant remains and identified charred tuber fragments from both manioc and sweet potatoes, along with corn, beans, peppers, and other domesticated and wild edible plants (Newsom and Deagan 1994). Elizabeth Wing (2001) undertook the analysis of animal bones. The samples proved to be amazingly diverse, with 60 vertebrate species from 47 families and 57 invertebrate species from 31 families. These species were captured in all of the habitats in the vicinity of the site. Rats (*Rattus rattus*) and pigs (*Sus scrofa*) were recovered from sixteenth-century deposits (most of them in the central mound structure). A more detailed accounting is provided in chapter 6.

Finally, Brad Ensor (personal communication, 2002) recently restudied the materials recovered from the main structure in the central plaza at En Bas Saline as part of his investigation into whether the Taínos were a tributary chiefdom (Ensor 2000). He observed evidence for a wide range of activities that indicated that the chief's household was not exempt from basic tasks. In other words, caciques like Guacanagarí may have been first among equals, but their households were still involved in the same kinds of tasks as were commoner households.

The site of En Bas Saline exemplifies the characteristics that we would expect to find at other chiefly settlements. The site is large, has an earthwork of human manufacture, contains a quantity of decorated ceramics and religious paraphernalia, and is connected to similar large settlements by a road. With regard to the more mundane aspects of survival, there is an accounting of food remains and evidence that chiefly households engaged in the same productive activities as did commoner households. These characteristics will be important when sites in the Bahama archipelago are scrutinized for evidence of the settlement at which Caonabó may have lived.

El Corral de los Indios (San Juan de Maguana)

After Caonabó was captured, the Spanish built a town called San Juan de Maguana in his village. This town has an extremely large plaza called El Corral de los Indios (Figure 3.7), more than 125,000 square meters in area. The second largest plaza in Hispaniola is Chacuey (35,721 square meters), and the third largest is Casa de la Reina (10,164 square meters). Given the lack of systematic archaeology in Haiti, it is likely that not all of the plaza sites have been identified. For instance, the village of Behecchio (in the vicinity of modern Port-au-Prince) has not been identified and may have been destroyed by historic development. Behecchio was at least as powerful as Caonabó, so it is possible that other large plaza sites existed in Haiti.

Nevertheless, El Corral de los Indios is by magnitudes the largest known village in the West Indies. In comparison, the largest ball court/plazas in Puerto Rico are all less than 4,000 square meters in area. Wilson (1990: 25) concludes that "this observation may suggest that there are significant differ-

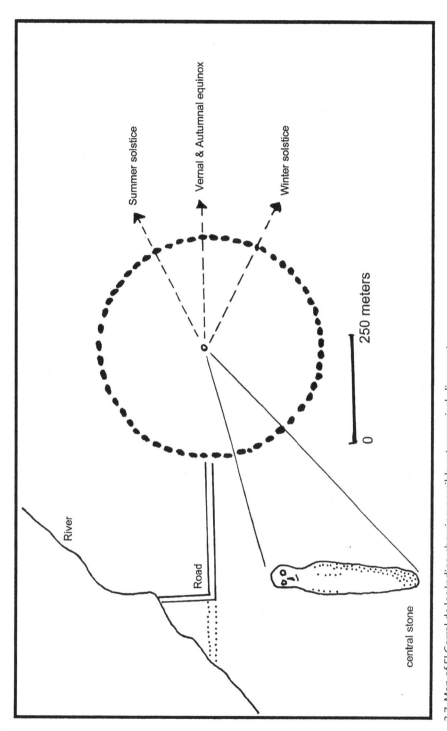

3.7. Map of El Corral de los Indios, showing possible astronomical alignments.

ences between the Taíno societies of Puerto Rico and Hispaniola," a conclusion that Curet (2003) supports.

El Corral de los Indios was first reported by Robert Schomburgk in 1851 (Alegría 1983: 33). Schomburgk reported that 15 to 25 kgs of rocks had been placed closely together to form a perfectly circular "paved road" 7 m wide and over 700 m in diameter. This was a single course of stones; they were not piled up as would be expected for a historic stone wall. At the center of the circle was a shaped granite rock 170 cm tall with a human head carved at the top. Although this rock was found on its side, it is believed to have been standing when the plaza was in use. Over the years there have been several efforts to reconstruct the plaza. It has been modified by agricultural activities, however, and its modern configuration does not exactly match either Schomburgk's descriptions or its appearance in 1492.

In addition to the circular enclosure, a paved pathway extends due west and then turns abruptly north to intersect a small brook. No petroglyphs are reported for this brook; but at other plaza sites in Hispaniola (for example, Chacuey) the road led to a brook or river where petroglyphs were carved on the rocks (Castellanos 1981; Weeks et al. 1996). At the Cerrado de Piedras plaza in Parque Nacional del Este (Dominican Republic), a road leads to the Mantiel de la Aleta, a sinkhole in which a wide variety of offerings have been recovered (Conrad et al. 2001; Guerrero 1981).

It is believed that these plazas were used for festivals, games, and ceremonies. At the plaza at Chacuey stones are aligned to mark the passage of the sun with regard to the summer and winter solstice (Castellanos 1981), but it is unlikely that the Antillean ball game (*batey*) was played here. In contrast to these circular plazas, ball courts have parallel-sided courts (Alegría 1983). Furthermore, there is no evidence for structures associated with the plaza, although very little archaeological research has been conducted at the site.

In sum, Caonabó lived at the largest-known village in the West Indies. We should expect nothing less for the man who was arguably the most powerful cacique on Hispaniola. Other plaza sites exhibit evidence for astronomical alignments and the presence of roads connecting them to important places, features that will be important in identifying Caonabó's homeland.

Lucayan Islands

Las Islas de los Lucayos (the Lucayan Islands) today include the Commonwealth of the Bahamas and the Turks and Caicos Islands (a British Crown colony). The etymology is traced to the Arawakan phrase Lukkunu Kaíri, which glosses as "island men" (Brinton 1871). The next chapter shows how Taíno social and political organization could allow for a "stranger king" to have come from the Lucayan Islands. The task at hand is to determine whether the culture history of these islands could have produced such an individual. Although it is possible that Caonabó could have come from a small village, it is more likely that he came from a settlement with demonstrable social, political, and economic ties to Hispaniola. In this regard, a Taíno outpost in the Lucayan Islands would seem to be the best candidate.

The Lucayans share a common ancestry with the Taíno societies that they separated from around AD 700, when people began to colonize the Bahama archipelago. There is no evidence that any other peoples preceded them. In other words, they were the first humans to settle on these islands. It was once thought that the Lucayan Islands were settled during one migration. The main justification for this belief is that the locally made pottery, Palmetto ware, is virtually indistinguishable in style and paste throughout the archipelago (but see Granberry and Winter 1995). Recent evidence suggests that there may have been several migrations from several different areas in the Greater Antilles (Berman and Gnivecki 1995). The presence of both pure Ostionan and pure Meillacan sites indicates that distinct cultural groups entered these islands on different occasions.

A Distillation of Lucayan Culture

Archaeological surveys have identified more than 400 pre-Columbian sites in these islands, ranging in size from isolated pot drops, farmsteads, and procurement sites to a settlement 6 km long on Delectable Bay, Acklins Island (Craton and Saunders 1992; Keegan 1997). Immigrants from Hispaniola and possibly Cuba first settled the islands beginning around AD 700. By 1492 all of the major islands and many of the smaller ones had been settled. Peter Martyr D'Anghiera reported that 40,000 Lucayans were enslaved and exported to Hispaniola and then to the pearl-oyster grounds off the coast of Venezuela in the first few decades after the Spanish invasion (Mártir de Anglería 1989). Slaving expeditions by Juan Ponce de León in 1513 and others in the early 1520s failed to encounter any native peoples in the Lucayan Islands (Keegan 1992), so it is generally accepted that the native population had been extirpated by that date.

The material culture of the Lucayan Islands is distinct from that of their Greater Antillean neighbors. These islands are built on a carbonate matrix composed entirely of limestone (Sealey 1985). Because there were no igneous or metamorphic rocks, all hard stone had to be imported from the Greater

Antilles. In addition, any pottery recovered from archaeological sites in the Bahamas that has quartz sand, igneous, metamorphic, or other noncarbonate tempers must have been imported from the Greater Antilles.

The locally made Lucayan pottery is called Palmetto ware after the Palmetto Grove site on San Salvador (Hoffman 1967). It was made from local iron-rich soils and burned and crushed conch shell (*Strombus gigas*) (Mann 1986). Some question remains as to where the recipe for Palmetto ware originated. The discovery on Grand Turk (GT-3) of shell-tempered Ostionan Ostionoid pottery imported from the Greater Antilles indicates that the first inhabitants of the Bahama archipelago were familiar with the use of shell as a source of temper. Similar shell-tempered wares also were common in the Virgin Islands at this time (Hoffman 1967). Palmetto ware shows clear continuity with wares manufactured in the Greater Antilles.

It is of special interest in Bahamian archaeology that over 90 percent of Lucayan settlements occur in pairs (Keegan 1992). These settlement pairs have been interpreted as reflecting social relations between these communities (Keegan and Maclachlan 1989). The basic argument (expanded in the next chapter) is that these settlements are the residences of intermarrying clans. Their location within 3 km of each other seems to reflect an effort by a matrilineal group to localize males within clan territories. Such localization of males occurs in sharp contrast to a matrilocal residence pattern, in which females are localized and males are dispersed.

Spanish records indicate that the Lucayans cultivated as many as 50 different plants, including 6 named varieties of sweet and bitter manioc (Hernández Aquino 1977), several varieties of sweet potatoes, cocoyam, beans, gourds, chili peppers, corn, cotton, tobacco, bixa, genip, groundnuts, guavas, and papayas (see Keegan 2000a for a review of Taíno foods). The carbonized remains of corn, chili peppers, palm fruits, tubers (probably manioc and sweet potato), and a gourd are among the plant remains identified in West Indian sites (Newsom 1993). As with most tropical horticulturalists, and given the absence of substantial animal prey, it is likely that at least 75 percent of the Lucayan diet came from plant foods. Manioc (cassava) was the staple, followed by sweet potato. Corn was apparently of limited importance.

Manioc (*Manihot esculenta*) tubers require special processing because they contain poisonous hydrocyanic acid. Sweet manioc has such small quantities of the poison that it can be peeled and boiled like sweet potatoes. Bitter manioc, however, requires more elaborate procedures that involve peeling, grinding or mashing, and squeezing the mash in a basket tube to remove the poisonous juices. After the juice was removed, the paste was either dried and sieved for use as flour or toasted into farina. The dried flour was spread on a flat clay griddle and cooked to make cassava bread. The flour and farina could be stored for up to six months.

The poisonous manioc juice was not discarded. It was boiled to release the poison and then used as the liquid base for *casiripe* or pepper pot. Pepper pot was made by adding chili peppers (*Capsicum* sp.), other vegetables, meat, and fish to the simmering manioc juice. In this way foods that would otherwise spoil could be preserved for several meals. The slowly simmering pot was available for meals throughout the day. Today in South America pepper pot is eaten by dipping cassava bread into the stew. Fragments of large ceramic vessels and griddles, which are associated with cooking pepper pot and cassava bread, are common in the archaeological sites.

The other portion of the diet came from land animals and the sea. The few land animals that were available—iguana (*Cyclura carinata*), crabs (*Cardisoma* sp.), and a cat-sized rodent called hutia (*Geocapromys brownii*)—were highly prized but were available in limited quantities. The major source of animal protein came from the coastal marine environment. Marine turtles and monk seals were available seasonally, at least during the initial settlement of the islands. The main foods, however, were the fishes and mollusks that feed in the grass flat/patch reef habitats between the barrier coral reef and the beach: parrotfishes, groupers, snappers, bonefishes, queen conchs, sea urchins, nerites, chitons, and clams. Fishes were captured with nets, basket traps, spears, bows and arrows, and weirs. Check-dams were built across the mouths of tidal creeks; these weirs allowed fishes to enter at high tide but prevented their escape when the tide changed. Meat and fishes were barbecued on a wooden lattice to preserve them, and leftovers were added to the pepper pot.

The number of ways in which Lucayans could satisfy their daily food requirements is noteworthy. It is difficult to imagine that anyone ever went hungry—a conclusion confirmed by the preliminary examination of human skeletal remains. These bones show little evidence of nutritional disorders, and it appears that the Lucayans enjoyed remarkably good health and nutrition (Keegan 1982; Winter 1991). They certainly did not suffer from the nutritional and diet-related disorders that plagued other horticulturalists in the West Indies and elsewhere (Coppa et al. 1995; Budinoff 1991; Vento Canosa and González R. 1996).

Oviedo y Valdés described the Taíno house as round to oval, with a high-pitched, conical thatched roof. It had a large center post and regularly spaced wall supports between which smaller branches were set or interwoven (Figure 3.8). In Hispaniola and Cuba these were large multifamily (or extended family) houses called *caneyes*.[4] Although it is probably an exaggeration, Bartolomé de las Casas reported that some houses in Cuba were occupied by 40 to 60

3.8. Re-created *caneyes* on San Salvador, Bahamas.

3.9. Depiction of Lucayan women cooking (after Benzoni 1857).

heads of household (roughly 250 men, women, and children). Households were formed around a group of related females. Grandmother, mother, sisters, and daughters lived together and cooperated in farming, childrearing, food preparation, and craft production. Men, by virtue of their absence from the village during periods of long-distance trade and/or warfare, were peripheral to the household. The importance of females as the foundation of society was expressed by tracing descent through the female line to a mythical female ancestor. The household's belongings were stored on the floor and in the rafters of the houses. Cotton hammocks for sleeping were strung between the central supports and eaves. Excavations of a house floor on Middle Caicos revealed ash deposits that may have been the remnant of a small, smoky fire used to control insect pests and to warm the house at night. Cooking was probably done in sheds outside the main house (Figure 3.9).

Most villages in the Lucayan Islands were composed of houses aligned atop a sand dune, with the ocean in front and a marshy area behind. These marshy areas quite likely provided ready access to fresh water before the islands were deforested. In addition many sites are located just offshore on small cays, such as Iguana Cay in Jacksonville Harbour, East Caicos; Major's Cay, Crooked Island; and Pelican Cay, Middle Caicos. These small cays were used for ceremonial purposes, perhaps even shrines, as indicated by the high frequency of highly decorated pottery and other items associated with rituals (for example, shell inlays for wooden statues).

The portrait that emerges from these islands is that the Lucayans were a smaller-scale version of the cacicazgos of Hispaniola. Most sites are less than 120 m long. I have estimated that there was one house per 30 linear meters of surface scatter, based on peaks in a histogram of site lengths (Keegan 1992). The few larger sites such as Pigeon Creek on San Salvador (which has an oval community plan) and Delectable Bay on Acklins Island may have been the seats of caciques who had hegemony over larger regional territories. All of the sites show evidence of exchange with the Greater Antilles in the form of imported pottery vessels and various hard-stone tools (for example, chert flakes and polished petaloid celts). It is likely that such materials entered the islands through ports of trade and were then dispersed down the line. In sum, the Lucayans of the Bahamas and the Taínos of Hispaniola reflect differences of scale, not significant differences in basic cultural characteristics.

Columbus's First Voyage

Twelve different Bahamian islands and Florida have been identified as Christopher Columbus's first landfall. The landfall island was called Guanahaní by the native peoples but was renamed San Salvador (Holy Savior) by Columbus.

Most of the debate concerning where he landed has centered on Columbus's descriptions of the first landfall island and his subsequent route through the Bahamas on the way to Cuba. Many of the proposed routes have only one or a few supporters—often individuals with a personal interest in a particular island. Three credible candidates, however, emerged in the years just prior to the Quincentenary: Grand Turk, Samana Cay, and San Salvador (formerly Watling's Island). As a part of more general surveys of the archaeology and geology of the islands, Steve Mitchell and I evaluated the geological and archaeological evidence for the main candidates in the mid-1980s (Mitchell 1984; Mitchell and Keegan 1987).

Grand Turk suffers a fatal flaw. Columbus clearly described the presence of Lucayan villages on the first landfall island. Archaeological research on Grand Turk conducted since 1989 has covered virtually every square inch of this tiny island. All attempts have failed to identify any archaeological remains that date later than AD 1300 (Keegan 1997). There is no evidence that anyone was living on Grand Turk at the time of Columbus's first voyage. Without Indians, the other problems with the Grand Turk track are moot.

In 1986 *National Geographic* magazine announced to the world that Samana Cay was the first landfall of Columbus. Using sophisticated computer modeling of the voyage, key flaws in Samuel Eliot Morison's (1942) reconstruction of the San Salvador route, and archaeological investigations to back up the proposed route, Joseph Judge presented a solid case. The Samana Cay track has various shortcomings; but the key point for the present inquiry is that Columbus departed for Cuba from the western coast of the landmass created by Crooked, Fortune, and Acklins Islands. Thus, even though I believe that this track is wrong, it does coincide with the Morison track in this key location: Crooked Island.

In my opinion a modified version of Morison's (1942) reconstruction of Columbus's route provides the best fit to descriptions in the *diario* (Keegan 1992). From the island today known as San Salvador he visited Rum Cay, Long Island, and Crooked Island and attempted to reach the lee shore of Acklins Island before departing for Cuba. From the beginning, Columbus was looking for gold. He associated gold deposits with tropical climes, as was common in Europe at the time. In addition he sought an audience with the Kubla Khan, reported by Marco Polo to be the ruler of China. (Columbus had not heard that the "gra Can" had been deposed almost 300 years earlier by the Ming Dynasty.) Columbus conscripted Lucayan guides and reported that he was headed with due haste to "Samaot . . . the island or city where the gold is."

When Columbus reached Crooked Island his native guides told him that this was Samaot. Because Columbus did not see evidence for a great king or much wealth, he interpreted their statement to mean that Samaot was across the island to the southeast. He therefore endeavored to cross the Bight of Acklins but soon gave up, with the realization that the waters were too shallow. Research near Delectable Bay on the west coast of Acklins Island has revealed a series of archaeological deposits extending along the shore for a distance of 6 km (Keegan 1992). This is the longest contiguous archaeological deposit in all of the Bahamas. Apparently the guides were correct. For although there was little gold in the Lucayan Islands (and it would have had to be imported), they were taking Columbus to the most powerful cacique in the area. Unfortunately, Columbus never gained an audience with this "king." After several days of waiting he followed his guides' directions and sailed for Cuba. Columbus's actions suggest that the people of the central Bahamas had stronger ties to Cuba than to Hispaniola.

Archaeology of the Southern Bahamas

Mary Jane Berman and Julian Granberry also have proposed a strong link between the central Bahamas and Cuba. Berman and P. L. Gnivecki (1995) have classified imported pottery at the Three Dog site on San Salvador as belonging to the Arroyo del Palo style of northeastern Cuba (Tabio and Guarch 1966). Because this pottery was found at one of the earliest dated sites in the Bahamas (eighth century AD), they further proposed that the first colonists arrived from Cuba. Moreover, lithic flakes found in the site were identified as consistent with the Cuban tradition of making and using microliths (Berman et al. 1999). In addition, John Winter and Mark Gilstrap (1991) used neutron activation analysis to document a connection between pottery found in the central Bahamas and Cuba. Thus the central Bahamas may have had a strong traditional social link to northeastern Cuba.

Julian Granberry (1991) used Lucayan toponyms to reconstruct links between the Lucayan Islands and the Greater Antilles. He interpreted the names for the islands recorded by the Spanish as having directional references. Thus Inawa (Great Inagua) is translated as "small eastern land" and Abawana (Grand Turk) as "first small country." The names indicate distinct associations between Cuba and Great Inagua "to the east" and between Hispaniola and the Turks and Caicos Islands. Granberry, like Berman and Winter, interprets the results of this analysis as evidence that Cuba was the source of the initial colonists of the central Bahamas. While their evidence suggests that such connections existed by the time of Spanish contact, it has not been determined when such contacts were first established. Therefore it is premature to conclude that there were two separate migrations into the Bahamas (Keegan 1997).

Whether the earliest colonists of the central Bahamas came from Cuba or not, by the time of Spanish contact these regions had strong ties. Pottery, microliths, island names, and the Lucayan guides who directed Columbus to Cuba all indicate a connection. The reason for this connection may be that Lucayans living to the south controlled access to Hispaniola. If the peoples of the southern Bahamas did control access to Hispaniola, then Caonabó's homeland must be in the southern Lucayan Islands.

The only candidates for Caonabó's homeland in the southern islands are Great Inagua, Mayaguana, and the Turks and Caicos Islands. I have conducted archaeological surveys on all of them. The entire coastline of Mayaguana was surveyed, and 10 pre-Columbian sites were found (Keegan 1992, 1997).[5] None of these sites were large villages; and although the sites were not excavated, nothing of significance was observed. Moreover, the most expedient route to Hispaniola from Mayaguana passes through the Turks and Caicos Islands.

Great Inagua is less well known. Although Mitchell and I walked from Southeast Point to just north of the Bahamas National Trust's turtle research station at Union Creek, we were not able to cover this vast area thoroughly in a short visit. Subsequent visits were made for Cultural Resource Management (CRM) evaluations at Aerostat and Federal Aviation Administration (FAA) installations, but the main stretch of the south coast merits further investigation. Based on present evidence, no sites on Great Inagua would fit the natal village of a Taíno cacique (Keegan 1997). In addition, Great Inagua is located between Cuba and Hispaniola (albeit to the north). Thus it is equally likely that the main influences on Great Inagua came from northeastern Cuba or western Hispaniola, which were outside the main contacts with the Spanish and beyond the territory that Caonabó controlled in Hispaniola.

Between 1976 and 1978 Shaun Sullivan, then a Ph.D. candidate at the University of Illinois, conducted an archaeological survey of the Turks and Caicos Islands (Sullivan 1980, 1981). Sullivan returned to Middle Caicos in 1981 and 1982 to excavate sites identified in his survey. Prior to his investigations Theodoor de Booy (1912) had visited the islands in the early 1900s as part of the Heye Foundation's Caribbean program and Charles A. Hoffman Jr. conducted an informal survey of Grand Turk in the early 1970s. Continuing this work, I began with Sullivan in 1978 and 1982, excavated the Pine Cay site in 1978 and 1979 (Keegan 1981), and directed surveys and excavations throughout the Turks and Caicos between 1989 and 2005. In addition, Brian Riggs, former manager of the Turks and Caicos National Museum, worked with Sullivan in 1977 and has lived in the islands since 1982. He has devoted a considerable amount of time to investigating unsurveyed areas and has discovered several new sites. The cumulative result of this work is that the Turks and Caicos

Islands are among the best known of all the Lucayan Islands in terms of archaeology. San Salvador certainly is the best known.

Sullivan identified Lucayan sites on Middle Caicos, Pine Cay, and Providenciales. The majority of his research was focused on Middle Caicos, where he discovered several large sites and a number of smaller ones associated with Armstrong Pond on the south coast. Sullivan claimed that that the majority of sites in the Caicos were located "inland," while most sites in the rest of the Bahamas were "coastal" (Sears and Sullivan 1978). This inland-coastal dichotomy was based on the prevailing belief at the time that early settlements favored inland locations with prime agricultural land and that later settlements were established on the coast (see Keegan and Diamond 1987). This belief has since been proven wrong (Bradford 2001; Haviser 1997).

Sullivan used the supposedly inland settlement pattern in the Caicos Islands to support his contention that these were the first islands colonized by peoples from Hispaniola. Yet the critical evaluation of settlement patterns in the Caicos Islands indicates that none of them were ever "inland" (Keegan 1995b). Sears and Sullivan (1978) reported that only one site in the Turks and Caicos was coastal. With the exclusion of sites in caves and those on the south coast of Middle Caicos, however, it is possible to throw a rock into the sea from virtually every other site. In addition, all of the sites on the south coast are located on the margin of the first permanently dry land above a broad tidal flat (salina). Studies of sea level fluctuations suggest that these sites would have been adjacent to the shore in AD 1492 (Valdés 1994). Even without a change in sea level, the salina is always wet; and storms from the south will push the waters of the Caicos Bank across the entire salina. Moreover, most of the supposed inland sites had fewer than 12 sherds, which suggests that they were pot drops associated with farming activities and do not represent village settlements.

Sullivan also missed the mark in another important respect. He failed to find any sites in the Turks group and concluded that these islands were too dry to support permanent human habitation (Sears and Sullivan 1978). Although he may have been correct in concluding that these islands were not permanently settled, 13 sites in all have now been identified on Grand Turk, Salt Cay, Cotton Cay, and several of the smaller cays in the Turks group. These sites are for the most part small and all have predominantly locally made Palmetto ware, except for the two main sites on Grand Turk (described below).

What is strange is that no archaeological sites have been identified on North or East Caicos, and only three very small sites were found on South Caicos. De Booy (1912) did report cave sites on North and East Caicos and described a series of mounds on Flamingo Hill (East Caicos) that he likened to the mounds on Middle Caicos. Yet despite repeated surveys of these islands, de Booy's reports have not been confirmed. More thorough surveys may be needed before this situation changes. It is also possible, however, that the inhabitants of Middle Caicos exerted sufficient influence over access to the Caicos Bank that no settlements were allowed on these neighboring islands.

Abawana (Grand Turk)

The archaeology of Grand Turk is illuminating, especially with regard to the initial settlement of the Bahama archipelago. The earliest archaeological site is the Coralie site (GT-3). It was first inhabited around cal AD 705 (Carlson 1999). The site is located on the western margin of North Creek at the north end of Grand Turk. It is about 1 km from "north wells," one of only two freshwater sources on the island. The archaeological deposit is composed of a thin stratum spread over a large area. Toward the creek the site is overlain by up to 60 cm of sand, which probably accumulated during a period of higher sea level that commenced after AD 800 (Scudder 2001). Radiocarbon dates indicate that the site was repeatedly occupied for four centuries and that different areas of the site date to different centuries. In addition, a Taíno canoe paddle was recovered underwater from a peat deposit in North Creek adjacent to the site. The paddle was radiocarbon dated to AD 1100 and is now on display in the Turks and Caicos National Museum.

All of the pottery in the site is classified as Ostionan Ostionoid. As mentioned, this subseries is associated with an episode of population expansion to the north and west that may have originated from Puerto Rico around AD 600. Moreover, all of the pottery in the site contains quartz-sand tempers, which indicates that it must have been imported from the Greater Antilles. In other words, the site represents a Hispaniolan outpost in the southern Bahamas and is not a true Lucayan settlement. It is also worth noting that the final phase of settlement at the site, which also contains only Ostionan pottery, has been dated to AD 1100. Because this pottery was imported from Hispaniola, the dates for the site indicate that Ostionan pottery continued to be manufactured for at least three centuries beyond the period recognized in the time-space systematics for Hispaniola (see Rouse 1992: 53). Here again is evidence for groups using different styles of pottery at the same time on Hispaniola (Meillacan and Chican styles also were being made on Hispaniola at this time).

The Coralie site contains a unique assemblage of fauna. The bones of green sea turtles (*Chelonia mydas*), iguanas (*Cyclura carinata*), and large fishes (5 to

20 kg) dominate the faunal remains. There are virtually no invertebrates in the site, except *Strombus gigas* shells that were used to make basin-shaped cooking hearths. The method of cooking is also unique in the West Indies. Turtle meat, iguanas, fishes, crabs, and lobsters were cooked together in the carapace of a green sea turtle. The site reflects what happened to the indigenous fauna after humans first reached an island (Carlson 1999). Within 200 years mature breeding turtles apparently had been extirpated, and fishing focused on juvenile turtles that probably fed on the seagrass flats in North Creek. Moreover, giant iguanas were taken during the initial occupation, but their size diminished in later deposits. There is a similar shift in birds through time: ground-nesting boobies (*Sula sula*) and flightless Key West quail doves (*Geotrygon chrysia*) were consumed first, and open grassland thick-knees (*Burhinus bistriatus*) were taken later. Finally, a native tortoise (*Geochelone* sp.) that was similar in appearance to the Galapagos tortoise and previously unknown for the island was targeted during the final phase of occupation. In sum, the first humans to exploit Grand Turk had a significant and irreversible impact on the local ecology (Carlson and Keegan 2004).

It is likely that the Coralie site reflects a sequence of seasonal or short-term occupations (Carlson 1999). There is evidence that people were living at the site, but the archaeological deposits are too thin to reflect long-term habitations. Moreover, the dating of different areas of the site to different centuries and the superposition of turtle carapace hearths reflect a shifting settlement pattern within a small area. The people who visited and lived at the site were clearly there to exploit the abundant marine resources, especially sea turtles. Nowhere else in the West Indies are sea turtle remains found in such abundance. The Coralie site shows that people living in Hispaniola knew about the Turks and Caicos by AD 700 and found it worth their while to travel 120 km by canoe to exploit the marine resources in the waters surrounding Grand Turk. It is likely that many more turtles and other marine and terrestrial animals were exported to Hispaniola than were consumed at the site.

At this point it is worth comparing the faunal remains at the Coralie site with those recovered from excavations on Île à Rat (Grouard et al. n.d.; Carlson and Keegan 2004). All of the fishes at Île à Rat were in the 1 to 2 kg range; there was a major focus on invertebrates, including both mollusks and echinoids. Moreover, the conchs in the site were all subadult, in the one-year to two-year age classes. The differences between these contemporaneous sites are stunning. They show that by AD 1000 the nearshore coastal environment of Haiti was already severely depleted, which may explain why the people of Haiti turned to the Turks and Caicos as a source of marine and terrestrial foods.

A second site on Grand Turk shows evidence for long-distance procurement activities. The Governor Beach site (GT-2) was first occupied around AD 1100. Again, all of the pottery in the site was imported from the Greater Antilles, as indicated by its noncarbonate tempers. At this site, however, all but one sherd can be classified in the Meillacan subseries. The one sherd that is different is a red-painted Ostionan sherd, which may suggest contact with the people at the Coralie site about 12 km to the north.

The Governor Beach site is located across the street from the second freshwater source on the island, "south wells." It was likely a temporary settlement established by people from Haiti to facilitate specialized craft production. The site was a shell bead workshop, at which disk-shaped beads were manufactured from the thorny jewelbox shell (*Chama sarda*). This shell is noteworthy because it is one of the few that retains its color for centuries. While the bright pink of the *Strombus gigas* shell's periostracum will fade to white in a decade, we recovered *Chama* shell beads that were a brilliant scarlet after 800 years of burial. Our excavations yielded more than 1,500 complete beads and more than 4,400 blanks, partially drilled beads, and beads broken during production. In addition, there were thousands of pieces of broken shell and other scrap from bead making. We also recovered the tools used in the manufacturing process, including *Strombus gigas* knippers used to break the *Chama* shells into a rough bead-like shape, manufactured concrete platforms made for the polishing of bead blanks, *Strombus* anvils for the bipolar flaking of imported chert used for drill bits, and over 550 pieces of chert, of which about 50 were spent drill bits (Carlson 1993).

Once again Grand Turk was not the location at which a long-term settlement was established. Instead people from Hispaniola visited the island for a short time and then returned to Haiti. At the Coralie site (GT-3) the emphasis was on high-ranked foods, while at the Governor Beach site (GT-2) the emphasis was on bead making. These beads were imbued with a value beyond the labor invested in making them. They were red, the color of life and male potency, and they came from a place far away, across the sea. The beads were exotic and thus of greater value than objects that could be fashioned locally on Hispaniola. Here we see the Turks and Caicos associated with the material corollary of the stranger king. In this case it was the value added to objects that come from across the sea and that differ in symbolic ways (for example, brilliant red color) from materials available at home (Roe 1982).

The Governor Beach site is something of an enigma. The site is interpreted as a seasonal settlement at which men from Hispaniola came to Grand Turk to make shell beads. An analysis of *Codakia orbicularis* clamshells from the area of the site dated to the early thirteenth century indicates that they were all

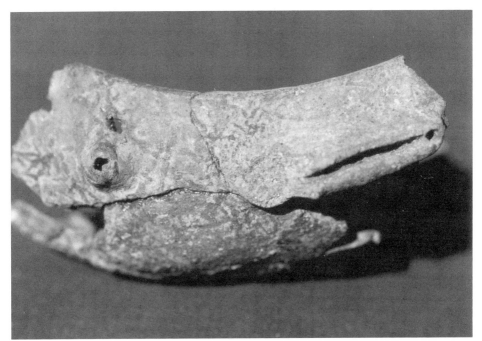

3.10. Porcupinefish effigy vessel from GT-2 (photo by Corbett Torrence).

collected during the same season (Irvy Quitmeyer, personal communication, 1995). These shells indicate a dry-season occupation (that is, people came to Grand Turk during the dry season when they were not otherwise involved in agricultural activities). But the material remains reflect a more complex situation. The pottery was of fine quality and included at least two effigy vessels. One is in the shape of a porcupinefish, and the other vessel has a bat on the side (Figure 3.10). Porcupinefish are interesting because they contain a potentially deadly neurotoxin. Their bones are found at sites throughout the islands, so it is apparent that the Taínos learned how to avoid the effects of this toxin. It is also possible that the toxin was used in appropriate doses to produce artificial death and hallucinogenic experiences. Porcupinefish is the main ingredient in the powder used by practitioners of Voudoun to turn someone into a zombie (Davis 1985).

The faunal remains in the site are significantly different from those identified at GT-3, even though these sites may have been contemporaneous toward the middle of the twelfth century. While the Coralie site contained mostly sea turtles, iguanas, tortoises, and large fishes, the Governor Beach site had mostly the head elements of the reef fish called a grunt (*Haemulon* sp.). It is possible that the people who lived at the Coralie site had extirpated sea turtles, iguanas, and tortoises before the Governor Beach site was established. Alternatively, because the focus of activities at the site was bead making, the people may have limited their efforts in food procurement to fishes for practical or religious reasons.

In addition, there is evidence for the sudden disruption of activities at the site. A variety of valued objects were abandoned or destroyed, including almost 400 complete shell beads (which were thrown into a fire), several effigy vessels (including the porcupinefish vessel), and exotic tools and other objects (Carlson 1993). For example, a Triton's trumpet (*Charonia variegata*) shell trumpet—which was so worn that it was possible to detect where the person who blew the trumpet had held the instrument—was abandoned. There is no reason to leave an object of such long use behind. The evidence suggests that a battle may have taken place, in which the Meillacan peoples were forced to leave the island for good. But whom did they fight? One possibility is that Lucayans who had been living in the Caicos Islands for about two centuries began to exert their authority over all of these islands at this time. This situation could reflect the competition between the Taíno chiefdoms in Haiti and their offspring in the Caicos Islands as part of their annexation of the southern Lucayan periphery. All that we know for certain is that there is little evidence that anyone lived on or visited Grand Turk after AD 1280.

Aniyana (Middle Caicos)

Things were happening elsewhere in the Turks and Caicos. By AD 1000 sites had been established on Middle Caicos at MC-8/10 on the south coast (Sullivan 1981; Sinelli 2001) and MC-12 on the north coast (Sullivan 1981; Keegan 1997). The predominant pottery at MC-12 is Palmetto ware. Thus by AD 1000 one element of an identifiable Lucayan culture had emerged. MC-12 grew into one of the largest villages on Middle Caicos. The other major settlements were MC-36 and MC-32. MC-36 is located near the modern town of Conch Bar, and very little archaeological work has been done there. MC-32 is 1.5 km east of MC-12. It is worth noting that MC-12 and MC-32 form a contemporaneous settlement pair after AD 1280. In fact, MC-32 may have been established by elites who had been living at MC-12. We will return to these sites in the following chapters.

One last settlement on Middle Caicos must be mentioned. It apparently was first reported by Theodoor de Booy (1912: 101):

> About four miles southwest of the Lorimers settlement, on the salina, and overgrown with guinea-grass during the greater part of the year, is found a large number of Indian mounds—not burial places as might

be supposed, but evidently erected as a shelter against the water on the salina and as a foundation upon which to build huts. These mounds average three feet high, eight feet wide, and about twelve feet long, and are built of pieces of coral rock. As a rule the mounds are arranged in a crescent, with not more than six mounds in a group.

Sullivan may have rediscovered de Booy's site in 1976, although he was reluctant to claim that his was the site that de Booy had reported. Even though it was located in approximately the same location, de Booy found far fewer artifacts on the surface than did Sullivan. In any case, Sullivan called his site MC-6. It is somewhat ironic that a site of such importance should have such a simple name. MC-6 means that it was the sixth site identified on Middle Caicos during Sullivan's surveys (Sullivan 1980). The site has revolutionized our understanding of the relationship between the Lucayan Islands and Hispaniola. Furthermore, MC-6 is far and away the best candidate for the settlement at which Caonabó grew up.

Conclusions

This chapter has continued the narrative of Columbus's first voyage through the islands and provided a brief introduction to archaeological research conducted in the area of interest. This account has four main objectives. The first is to demonstrate that the conventional ceramic chronology for the islands is inaccurate. The prehistory of the region is not simply the outcome of migrants from Puerto Rico establishing an Ostionan outpost in Hispaniola and the islands to the north and west. Pottery had long been a component of the Archaic toolkit, and the Taíno cultures that had developed by the time of European contact reflect the complex interactions of multiple social groups. In fact, several of these groups (for example, the Macorix, Ciguayo, and Nuhuirei) maintained regional polities alongside those of the traditional Taínos. In this regard, the ethnohistory of Hispaniola may not be directly transferable to the archaeology of Puerto Rico or other islands in the West Indies (for example, Las Casas described four different cultures inhabiting Cuba).

Second, archaeological investigations at a number of village sites in Hispaniola illustrate the characteristics of chiefly settlements, including large size, a circular to oval plan, artificial earthworks, roads connecting the settlement to important places, astronomical alignments, objects of wealth, and evidence for feasting. These features will be important in the search for Caonabó's homeland in the Lucayan Islands.

Third, the general characteristics of Lucayan culture provide a backdrop to the society from which Caonabó reportedly came. In general Lucayan culture seems to have been a smaller-scale version of the culture described for the Taínos. Evidence from Grand Turk indicates that peoples in Haiti knew of and exploited these islands from the eighth century on. The initial use of these islands involved temporary settlements for the procurement of marine resources, which probably were exported to feed the growing population on Hispaniola. Somewhat later, craftspeople from Haiti went to Grand Turk to make shell beads. These beads were of special significance during the protohistoric period, when they were being woven into beaded belts. Finally, permanent settlements were established in the Caicos Islands after about AD 1000.

Finally, the islands of the Bahama archipelago have been evaluated with regard to their potential as Caonabó's natal home. At least by the time of Spanish contact the central Bahamas had closer ties to Cuba than to Hispaniola. Great Inagua and Mayaguana were in less favorable geographical locations and therefore likely had less direct immediate access to the cacicazgos of Hispaniola and specifically to those associated with Caonabó. By this process of elimination the Turks and Caicos Islands have come to the fore as the best candidate for Caonabó's homeland. More specifically, MC-6 on Middle Caicos is so unique that it is the only known settlement in all of the Lucayan Islands that could have reared a cacique who would return to Hispaniola and share control of over half the island. The first piece of the puzzle is in place. MC-6 fits the bill as a Taíno-influenced gateway community with direct ties to Hispaniola. Chapters 5 and 6 examine the specific characteristics of MC-6 and neighboring sites.

Of course all of this hinges on the assumption that Las Casas was correct in calling Caonabó a Lucayo who came from the Lucayan Islands. But before looking at the archaeological evidence from MC-6, we will explore the characteristics of Taíno society in greater detail. The next chapter reviews Taíno social and political organizations to show that they were flexible enough to allow for the coronation of a stranger king.

4

Kinship and Kingship

Sometimes parody is the best way to capture the essence of reflected reality. Take the following scene from *Monty Python and the Holy Grail*:

> Woman: "Order, eh? Who does he think he is?"
> King: "I'm your King."
> Woman: "Well I didn't vote for you!"
> King: "You don't vote for Kings."
> Woman: "Well how'd you become King then?"
> King: "The Lady of the Lake, her arm clad in the purest shimmering samite, held aloft Excalibur from the bosom of the water signifying by divine providence that I, Arthur, was to carry Excalibur. That is why I am your King."
> Dennis: "Listen, strange women lying in ponds distributing swords is no basis for a system of government. Supreme executive power derives from a mandate from the masses, not from some farcical aquatic ceremony—"

There is nothing in the anthropological literature that captures the philosophical essence of human agency in such pure form. I would, however, give Kent Flannery (1976) a close second for the scene in his parable in which ideas are offered in exchange for a huge ball of jade. In the *Monty Python* scene it is Dennis (the "peasant") who spouts political theories for the rule of the masses, while King Arthur appeals to a mythical justification for the position, role, and status that he holds. In both examples we have modern stories offered as satire that take our search for absolute answers to (il)logical extremes.

Modern frameworks, paradigms, perspective, and myths such as cultural materialism, evolutionism, scientism, Marxism, postmodernism, and other "isms" all claim to be the r^2 of cultural practice. In other words, they incorporate the variables that explain the major part of the circumstances. Yet the foundation of human culture is social interaction. People live in aggregates or groups. The relations that regulate social interactions are the key to understanding human culture. These interactions are the basis of kinship. Although most archaeologists deny any role to kinship in complex societies, they do so at their own peril (see Ensor 2003; Gillespie 2000a). Kinship relations define a society, be they between parent and child, husband and wife, in-laws, clan members, ancestors, friends, or even subject and king. (Even the notion of "subject and king" reifies the modernist dichotomy and the structuralist dialectic.)

Sahlins (1985: 78) suggests that the transition to kingship implies a rejection of kinship: "great chiefs and kings of political society are not *of* the people they rule." The king, as divine (and benevolent or oppressive dictator), is a foreigner who is not bound by social conventions. Yet even where the myth of the stranger king is used to justify leadership, the current ruler is only *l'étranger* because of genealogy tracing back to a foreign ancestor from sometime in the distant past. Thus the king must also justify his or her position through reference to kin relations with the ancestors. Even if the king's kinship is distinct from the kinship of others, it is still kinship.

It has been said that ordinary Hawaiians were not permitted to trace their genealogy. While this may satisfy an anthropologist's etic curiosity, I find it hard to believe that commoner Hawaiians did not know who their kin relations were and where they fit in the overall social hierarchy. A rule that forbids commoners to trace their ancestry first identifies that this practice existed, and the maintenance of the rule indicates that it continued to be practiced despite prohibitions.

Kinship theory, especially in anthropology, has endured a period of abuse versus use. The critiques made by (1) Sahlins and others in an effort to distinguish between the social economy and the political economy; (2) Ward H. Goodenough (1955), David M. Schneider (1984), and others who observed that anthropological models of social organization were too rule-bound and structured (classificatory); and (3) agency theorists who focus on individuals have all conspired to subdue kinship theory. These critiques reflect a general anthropological dissatisfaction with social organization as defined by George Peter Murdock (1949). Furthermore, despite efforts by James Deetz (1968), James N. Hill (1970), and William A. Longacre (1970), or perhaps due to their efforts, archaeologists have turned away from social organization because social structures are "impossible to excavate."

The current trend in archaeology is to look for "house" societies based on the concept introduced by Claude Lévi-Strauss (1982, 1987). By focusing on houses, kinship can be recast in a corporate or economic model, eliminating the need to deal with the intricacies of social relations (Joyce and Gillespie 2000). I agree with the critiques that consanguinity has been overemphasized in kinship studies. Moreover, this emphasis is based on Western notions of bloodlines and blood relations. Nevertheless, it is still possible to investigate how individuals navigate the tendencies of lineality, descent, residence, and marriage.

It would be easy for me to jump on the house society bandwagon, especially given one translation of Caonabó's name as "golden house." Yet Lévi-Strauss never meant for *société de maison* to be the exclusive category of identity. In keeping with the perspective presented in chapter 1, social organization is chaotic. It is especially chaotic when we try to track relationships, roles, statuses, and other interactions that define ego's notion of self-identity. Yet chaos is not random. There are deeper structures that can be expressed by renovating Murdockian organizational concepts. An excellent example is Per Hage and Frank Harary's (1983, 1996) use of structural models developed in graph theory. In sum, while our goal should be to adopt a processual perspective (Gillespie 2000a: 1), processes are responsive to underlying structures. And if these structures can be given names, and thereby used to classify social groups, have we not come full circle?

Postprocessual archaeology initially adopted Murdock's language and tried to apply it to archaeological contexts, and I applaud these efforts. Nonetheless, there are pitfalls that come from an incomplete understanding of how social relations are expressed in practice. An excellent example is Ian Hodder's (1979) study of the relationship between residence patterns and burial practices among the Mesakin who live in the Nuba Hills of the Sudan. Abraham Rosman and Paula Rubel (n.d.) are critical of Hodder's conclusions because they feel that he is not adept in the intricacies of social organization. They conclude: "Since Hodder does not understand the way in which a matrilineal avunculocal society operates, he naturally draws incorrect conclusions from the Mesakin data." Clearly I side with Rosman and Rubel.

Archaeologists can detect social relations, social structure, and even individual behavior if the data are available. Moreover, all societies have some notion of inheritance and descent, practice patterned forms of residence, and have elaborate rules to identify a potential spouse. Does every society have hard and fast rules for each of these categories? No: to repeat my litany, just because culture is chaotic does not mean it lacks underlying structures. Archaeologists need a more thorough grounding in theories of kinship and social organization and must endeavor to find ways to observe these in the archaeological record (for example, Ensor 2003).

Taíno Social Organization

In the present case, the mythical realm from which the Taínos emerged is charged with relations among kin. The Oedipal conflict between father and son, the reference to the mother with five names (indicating multiple female roles) and her brother (emphasizing matrilineal ties), the story of Deminán and his three brothers, the murder of Guahayona by Anacacuya (brothers-in-law) in order to take all the women for himself, and the mythical islands of women (Matininó), men (Carib) and sexual union (Guanín) all attest to the importance of kinship. Moreover, in these mythical relations we can also see the foundations of Taíno social organization. In other words, the belief system, as recorded by Ramón Pané, both reifies and proscribes relations among kin. It is from these relations that kingship emerged.

The present discussion is complicated, because I need to present the information in a linear format, when in fact the topics are multidimensional and codetermined. I have decided on the following sequence. First, the basic patterns of Taíno social organization as described by the Spanish are outlined in terms of descent, residence, and marriage patterns as well as the membership of individuals in different kin groups. Second, a hypothesized sequence for the evolution of kin relations in the West Indies is presented. Third, the political agenda is rehearsed in regard to general theory concerning chiefdoms, with specific reference to Taíno cacicazgos. Finally, I show how kinship relations make it reasonable to conclude that Caonabó was truly a stranger king and that he actually came to Hispaniola from the Lucayan Islands.

Spanish Accounts

The Spaniards who conquered the West Indies at the turn of the fifteenth century were fascinated by the ways in which native West Indian societies were organized. Although they detected many differences, the chroniclers also reported that the Taínos had a hierarchical social organization that mirrored Spanish feudal society. Such descriptions certainly over-Hispanicized Taíno social organization, and the chroniclers were inaccurate in some of their interpretations of the Taíno social formation (Moscoso 1986; Wilson 1990). Nevertheless, their accounts are sufficiently detailed to provide the historical continuity needed to create a model of Taíno society at contact.

The Spaniards who recorded Antillean cultures made the majority of their observations among the Taínos of Hispaniola. They reported that the Taíno traced descent through the female line (see Keegan and Maclachlan 1989). This report is supported by the Taíno myth of an immortal being who had a mother with five names and a maternal uncle (Rouse 1948). In practice, matrilineal descent was expressed in the inheritance of rank through the female line, with females sometimes inheriting chiefly positions (Sued-Badillo 1979; Wilson 1990). Cemíes, in this case the physical representations of the lineage's spirits, were passed through the female line (Rouse 1992). Women also are reported to have been both the producers and the distributors of certain high-status goods. When Bartholomew Columbus went to Xaragua to demand tribute, the principal male cacique Behecchio offered foodstuffs, while his sister brought Columbus to a warehouse where she made gifts of high-status goods fashioned in wood and cotton (Las Casas 1951; Wilson 1990; also see Petersen 1982).

Personal property is not reported as an important item of inheritance among commoners in Taíno society. The Spanish said that the Taínos who accompanied them from the coast during the first entrada in the Vega Real helped themselves to goods in other villages. Although the Spanish thought that the people must be related, that idea was based on notions of proper conduct in medieval Spain. There are other examples of the Taínos taking goods from the Spanish without asking for permission to do so. In reading the chronicles, it appears that access to corporate resources was the primary good obtained through matrilineal inheritance. In fact Ramón Pané translated the Taíno word *conuco* as "the lands of his inheritance." Today we use the term as a general reference to agricultural fields.

Curet (2002) has made an important distinction between the inheritance of goods and the inheritance of statuses and roles. He goes on to note that the Spanish were inconsistent in their description of succession. With regard to the inheritance of leadership positions (succession), one of the Spanish accounts indicates that the eldest son would on occasion inherit the rank of lineage chief from his father (Rouse 1948; Alegría 1979). This observation does not necessarily contradict the preceding conclusion that inheritance among the Taínos was matrilineal. Such inheritance could result from patrilineal descent, but this option appears to be an exceptional practice that may have been brought about by the Spanish disruption of the indigenous social system (Curet 2003; Sued-Badillo 1985). The multiple interpretations of Taíno succession in Spanish accounts point to a main goal—to keep the position of chief within the cacique's family—and indicate that matrilineal descent was the most common way in which this was accomplished (Keegan 2006a).

A patrilocal residence pattern was reported for the Taínos (Rouse 1948). Yet this pattern of residence is not consistent with the residence possibilities of matrilineal systems (Aberle 1961; Fox 1967). Moreover, the Spanish identification of patrilocal residence easily could have resulted from confusing where the wife resided with where the husband-and-wife resided in relation to the husband's lineage. Thus, although the wife may have moved to her husband's village, the husband had already moved as a youth to reside avunculocally with his mother's brother in the village of his lineage. This viri-avunculocal residence pattern also was recorded among the Trobriand Islanders of Melanesia; the Haida, Tlingit, and Gitksan of British Columbia, and the Longuda of Nigeria (Adams 1973; Malinowski 1978; Murdock 1949; Rosman and Rubel 1971).

In sum, the Spanish accounts can be interpreted as indicating that the Taínos practiced matrilineal inheritance of corporate resources, that descent was traced through the female line, and that most people resided matrilocally. The caciques and Nitaínos (elites) were different. Their case involved significant resources, in terms of both goods and property that were passed on through inheritance. Moreover, efforts to localize and control these resources would have promoted an organizational configuration that localized elite males. Thus the elite members of the society probably practiced avunculocal residence. In this regard the Taínos are similar to the cultures mentioned above.

These conclusions are not drawn to classify Taíno society or to indicate that all members followed avunculocal rules. In fact avunculocality could not exist without accompanying and alternate residence strategies. The issue is one of process, for which we need labels to communicate. In the Taíno case this involved the process of transforming society from a dominant female domestic economy to a predominant male political economy in which the domestic (subsistence) economy was subsumed.

Agents of Stasis, Agents of Change

Sometimes the path from chaos to structure is the easiest one to follow. Therefore I begin with the chaotic social relations as viewed from the perspective of a single individual ("ego"). Membership in social groups began at birth. Soon after birth ego was given a name that identified ego as a Taíno—a human being (Fewkes 1907: 47). Already ego belonged to a nuclear family, an extended family, a matri-clan, a matrilineage, and a cacicazgo. Gender and membership in these groups had consequences for ego's entire life. We also need to consider ego's personality, which would be apparent to the members of a small-scale group within a few years.[1] Moreover, if we view ego as attempting to achieve the most advantageous position in the culture, then we need to recognize that some would prefer the status quo while others would attempt to change the system (structure). Change and stasis are both processes of structuration (Amodio 1999).

Although there are no records of lateral kin terms in the available ethnographies or histories, Bryan Byrne's (1991) cross-cultural analysis suggested that the Taínos used Crow-like kin terms, a conclusion reached independently by Ensor (2003). In the bifurcate-merging Crow system female patrilateral and matrilateral cross-cousins are differentiated from each other, from siblings, and from parallel cousins, while patrilateral daughters are lumped with patrilateral aunts and matrilateral daughters are lumped with their brother's daughters (Murdock 1949: 224). More recently, Ensor (2003) has shown how Crow kin terms and marriage patterns structured both marriage practices and the layout of villages. He suggests that the circular to oval pattern of settlement that is characteristic of West Indian settlements can be viewed as an outcome of Crow/Omaha kinship. Omaha kinship is basically the patrilineal equivalent of matrilineal Crow kinship. Ensor (2003) argues that both have similar consequences for the societies they describe.

Ego's world was dominated by his or her mother's kin, especially the female kin with whom ego lived. The most important male was ego's mother's brother. Between birth and puberty ego was socialized in the rights and obligations that accompanied group memberships. Life passages were marked by participation in various ceremonies, including a hair-cutting ceremony in which ego was the focus (Lovén 1935). The passage from child to adult was celebrated at puberty. Unless they were already married at this time, girls remained in the village of their mothers. Boys, particularly those who were expected to participate in leadership roles in their clan, moved to the village of their designated maternal uncle.

Marriage marked passage to full adulthood. Commoner males were expected to compensate the wife-giving lineage by providing bride-service (Fewkes 1907: 48). The husband moved to the village of his wife, where he worked for his in-laws for several years. It is not clear how long bride-service lasted, but in some societies the end of bride-service (sometimes called suitor-service) coincides with the birth of a child. In effect, bride-service ends with the production of a new member of the wife's clan. The couple would then set up their own household in the most advantageous location. After marriage and bride-service most commoners would pass through various roles and positions within their lineage and other less formal groups. In addition, certain individuals would receive training as craft specialists or as healers and shamans (*behiques*).

In contrast, it is reported that high-status males compensated the wife-giving lineage with payments rather than with service. The husband would accumulate a variety of wealth items with the help of his clan and pay these to the wife-giving clan. The wife would then move immediately to live viri-avunculocally with her husband. High-status males were also polygynous and were able to take as many wives as they could support. It may actually be worth reversing the sequence of cause and effect. Elite individuals who engaged in polygynous marriage alliances may have been expected to support as many wives (denoting allied communities) as they could.

Such multiple marriages had an important integrative effect for the society. High-status women from one clan or lineage were given in marriage to a high-status male from another clan or lineage, thus creating a bond between these groups. All offspring were members of the wife-giving lineage, which strengthened the bond. Moreover, Marvin Harris (1979: 145) notes that "bride-price and suitor-service tend to occur where production is being increased, land is plentiful, and the labor of additional women and children is seen as scarce and as being in the best interests of the corporate group." His comments certainly characterize Hispaniola during the rise of the Taíno cacicazgos (Ensor 2003; Keegan et al. 1998).

The highest position a high-status individual could achieve was that of cacique. In preparation, a male joined an assembly of nephews in the village of his cacique uncle. There he would have been instructed in the duties of the position until the moment of succession. Moreover, there were several grades of cacique: from clanlord or headman in a village, to district chiefs who counted a number of villages as allies, to *matunherí*, who were the paramount chiefs of the major provinces in Hispaniola (Redmond and Spencer 1994). Obviously the individuals who assumed these different roles went through different processes of education.

The final passage was death, which was celebrated by a variety of ceremonies, depending again upon the age, rank, and gender of the individual. For example, it is reported that a cacique was buried in a specially prepared tomb in which he was seated on his wooden stool (*duho*) and that at least some of his wives were buried with him (Fewkes 1907: 70). In addition, some individuals lived beyond death; their bones were curated in shrines to reflect a reverence for the ancestors, just as Yayael's bones were preserved in the origin myth. Columbus reported that human bones were kept in baskets hung from the rafters of Taíno houses. Although some Spaniards attributed this practice to cannibalism, Columbus noted that it was done out of respect for the ancestors.

In sum, every individual was born into circumstances that differed from those of every other individual. Ego certainly negotiated through a maze of relations (economic, social, ritual, political, and so forth). For those favoring economic maximization as the main motivation, ego would have tried to make the most out of life. We must also consider the possibility that ego was simply along for the ride. Thus the notion of a methodological individual may serve to characterize general trends in a society, but it has no hope of capturing the chaos that was the lives of particular individuals.

Initial Conditions: Islands of Chaos

The other main component of chaos theory is that outcomes are strongly dependent on initial conditions. Thus we need to investigate who colonized the West Indies and who were the ancestors of the ethnohistoric Taínos. Groups of pottery-using horticulturalists, called Saladoids after the Saladero type-site in Venezuela, entered the Antilles from coastal Guiana and the Orinoco River Valley prior to 400 BC (Haviser 1997; Rouse 1992; Siegel 1992). Their migration is easily traced by the distinctive ways in which they decorated their pottery vessels. Yet the manner in which they colonized the islands is very much the subject of conjecture and debate (Bradford 2001; Keegan 2004).

The traditional model of island colonization implied that a single propagule reached Grenada and that thereafter each island was colonized in turn. This characterization fits traditional models from island biogeography (Keegan and Diamond 1987), because after Grenada was discovered there were islands visible to the north all the way to the U.S. Virgin Islands. This view of island colonization also made good economic sense. Despite their small size, every island in the Lesser Antilles could have supported a substantial population. Thus the motivation to move to the next island in the chain would only occur when the resources on the inhabited island had been depleted. In fact island colonization was such a no-brainer that until recently few Caribbean archaeologists even considered it to be an issue worth investigating (Siegel 1991).

Reality has a funny way of deflating our logical models. In the first place it was impossible for one propagule to procreate at a rate that could account for the colonization of Puerto Rico by 400 BC (Keegan 1985). Second, plotting Saladoid settlements on islands according to their chronology showed that only after AD 200 did every island have at least one Saladoid settlement (Haviser 1997). Third, recent evidence suggests that the earliest Saladoid sites in the West Indies were in Puerto Rico and the Leeward Islands. This distribution indicates that most of the Lesser Antilles were bypassed during the initial migration(s) such that arrival in the Greater Antilles was almost simultaneous with departure from South America (Bradford 2001; Keegan 2004).

It can be argued that economic factors were not the main dimension in structuring the Saladoid expansion. Take Grenada, for example. The population of Grenada in 1990 was estimated to have been slightly more than 84,000. Obviously Grenada today is part of a world economy, so the population could exceed that which could be supported by local resources alone. Nevertheless, it is impossible to justify on economic grounds alone the fact that there were only two major settlements on Grenada, one in the southwest (Grand Anse) and one in the northeast (Pearls) at AD 200. Even giving very generous estimates for their populations, it is difficult to imagine that fewer than

1,000 people could have taxed the resource base of the entire island. Furthermore, many of the earliest settlements are actually on the smaller islands of the Lesser Antilles (Bradford 2001). Why settle a small island like Carriacou (in the Grenadines just north of Grenada) when most of Grenada was unoccupied?

We can address this issue by applying several different measurements of distance. Let us start with economic distance. Studies of resource use in the West Indies indicate that the majority of food resources in archaeological sites were obtained within 5 km of a site (Wing and Scudder 1983; Wing 2001). Therefore we would expect that the minimal distance between settlements with no direct competition for resources would be 10 km. Going back to our Grenada example, there could have been more than a dozen sites on Grenada without substantial competition for resources. Yet we need to factor several other variables into the equation. First, not all resources are evenly distributed, so a small number of key, "patchy" resources would expand the minimal range (for example, the distribution of potable water sources is often mentioned in this regard). Second, if travel time versus absolute distance is factored in, then sites along easy pathways (for example, watercourses for people adept with canoes) would have a longer catchment dimension than do those separated by less navigable terrain (for example, steep mountain ranges). Finally, anthropological notions of carrying capacity are typically based on groups that have occupied an area for a substantial length of time. It is likely that the first people to reach an island rapidly consumed resources that were not previously subject to predation and that they rapidly moved to new locations at which these high-ranked resources were more abundant (Carlson 1999; Carlson and Keegan 2004). In other words, during an initial period of exploration and exploitation people moved rapidly through the islands in order to exploit the best resources (Berman and Gnivecki 1995; Irwin 1992; Keegan 2004). Because such sites were ephemeral, they are the most difficult to locate.

A second measure is demographic distance, which is defined as the minimal distance required to maintain a reproductively (procreative) viable population. Small groups of colonists are subject to substantial stochastic risk in terms of the production of offspring, and a gender balance must be achieved to maintain an adequate spouse pool. Demographers abandoned this question years ago when it was demonstrated by a Monte Carlo simulation that one man and two women of prime reproductive age could have peopled all of Australia 50,000 years ago. Minimum numbers were clearly not of value. John Moore (2001), however, has demonstrated by simulation that the viability of a colony was greatly enhanced by maintaining ties to one other settlement from which spouses could be recruited. In other words, relations between parent and daughter communities made reproductive survival much more likely. The issue is the maximum demographic distance that would allow groups to maintain sufficiently close ties to another community from which spouses could be recruited.

Ceremonial distance provides yet another dimension. Ceremonial activities serve to reinforce the sense of group identity and to legitimize positions of leadership. What is the maximum geographical distance over which members of a "ceremonial group" successfully can be maintained? There must be a point at which the paramount leader has no meaningful role in ritual activities of a community. In this regard, peripatetic leaders visit distant communities not only to support their retinue by the largesse of their distant followers but also to reinforce the notion of ritual urgency (Earle 1997). In other words, rather than bring staples to the chief, the chief goes to the staples; and the chief brings the immediacy of their dominion to the community and supplies it with divine blessings.

Political distance is embedded strongly in ceremonial distance. Again, the question is how far leaders can extend control beyond the village in which they live. This is one of the main problems discussed in the previous chapter with regard to the boundaries of the Taíno cacicazgos. These boundary areas were fuzzy zones that were never hard and fast (Wilson 1990).

A final dimension is social distance: what is the maximal distance between settlements that still allows the members of a social group to exercise their rights and fulfill their social obligations? The members of a social group who reside in the same or nearby village will experience fewer impediments to participation than will those who come from more distant communities. When individuals move at marriage to live in the village of their spouses, and when a village fissions and some members move to form a new village, the individuals will no longer have immediate access to their former social network, especially when such moves are over long distances. In this regard social ties will influence the distances over which such moves will take place. In the present case, I argue below that Taíno society evolved from an initial condition in which matrilineal descent and matrilocal residence were the predominant organizational patterns. For this reason I focus on the maximum social distance for such groups (the minimal distance is residence within the same community).

In matrilineal and matrilocal societies females are localized and males are dispersed. William Divale (1974) has argued that this form of social organization is particularly well suited to situations in which a group actively is colonizing new territories. Female productive activities are localized, thus maintaining continuity in the base group, while men are free to pursue visiting, trading, and raiding (see Ember 1974). Men are married into the villages of their wives. They are outsiders, and their primary allegiance and responsibilities are to their kin who live in other villages. Remember that we are not talking about marriages based on love; we are dealing with marriages based on alliances between extended families and their connections to larger social groups. Per Hage (1998, 1999; Hage and Marck 2003) has shown that the initial colonists of Island Melanesia and western Polynesia practiced matrilineal descent and matrilocal residence. This conclusion runs contrary to the patrilineal conical clan model for the Lapita expansion into the Pacific (Kirch 2000). Yet Hage's conclusions make perfect sense and serve to explain both the long pause in western Polynesia and the social foundations for this pause.

Each of these means for defining distance is embodied in the model of circulating reference. For example, marriage (social) requires ceremonies (ritual) that require the accumulation of goods (economic) for the purpose of alliance (political) and procreation (demography). Clearly we cannot define the accumulation of wealth without reference to political, ritual, social, and economic relations; marriage is not simply the union of two people; children are not defined by who contributed their DNA; there is a multiplicity of dimensions and chaos along every fractal. This is what I mean by the harmonics of life. Even if we pluck one violin string, there are still undertones and overtones. But when we play a chord and add to it the orchestra of brass, woodwind, and percussion, we produce sound waves that may be symphonious or discordant to our sense of hearing. The challenge is to find ways to represent the music of life within the confines of language.

The preceding is an example of what I call the harmonic reality of hermeneutic chaos. At every moment our interpretive senses are overwhelmed, and it is only the selectivity of our brain that saves most of us from descending into chaos. What creates meaning? Can meaning be categorized as social, economic, demographic, ecological, or something else? Is it a product of our individual brains, and can we really comprehend how others have described it? What meanings underlie our understanding and the understandings we attempt to communicate? The answers to these questions require a new form of thinking—a horizontal form of thinking. If our linguistic expressions are of necessity linear, then our line must crosscut dimensions. We need to move away from a philosophy based on hierarchy ("hermeneutic spirals") and develop a complementary theory of heterarchy. Rather than engaging in a contest of taste ("It is chicken, fried, and I taste 11 herbs and spices"), this should be a contest of comprehension. We do not need to deconstruct the ingredients to recognize Kentucky Fried Chicken. We need to embrace harmony and use it to further the philosophy of interpretation.

It seems logical to start with the melody.

Let us then focus on a particular set of historical contingencies. It is impossible to track all of the different dimensions influencing the emergence of the peoples we call Taínos, so my circuit starts with and focuses on social distance, which to me seems to be the most important factor for understanding the Saladoid colonization of the West Indies. Although we cannot identify the sequence in which sites were established, it is clear that they were widely scattered during the initial phase of settlement. Moreover, expansion to the west seems to have been cut off for as yet unknown reasons, so the entire Saladoid period can be viewed as reflecting the colonization of the Lesser Antilles, along with Puerto Rico and the Virgin Islands.

During the initial phase of island colonization the population grew at very rapid rates as groups moved quickly through the islands. Opportunities for individuals to assume positions of leadership would have been common but short-lived. These initial colonists likely practiced matrilineal descent and matrilocal residence, because these patterns of residence and descent characterize the mainland Arawakan peoples who today live closest to the river mouths from which the ancestors of the Taínos departed (Steward and Faron 1959: 300–301), because matrilineal descent is usually accompanied by a preference for matrilocal residence (Aberle 1961: 666), and because this residence preference is necessary for avunculocal residence to emerge (Fox 1967; Murdock 1949). Furthermore, as already mentioned, ethnohistoric reports suggest that matrilineal descent and avunculocal residence were one form of practice among the Taínos of Hispaniola at contact (Alcina Franch 1983; Keegan and Maclachlan 1989: 623; Keegan 2006a).

Within these social arrangements males filled the major political roles as leaders of the matrilineage (Schneider 1961: 5). Male leaders would have come forward in a number of instances, for example: (1) in the formation of marriage alliances with other matri-sibs, which were needed to ensure reproductive continuity; (2) during the fissioning of local settlements and the movement of people between islands; (3) in the management of economic and demographic risk inherent in island colonization through the continuation of interisland trading and visiting; and (4) in relations (whether hostile or benign) with Archaic groups already in residence on at least some of the islands. These and other opportunities for leadership were short-lived and could be abrogated through the fissioning and moving away of dissatisfied individuals and their supporters.

According to conventional wisdom, there was a pause of almost 1,000 years before population expansion continued out of Puerto Rico and into the west and north (Rouse 1986, 1992). By the time a second wave of expansion began around AD 600, the pottery style in western Puerto Rico had changed so much that the people living there were considered culturally distinct from their Saladoid ancestors. These people were called Ostionan, a name derived from the type-site of Punta Ostiones in western Puerto Rico. This second wave of Ostionan expansion moved rapidly westward along northern and southern routes to colonize Hispaniola, Jamaica, eastern Cuba, and the Bahamas (Rouse 1992). I have proposed an alternate view for the settlement of Hispaniola and Cuba (see chapter 3). In this scenario, pottery making and horticulture moved across the Mona Passage at an earlier date (circa 350 BC), and the Ostionan peoples confronted other Ceramic Age horticulturalists when they began to colonize the islands west of Puerto Rico. Faced with mounting evidence, I now suspect that Ostionan peoples first developed in some of the Archaic groups of eastern Hispaniola (Keegan 2006b).

David Watters (1982, 1997) has long maintained that Caribbean archaeologists would do well to follow the trail blazed by our colleagues in Oceania. Allaire (2003: 198) recently has suggested that comparing the Caribbean Islands to those in the Pacific may be "misleading when we consider that the Lesser Antilles are not distributed as a scattering of widely dispersed isolates in the immensity of the Pacific Ocean." Yet his suggestion is based on a misunderstanding of the geography of Oceania. Island Melanesia, Micronesia, and Western Polynesia are not the widely dispersed isolates of which he writes; they are composed of a series of archipelagos that share much in common with the West Indies (for a comparison with the Mediterranean islands, which he proposes as more appropriate, see Keegan and Diamond 1987).

I too have been reluctant to follow the trail charted by Watters, because the Lapita peoples who were the earliest colonists of western Polynesia have been described as having a form of social organization characterized as a patrilineal conical clan (Goldman 1970; Kirch 2000; Sahlins 1958). In contrast, the Ceramic Age colonists of the Caribbean seem to have based their social organization on matrilineal principles. It might seem logical that these forms of organization are mirror images, in which one simply substitutes a woman (matri) for a man (patri); yet in both forms of descent reckoning it is males who assume the leadership positions that require interaction with foreign groups (Schneider 1961). Thus a matrilineal organization adds a twist: it is an individual's mother's brother who wielded supreme authority. In other words, these forms of social organization can have very different expressions.

The tables seem to have turned. In a series of articles that have led to the reinterpretation of the social arrangements of the peoples who colonized Oceania, Per Hage (1998, 1999; Hage and Marck 2003) has demonstrated how groups with matrilineal descent and matrilocal/avunculocal residence were the initial colonists of Oceania. Thus both sets of colonists are now viewed as practicing matrilineal descent and matrilocal residence. By a further strange coincidence, Saladoid colonists had reach Puerto Rico by 400 BC but did not expand further west for over 1,000 years, and Lapita colonists reached western Polynesia by 2500 BC but failed to settle eastern Polynesia for perhaps 1,500 years. Could the "long pause" in the Caribbean and in Polynesia share a common foundation? From eastern Polynesia the archipelagos are markedly different. While Puerto Rico is hardly more than a stone's throw from Hispaniola, the distance from Samoa to the next inhabitable island is greater than the distance from South America to Puerto Rico and from Puerto Rico to both Florida and the Yucatan. Yet geographical distance may be of somewhat less importance, because the people of the Pacific had sailing canoes, while the people of the West Indies paddled dugout canoes.

Nevertheless, there appear to be important parallels. In both cases the organizational characteristics of the colonists were not sufficient to allow for further expansion. In the Caribbean it is likely that the rapid settlement of Puerto Rico placed a strain on matrilineal relations for peoples who traveled by canoe and were distributed over 1,000 km of islands and sea. Moreover, groups that already inhabited Hispaniola may have made westward expansion less inviting than was the settlement of uninhabited islands to the south. It was only after emerging caciques began to assert control over other villages that the Ostionan peoples of western Puerto Rico moved on. A similar situation obtains for the settlement of eastern Polynesia. Matrilineal and matrilocal organizations require "short" marriage distances so that dispersed males who are living in their wife's village (uxorilocal) can easily return to their natal village and participate in clan activities. In other words, it is extremely difficult to assemble a matrilineal/matrilocal group that is willing to strike out on its own with only limited potential for maintaining close ties and interactions with the matri-clan. The more substantial distances between west and east Polynesia halted the matrilineal/matrilocal Lapita peoples in their tracks (Hage 1998, 1999; Hage and Marck 2003).

Here again, the social organization could not tolerate the vast distances between parent and offspring community. It is these social consequences that led to the demise of Lapita Culture in western Polynesia (and to the end of Saladoid Culture in Puerto Rico). It was only after the populations on Fiji, Samoa, and Tonga had grown to the point at which first avunculocal men became rulers and later ranked patrilocal men assumed these roles that an acceptable social means for fissioning became possible.

The shift from matrilineal to patrilineal organization occurs in settings where males are no longer absent for long periods (for example, episodes of exploration and exploitation of distant resources and/or the practice of long-distance exchange). Various forms of social organization began to emerge after the main trading corridor became limited to Fiji, Samoa, and Tonga. My colleagues in the Pacific might claim that there were many islands available for settlement at low population densities, especially in the Fiji and Tonga archipelagos. Yet work in the Caribbean has demonstrated that mobile peoples will tolerate far lower population densities than people of urban ilk are accustomed.

In essence, there was nowhere left to go. As men became settled, and their control of local resources was more firmly in hand, then some means of inheritance had to be practiced in which males played a more immediate role. With men at home they tend to try to dominate both the political economy and the domestic mode of production. When we consider that we are dealing with more than 1,000 years, it is not unreasonable to propose that male domination came to be expressed in the patrilineal conical clan. This form of social organization emphasizes descent and primogeniture. Thus with every generation, and as resources became increasing carved up among family members, the junior members of the lineage were increasingly marginalized. As the junior members of the patrilineal conical clan ("ramage") were increasingly disenfranchised, escape and long-distance expeditions became an increasingly attractive option. Moreover, the conflict between male participation in their clan was no longer an issue. A patrilineal organization consolidated its male members, all of whom shared similar potentials, and females were simply purchased from the wife-giving clans. A final consideration is that colonies have a substantially higher potential for success if they maintain contact with one other community (Moore 2001). I mention this because Geoff Irwin's (1992) model of safe sailing and return voyaging also makes practical sense from a demographic perspective.

Returning to the West Indies, all of the islands were occupied eventually at relatively low densities. In the first phase all of the archaeological sites contained common material threads (for example, white-on-red painted pottery, exotic stone pendants and amulets, and common religious paraphernalia). The next phase is characterized by semiautonomous developments on a subregional scale. This intermediate phase is reflected in divergent regional pottery styles (Rouse 1986). In the final phase, Chican styles of pottery emerged and spread widely through the Greater Antilles and into the northern Lesser Antilles and the Bahama archipelago. These styles are associated with the ethnohistoric Taínos.

Trade networks were always the bloodlines of West Indian peoples. During the Saladoid these networks connected South America and Puerto Rico; but with the rise of the Taíno chiefdoms, a very broad area encompassing all of the Greater Antilles, the Bahamas, and the northern Lesser Antilles as far south as Saba came to be integrated in a Taíno interaction sphere. Trade networks through the rest of the Lesser Antilles brought exotic and ritual goods from South America to the cacicazgos of Hispaniola. Moreover, the Taínos did not simply engage in exchange. Excavations on Grand Turk have revealed that seasonal expeditions came from Hispaniola to extract the resources in the southern Bahamas. The best example is the specialized shell-bead production center at the Governor Beach site on Grand Turk that was in operation in the twelfth and thirteenth centuries (Carlson 1993). In addition, some researchers have suggested that there was also contact with Mesoamerica, based on similarities in the ballgames played there and in the Greater Antilles (Alegría 1983; compare Walker 1993).

Cacicazgo: The Model for Chiefdoms

Elsa Redmond and Charles Spencer (1994) have noted that before chiefdom was a stage of cultural evolution it was the manner in which West Indian peoples organized themselves. In this regard there is some tension between the theory of chiefdoms and the reality of cacicazgos, especially given the ways in which the notions of chiefdom have been generalized. It is therefore worth considering general models of chiefdoms before attempting to describe the reality of Hispaniolan cacicazgos at the time of European contact.

I was a student of Tim Earle and Allen Johnson, so my definition of chiefdoms has tended to follow their lead (Earle 1978, 1987, 1997; Johnson and Earle 1987). They defined chiefdoms as regionally integrated polities in which the interests of a dependent population are balanced against those of an emerging aristocracy (Earle 1987: 297). Earle further distinguished between simple and complex chiefdoms, a distinction of size versus scale. Chiefdoms, in contrast to "Big Man" or "local group" polities, are regional in the sense that they extend beyond the village or local group (Johnson and Earle 1987). To a large degree the main difference between simple and complex chiefdoms is that simple chiefdoms have fewer members. Because they both use similar mechanisms to integrate regional populations, they share more with each other than they do with similar-sized local group polities. In other words, a simple chiefdom with 1,000 members is more similar to a complex chiefdom with 10,000 members than it is to a Big Man polity with 1,000 members.

Earle (1987: 291) reports that almost all efforts to explain the rise of chiefdoms have stressed the importance of economic relations. These relations are characterized as either managerial (in which the chief organizes and manages aspects of the economy) or controlling (in which there is differential access to productive resources and/or exchanged wealth). Johnson and Earle (1987) have shown that such hierarchical relations of production should be viewed as complementary behaviors constituting the economic role of chiefs.

I view Earle's dichotomy of "management" and "control" as representing mechanisms for achieving a more basic objective. This objective is economic growth under conditions of locally diminishing marginal returns to production. Chiefdoms emerge from subsistence economies. The economic goal of subsistence production is usually given as the satisfaction of needs or wants using a cost-minimization strategy (Johnson and Earle 1987). For a cost-minimization strategy to be effective, however, some other aspect of the economy must be satisfied, optimized, or maximized. I propose that the major goal of horticultural economies is population growth through either the production of offspring or the recruitment of new members. This goal should not be surprising, given that labor is typically the major limiting factor in horticultural economies. Yet this explanation is likely too materialist, in a vulgar sense, for my Marxist colleagues.

The current trend in archaeology is to describe chiefdoms in terms of agency theory, as involving either corporate or network strategies. Corporate strategies emphasize staple finance, collective ritual, and communal burials (Blanton et al. 1996: 6). This strategy promotes monumental architecture, comparative egalitarianism, wealth equality, communal ritual, and a lack of evidence for powerful individuals. In contrast, the network strategy involves elites who emphasize exchanges in prestigious marriage alliances, exotic goods, and specialized knowledge in extralocal networks (Blanton et al. 1996: 4–5). This strategy promotes an emphasis on the production and exchange of prestige goods controlled by elites and the development of dependent commoners. Although all chiefdoms are recognized as practicing both strategies, it has been proposed that one strategy was dominant in every chiefdom. It must also be remembered that these behaviors represent elite strategies and are thus not characteristic of societies as a whole. Yet there are strong correlations between corporate strategies and complex chiefdoms and between network strategies and simple chiefdoms (Ensor 2003).

This corporate-network model has been applied to the Taínos of Puerto Rico by Antonio Curet and José Oliver (1998). They propose that changes in domestic structures (houses) represent the gradual dismantling of kinship relations and communal institutions by emerging elites. In the same vein, Siegel (1997) argues that chiefs and shaman gained power by controlling the rituals and ceremonial spaces that maintain and reproduce society. Following Ensor, I prefer to downplay elite agency and look at the structures in which they emerge and negotiate their status. The issue that is largely ignored is: where do elites come from? "Leaders in non-class societies do not appropriate for power, they reciprocate for power. Power, prestige, labor and resources are given by commoners having their own ambitions" (Ensor 2003: 148–149).

In structural terms I view chiefdoms as hierarchically organized, kinship-based polities that are organized to promote economic growth. Economic growth occurs through the recruitment of new members by immigration and procreation. In a sense, chiefdoms can be compared to an inverted pyramid in which the cost of membership is not severe, and everyone benefits as long as growth continues. When population size exceeds the organizational capabilities of the kinship system or when growth stops, however, the inverted pyramid collapses under its own weight (often with a shove from a neighboring competitor). This is a slightly modified description of a system of staple finance, a type of finance that is sometimes referred to as "redistribution" (Earle 1987).

The use of staples to create a financial institution begins in economies in which the subsistence output of every household is autonomous. In order to make certain that needs are met, every household must produce somewhat more than it actually uses. When a leader emerges who is able to mobilize the overproduction of individual households, the opportunity for political action also emerges. In other words, the initial step involves appropriating the surfeit of staples that households produce in order to maintain a certain standard of living.

In return for people's otherwise unused produce the leader must provide at least the same level of subsistence security as was represented by the appropriated surplus. By accepting responsibility for their security and managing subsistence risk, the leader obtains the means to finance other activities with no additional cost to the individual households, and the surfeit is turned into a surplus that is employed for political action.[2] For such a system to work there must be trust among the participants. The producers must trust their leader to bail them out in times of subsistence stress, and the leader must trust the producers to maintain the same level of subsistence overproduction. Such trust—what sociobiologists would call reciprocal altruism—is achieved through the manipulation of kinship relations. In this initial phase of a zero-sum game, both leader and follower relinquish their autonomy.

From this initial economy of scale the jump to a regionally integrated economy is easily achieved. First, the basis for collaborative effort is already in place, because kinship relations typically extend over a wide area. Through marriage alliances, and the more formal expression of rules of residence and descent, the social fabric is ever more tightly knit. Second, subsistence security is more easily maintained over a larger area and with a more diversified economy. In fact the initial basis for the redistributive model was the Hawaiian practice of dividing the island into pie-shaped wedges that gave each "king" access to a complete set of resources from the interior mountains to the coast (Sahlins 1958). Shortfalls in one area could then be offset by the allocation of excess products from other areas. So long as crop failures and other disasters were localized and not severe, the economy could grow at a rapid rate for no additional investment in subsistence production. Finally, as the economy grew the household was ever more distant from the leaders who appropriated their excess production. In the process, the surplus was converted from a household need to a political necessity.

Competition between households and larger aggregations (clans, lineages, and so forth), the intensification of wealth finance as a means to integrate the ever growing regional polity (D'Altroy and Earle 1985), and increasing demands on the organization and output of household production all contributed to the emergence of chiefdoms as a recognizable social formation. At their inception, simple chiefdoms provide benefits to most, if not all, of their members. Moreover, by the time hierarchical inequalities have developed, the household may have no option other than to accept the dictates of the emerging elites.

The crucial first step involves engaging kin. Once an economic base is established, kin still form the most reliable group of ardent supports, including both cognates and affines. Yet kinship may be subverted in order to privilege individuals who possess personal attributes that are of use to the leader. In this regard, Ensor (2003) views marriage alliances as critical to the emergence of social stratification. First, he concludes that a focus on marriage alliances, including nonelite strategies, provides a larger perspective on and complementary model of social stratification. Marriage alliances are considered in the next section, but it is worth emphasizing that this approach is based on the recognition that kinship is fundamental to the emergence and maintenance of social stratification. Second, Ensor notes that the intensification of production in chiefdom societies typically involves additional labor on the part of females. Thus the emergence of social stratification begins with gender inequality and is only much later followed by class inequality. The demands on women are intensified by social relations that free men from participation in the domestic mode of production.

Avunculocal Chiefdoms

In defining chiefdoms as regional-scale growth economies that are organized by principles of kinship, kinship becomes the key element in the emergence of chiefs. It is impossible to understand the political formation called chiefdoms without first understanding the social foundations in which their political economies are imbedded. With regard to the Taínos, Spanish descriptions leave little doubt that the Taínos in Puerto Rico, Hispaniola, and eastern Cuba were complex chiefdoms by the date of European contact (Keegan 1992; Siegel 1997; Wilson 1990). In addition, the archaeology of the Bahamas, Jamaica, central Cuba, and possibly the Leeward Islands indicates that populations on these islands were within the Taíno political sphere and were characterized by simple chiefdoms (Allaire 1987; Delpuech and Hofman 2004; Keegan 1997; Rouse 1992).

It is my contention that the Taínos represent one of the clusters of societies in which conditions favoring the avunculocal chiefdom occurred. Avunculocal chiefdoms are interesting for at least two reasons. First, they are comparatively rare, yet they evolved in a series of widely separated areas of restricted size and with a remarkable degree of similarity. Thus it is a matter of theoretical interest to understand why disparate, unrelated peoples should arrive at this unusual and complex pattern of kinship organization. Second, avunculocal chiefdoms serve as an excellent vehicle for illustrating the ways in which economic relations and social organization evolve in concert.

The notion of infrastructural primacy that underlies the cultural materialist perspective is often misunderstood to mean a mechanical materialism in which certain material conditions are viewed as leading inevitably to similar social organization and ideology (Harris 1979). In fact the primacy attributed to infrastructural determination suggests instead that infrastructural stability promotes social stability whereas infrastructural change regulates social change, with the character of the change reflecting prevailing cultural patterns. Thus it is hardly surprising that chiefdoms are found with cognatic, matrilineal, and patrilineal descent and several patterns of marital residence. The question is why societies take one turning rather than another in their development in response to comparable infrastructural change. Part of the answer lies in the antecedent social organization on which infrastructural change goes to work.

The idea that infrastructurally driven social change is mediated by a society's antecedent structure is illustrated by Melvin Ember (1974; Keegan and Maclachlan 1989). Matrilocal residence and the subsequent development of matrilineality, he suggests, emerge from external warfare. With men absent much of the time, women are obliged to rely heavily on one another, resulting in extended households centered on groups of related women. Internal warfare and heavy reliance on male labor, by contrast, favor patrilocal residence. Avunculocal residence is seen as a response to internal warfare emerging in a previously matrilineal and matrilocal society as powerful men rally their clansmen around them to form extended households of matrilineally related men.

This argument would seem to imply an incompatibility between matrilocal residence and the competition of men for control of local resources. It is not difficult to see how this might be so. Divale (1974) has viewed matrilocality and external war as elements in an expansionist migratory strategy such as that of the Bantu-speaking peoples in Africa. The matrilocal family is also congenial with a pattern of low intensity-horticulture reliant on female labor coupled with hunting or fishing by men over large areas. Absent men and the relatively high divorce rates typical of matrilocal societies may also inhibit population growth. In any case, the matrilocal pattern seems suitable to a society that can deal with the crowding of local subsistence resources by migration or expansion of catchment areas. This pattern of residence, however, is not suited for the intensification of labor in farming or growth in population density. First, the intensification of effort requires the labor of previously absent men; and second, population pressure on local resources suitable for intensified production engenders internal conflict.

Here we observe the structural mediation of infrastructurally driven processes quite clearly. When infrastructural conditions conducive to the emergence of Big Men and then chiefs occur in a previously patrilocal society, no change in marital residence takes place, because the existing pattern is compatible with new political and economic realities. In the matrilocal case, the existing pattern deprives the male would-be entrepreneur of both a domestic group of related males and the resource base he needs to advance his interests. Something has to change.

Observations concerning what chiefs do to transform slow-growth matrilineal societies into societies with denser populations and higher productivity remain to be added. In this regard the work of Rosman and Rubel (1989) is of great importance. They employed a controlled comparison to the Southwest Pacific and the Northwest Coast, somewhat similar to that employed for the Taínos (Keegan and Maclachlan 1989). In addition, they have demonstrated how an avunculocal chiefdom used the potlatch to reinforce the status of an entire community (Rosman and Rubel 1971). It is likely that the Taínos practiced a similar form of community-sponsored feasting (Lovén 1935).

Rosman and Rubel point to the marked similarities between the Trobriand Islanders on the one hand and the Haida and Tlingit on the other. In both areas there is an aristocracy of chiefs with avunculocality, and matrilineal descent, as well as Crow kinship terminology and patrilateral cross-cousin marriage. They then address the question of how these societies reached this state by comparing them to their culturally related neighbors, on the assumption that they may reflect both an antecedent baseline state as well as transitional states on the path to an avunculocal chiefdom. In one case these are neighboring Melanesian horticulturalists, and in the other they are Athapaskan hunter-gatherers. In both instances the baseline state involves a matrilocal society that practices direct marital exchange (usually bilateral cross-cousin marriage), and the transitional stages involve growth in matrilineal kinship, in political integration, and in the frequency of avunculocal residence.

Rosman and Rubel (1989) describe their comparisons as the investigation of developmental potential in two contrasting environments. They demonstrate that the sociopolitical organizations of the Trobriand and the Haida and Tlingit are virtually identical, despite dramatic differences in their ecology and economy. The results undercut traditional materialist theories, which view ecology and/or economy as the major determining factors. It thus appears that structural principles have priority in the evolution of social complexity. How else can we explain identical sociopolitical organizations in such radically different environments (Arctic versus tropical island) and among people with radically different economies (hunter-gatherers versus horticulturalists)?

Such macrocomparisons of ecology and economy overlook more basic similarities. If we reconstrue their data in terms of differing potentials for economic and demographic growth in relation to their neighbors, what matters are not the differences between Melanesian horticulture and Northwest Coast foraging but the distinct advantages that the avunculocal chiefdoms in both areas enjoyed over their neighbors due to superior subsistence resources and strategic locations for trade. Thus the features of infrastructure that may be most important in the transformation of relatively egalitarian matrilineal societies into aristocratic avunculocal chiefdoms have less to do with the character of subsistence technologies or environments than they do with the locational concentration of resources within regions and factors circumscribing the opportunities of individuals and groups (Carneiro 1970). In materialist terms, the means and mode of production as expressed in the organization of labor are crucial.

Occupation of a regionally advantageous position opens the way for the development of social organization capable of controlling resources and arranging them in a way leading to the economic and population growth that consolidates the advantaged group's regional position. It should be remembered that throughout this process these societies are not simply responding to the independent growth of their population but are actively promoting the production of offspring. At the same time, the process is attended by growing differences of rank and privilege within the advantaged society. The less advantaged are members of an advantaged society, which may be what holds them in place if indeed they have some place else to go. Migration may entail unacceptable opportunity costs, such as those suggested as the bases for long pauses in western Polynesia and Puerto Rico. Better to be a low ranking Trobriander or Haida than the tiller of an impoverished atoll or a nomadic hunter.

Taíno Political Economy

At contact the Taínos lived in a ranked society whose primary division was between the aristocratic Nitaínos and the commoners and *naborias* (see Harris 1994; Moscoso 1981). As with other ranked societies, it is likely that there were numerous divisions within these primary ranks. With the exception of *naborias*, there is little discussion of the divisions within the commoner class. Previously, *naboria* was translated as "personal slave"; however, as Las Casas explained, the Taíno treatment and meaning of "slave" were very different from its European use (Harris 1994: 18). To the Taínos *naboria* meant personal service, being a war-captive, and having lower status than commoners, but it did not imply personal ownership (Moscoso 1981: 260–261).

Divisions within the Nitaínos included, for example, caciques (chiefs), *behiques* (shamans), and clanlords. The highest rank was held by the paramount cacique, a ruler whose leadership extended over a substantial territory (Redmond and Spencer 1994). The Taíno lineages were further grouped into cacicazgos. Each cacicazgo was headed by a paramount cacique who had the support of a large number of district caciques and village clanlords. For example, the thirty wives and multiple names ascribed to Behecchio, the paramount cacique of Xaragua, represent villages allied under his leadership (Fewkes 1907: 34; Wilson 1990: 117–118).

One interpretation of the chronicles is that caciques had overall command of the processes of production, including agriculture, fishing, hunting, and handicrafts, with surplus products stored in the caciques' warehouses (Moscoso 1981). Ordinary (commoner) Taínos were reportedly extremely obedient to their caciques. The Spanish noted that ordinary Taínos would suffer torture or commit suicide if this would best serve their cacique (Las Casas 1951: vol. 2, 312; Mártir de Anglería 1989: 592). Harris (1994) has argued that such obedience reflected their belief that caciques were divine. Their status was reflected by the use of specially carved wooden stools (*duhos*), by their transport on litters, by their ability to communicate with the spirits through the *cohoba* ritual, and by their mythic association with *cemíes* (Roe 1997). Yet what is the boundary between respect and subjugation?

In initial dealings with the Taínos, Columbus demanded a set level of tribute from each of the caciques. The caciques were responsible for collecting the tribute from their followers and delivering it to the Spanish (Moscoso 1981; Wilson 1990). Later, when the Spanish began to allocate Taíno communities in encomienda grants, the caciques were exempt from service and other Nitaínos served as supervisors and overseers. These roles may reflect the precontact positions of a certain class of Nitaínos in the tributary chiefdom (Moscoso 1981: 234), or they may reflect Spanish notions of the proper treatment of feudal lords (Ensor 2003).[3] Whether or not the Taínos had a tributary economy is still debated.

The Spanish chronicles regarding tribute among the pre-Hispanic Taínos have been interpreted in contradictory ways (Ensor 2000). On the one hand, a tribal-tributary mode of production has been proposed, in which caciques oversaw all labor and how all products were collected and redistributed (Moscoso 1981: 77, 2003; Siegel 1997: 209). On the other hand, the cacique is viewed as sponsoring community based "potlatch" ceremonies in which resources were collected from communal autarkies (self-sufficient villages) with no exploitative relations (Cassá 1992). In this way caciques manipulated ceremonial activities to enhance their prestige and power (Curet and Oliver 1998; Oliver 1998; Roe 1997). Was such prestige and power associated only with the cacique, however, or did the general populace gain advantages as well? The latter seems to be the case. In his restudy of evidence for production within the chiefly domestic refuse at En Bas Saline, which has been identified as the village of Guacanagarí, Ensor (2003) found evidence for multiple production activities. Thus it appears that the cacique's household was involved in the same activities as other households in the village.

The Emergence of Caciques

Hereditary ruling classes, headed by a cacique or chief, emerge in stratified societies based on unequal access to the means of production. Johnson and Earle (1987) have summarized the four main pathways by which social stratification is achieved: (1) surplus production for the management of risk, (2) facilitation of large-scale infrastructure (for example, irrigation projects), (3) warfare, and (4) long-distance trade. These pathways received varying emphasis in different societies, as is clear from competing theories regarding the origins of the state (for example, Wittfogel 1957; Carneiro 1970; Rathje 1971). Furthermore, it was not necessary for a society to pursue all four pathways, and the context in which these pathways were pursued was as important as the pathway itself. It is my contention that in chiefdom-level societies the ultimate objective is population growth (a sort of incipient mercantile economy), that this objective was pursued in competition with like groups, and that production and reproduction were organized by kinship relations.

Those pathways reflect the basic structures around which chiefdom-level societies are organized. In every case they involve the movement of goods and services toward the chiefly core. Yet this structure is submerged beneath a surficial, topological chimera in which rite and ritual proclaim the divinity of the ruler, the right of the ruler to rule. ("How do you know he's a king? Because he hasn't got shit all over him.") I am not denying that ritual, dress, mannerisms, oral histories, myths, and like behaviors are significant. In fact enormous amounts of corporate resources have been consumed in maintaining the divinity and authority of gods and kings. For the West Indies, Antonio Curet (1992a), José Oliver (1998), Peter Roe (1997), and Peter Siegel (1997) have done an excellent job of documenting how beliefs and rituals first supported the emergence of caciques and then served to maintain their authority.

Yet I am also mindful of Henry Petitjean Roget's (2001) foray into psychological archaeology. Noting that the end of the Saladoid period coincided with a period of hyperaridity in the West Indies, he suggests that the failure of the old gods (and leaders?) to maintain the environment of the past led to their overthrow and replacement with new gods and new leaders. Petitjean Roget would never in a million years portray himself as a cultural materialist. Yet his compelling prose concerns people living on Guadeloupe who were faced with the catastrophe of rivers running dry, crops withering, and other environmental disasters. Obviously their leaders and the gods had abandoned them.

The Taínos exhibit all of the characteristics identified for chiefdoms. Evidence shows that the population was growing rapidly until at least AD 1200 (Curet 1992a; Keegan 1992). There is clear evidence for the intensification of food production through mounding, terracing, and irrigation (Moscoso 1981, 1986; Ortíz Aguilú et al. 1991; Sauer 1966) along with the domestication of animals and the elaboration of fishing technologies (Keegan and DeNiro 1988; Wing 1993) and the production of surplus handicrafts (Wilson 1990). Specialized craft production tied to long-distance exchange is now dated to AD 1100 between Hispaniola and the southern Bahamas (Carlson 1993); large ocean-going canoes were observed by Columbus in both Cuba and the Bahamas (Dunn and Kelley 1989), as were daily "commuter flights" between Puerto Rico and eastern Hispaniola.

Warfare is reflected in a variety of references. L. Hernández Aquino's (1977) dictionary of Taíno words includes multiple references to warfare and weapons (for example, Nihuche or Nihucto is glossed as the Igneri word for war).[4] Weapons, military adornments, and "war dances" (arietos) were observed, and the Taínos were able to assemble, in very short order, large armies to fight the Spanish (Harris 1994; Stevens-Arroyo 1986). Moreover, Guacanagarí is reported to have sent warriors with Columbus during the "pacification" of the Vega Real. In addition, Wilson (1990: 116) notes that in the summer of 1496 Bartholomew Columbus encountered Behecchio along the Río Neiba, where he had launched an expedition to conquer the villages in this area as well as some other caciques of the island. In sum, all of the evidence supports the conclusion that the northern West Indies functioned as a system of competing, regionally integrated cacicazgos, with interactions between them over substantial distances.

In kinship terms the Taíno political machine is best described as an avunculocal chiefdom. This term is used because a chiefdom can be organized through avunculocal residence without the entire society following this practice. Avunculocal residence seems to emerge in previously matrilocal, matrilineal societies that have experienced a recurrence of internal warfare (Ember 1974). Because marriage distances are usually short in matrilocal societies, the men of the matrilineage can routinely assemble for political and ritual activities. As internal conflict commences, outbreaks of warfare with nearby neighbors are often intermittent with periods of alliance and trade, which makes them difficult to anticipate. Constant readiness is required, because political leaders must always be mindful of potential threats as well as offensive opportunities. Under these conditions the incentive to assemble the men of a matrilineal group more often and for longer periods increases. It is not possible to localize all of the men all of the time, however, so clanlords would have had to assemble a retinue of capable and loyal followers from among their matrikin.

Spanish accounts make no specific mention of warfare between cacicazgos. In fact the Taíno caciques seem to have been amiable to a remarkable degree. This situation is surprising, because avunculocal chiefdoms tend to develop in an environment of intragroup hostility. In other words, it is likely that the Taíno chiefdoms were sociopolitical groups that at one time waged war on each other (Stevens-Arroyo 1986). The reason for their apparent peacefulness may be that at the time of European contact the Nitaínos (elites) were forming marriage alliances between themselves while at the same time increasing the social distance between themselves and commoners. There is tantalizing evidence that the Taíno elite practiced patrilateral cross-cousin marriage in which spouses were exchanged between the paramount cacicazgos. Second, there is compelling evidence that the Taínos used Crow-type kinship terms (Byrne 1991; Ensor 2003). Third, military entrepreneurship and political entrepreneurship were the key elements in the emergence of avunculocal chiefdoms (Keegan and Maclachlan 1989; Keegan et al. 1998). Faced with a military standoff in which each cacicazgo marshaled roughly equal military forces, an alliance among the Nitaínos would foster peaceful relations that would increase the productive capacity within each cacicazgo. This standoff may be reflected in the spatial distributions of the 21 known ball courts on Hispaniola and the 65 ball courts on Puerto Rico (Wilson 1990: 22–27). Gary Vescelius noted that in Puerto Rico the most elaborate ball courts seem to be located along the boundaries between cacicazgos, where they served as an outlet for competition between the polities and a means for defining the will of the gods (Alegría 1983; Rouse 1992: 15).[5]

The underlying factor in the emergence of caciques was the creation of a power base through the localization of males who were previously dispersed at marriage. The localization of males provided an underutilized labor force for the intensification of subsistence production, a military force for defense and expansion of territory, and organized long-distance trading expeditions for the purposes of creating and maintaining alliances that were cemented through the exchange of women in marriage. Succession is of supreme importance under these conditions. It thus became institutionalized in the social formation that Maclachlan and I called the avunculocal chiefdom (Keegan and Maclachlan 1989).

Finally, with regard to the status of women, we are faced with the issues of rank, power, status, autonomy, and authority. It is reported that most caciques were men, but there are records of women who ascended to this role (Sued-Badillo 1979, 1985). More importantly, women are the power behind the throne in avunculocal chiefdoms. Anacaona, the sister of Behecchio, was married to Caonabó, the paramount cacique of Maguana. This marriage cemented the alliance between the two most powerful Taíno cacicazgos in Hispaniola. Moreover, Bartholomew Columbus reported that Anacaona controlled both the production and distribution of a wide variety of high-status goods. It is only by adopting the marriage alliance approach advocated by Ensor (2003) that the statuses of men and women in Taíno society make sense. Elite men were not independent agents; their status was determined by their wives (and the alliances they represented), their inheritance came first through their mothers, and the status of the cacicazgo was determined by the productive capacity of women in terms of both subsistence production (staple finance) and the production of high-status goods (wealth finance).

One of the unique characteristics of the avunculocal chiefdom is that at each succession a stranger king arises, because the sisters of the cacique in one village are married to caciques in other villages in order to cement alliances. These sisters move to the village of their cacique husband. "Move" is used here in a relative sense. It is possible that a cacique's married sisters physically moved to live in the village of their husband. It is also possible that such moves were conceived in a symbolic sense that did not involve actually living in the husband's village. I make this distinction because Anacaona was married to Caonabó, yet she maintained workshops and storehouses in her brother's cacicazgo. In addition, after her husband died she returned to her brother's village; and after her brother died she became cacica of her brother's cacicazgo. Although Anacaona may be an exceptional case, it is important to retain flexibility when conceptualizing the dichotomy of mobility and residence.

The children who were born to these unions belonged to their mother's clan and thus owed primary allegiance to their mother's brother, who resided in another village. At puberty the boys would return to the village of their mother's brother, where they competed to put themselves in the most favorable position to succeed their uncle and to become cacique. Because some, if not all, of these boys arrived as "adults" from other villages, each would be received as *l'étranger* (perhaps a better term is *l'inconnu*).

Summary

We have now completed the third cycle of circulating reference. We began with the legend of Caonabó and his mythical associations, suggested a specific location for his youth (Middle Caicos), and have now explored sociological factors. As we have traversed mythical, political, social, demographic, and economic terrains we have also confronted anthropological concepts of chief and chiefdom and explored the degree to which these may have matched Taíno beliefs.

The circular to oval villages of the Taínos and their ancestors conform to the community plan that Ensor (2003) has identified for peoples practicing Crow/Omaha marriage alliances. During the Saladoid period the centers of some of these villages (primarily in Puerto Rico) were cemeteries in which the ancestors were buried, in order to allow them to participate in village life on a daily basis. This situation changed during Taíno times, when the chiefly household came to occupy the center of a prepared plaza. Thus specific individuals who were awarded the status of cacique came to be the focal point of the community. The caciques were supported by their kin, who lived in the houses that surrounded the plaza. From this position they could scrutinize the activities of the cacique and the cacique's household. If it is necessary to classify this type of arrangement, then it most closely resembles a network strategy in which the power of the group is expressed through the cacique's ability to accumulate goods for ceremonial feasts or potlatches. Clearly a cacique living at the center of a village was living in a glass house. It is very unlikely that the caciques could act as independent agents with so many eyes focused in their direction.

Yet there is also evidence for an emerging aristocracy. Where caciques and shamans (*behiques*) apparently once *shared* the ability to communicate with the ancestors and spirits, by Taíno times the cacique had abrogated the power of the *behiques*. Although shamans may have continued to serve as healers, it was only through the cacique that the spirits and ancestors could be approached. The mythical characteristics attributed to Caonabó attest to the emerging sense of cacical divinity. Moreover, marriage alliances between caciques at all levels not only served to establish peaceful relations but also provided the nexus around which a separate identity, a social class if you will, was beginning to emerge among elites. Thus Behecchio and Caonabó were able to assert their authority over half of Hispaniola, and Behecchio maintained control of Xaragua through his marriage to 30 wives from allied villages.

It must also be recognized that caciques did pursue corporate strategies as well. The independence of chiefs beyond elite marriage alliances is evident in Caonabó's attack on Guacanagarí's village and when Guarionex sought refuge from the Spanish in the village of Mayabonex (Macorix de Arriba). Guarionex was surprised that the Spanish continued to pursue him even after he went into exile. After all, he was only one man, and he had lost the support of his followers. It was only the Western mindset that reified an association between an individual ruler and people he ruled. In other words, the leader must be punished personally for the intransigence of his people.

If we accept simple dichotomies such as corporate and network or managerial and control, then we must conclude that the Taínos of Hispaniola were living on a cusp. Wars had been fought to establish their territories and marriages had been arranged to solidify alliances; yet the caciques still lived at the focal point of their villages. The entire island was viewed as a giant female beast, and the complementarity of cacicazgos was sanctioned by shared belief. The caciques were also consolidating their power through intermarriage, by subjugating the *behiques*, and by claiming divine status and exclusive access to the gods. How can we put a single label on such dynamic processes?

Conclusions

It is also possible to suggest several more general conclusions. First, chiefdoms (cacicazgos) emerged in societies that are experiencing economic and demographic growth under conditions of locally diminishing marginal returns to production. The specific manner in which these societies develop depends on the ways in which production and reproduction unfold within the society's social matrix. In turn, this social matrix is itself subject to change in concert with the evolving infrastructure. Greater emphasis should be placed on identifying the social relations of production and reproduction that provide structure to the political economy. In sum, explaining the emergence of a chiefdom requires knowledge of the antecedent social organization. It is not sufficient simply to name pathways (for example, risk management, technology, warfare, and trade) because these have variable effects, depending upon the social arrangements through which they are expressed.

Second, as Rosman and Rubel (1989) have shown, the environment and macroeconomy are not determining variables in the emergence of chiefdoms. Social organization, with regard to the organization of production and reproduction, is the crucial factor. While recognizing the significance of their work, we must also consider relations with neighboring groups (for example, alliances and competition). Thus social and political relations of the entire polity and the polity's relations with neighboring groups and other intergroup relations must be defined.

Third, the evolution of social and political systems requires the collaboration of archaeological, ethnohistoric, and cross-cultural ethnographic data evaluated in a well-structured theoretical framework. Having identified the Taínos as an avunculocal chiefdom, it has been possible to ask specific questions of the different data sets and to refine our understanding of Taíno society. For example, the excavation and dating of settlement pairs on Middle Caicos and the excavation of the shell-bead manufacturing center on Grand Turk were both undertaken with their larger significance in mind. In addition, we can return to the original chronicles with a clearer notion of the kinds of data that would support or refute the proposed model of Taíno social organization. Without such structure, investigations of political evolution are doomed to reinventing the wheel or imposing ethnographic models on the empirical data. Understanding human culture can only be advanced by casting aside such ethno-tyrannies (Maclachlan and Keegan 1990).

5

MC-6 and Its Milieu

One outcome of the postprocessual movement in archaeology has been the promotion of a supposedly new form of field research called "reflexive archaeology" (Hodder 1999, 2000; compare Gero 1990; Leone et al. 1987). Apparently British archaeologists do not often work with untrained volunteers. If they had, they would have realized that all archaeology is reflexive when archaeologists have individuals on site questioning their every move. I thank the Earthwatch Institute (Center for Field Research) for supporting my research with volunteers who have provided me with a reflexive experience. A colleague who read the first draft of this book objected to my equating "reflexive archaeology" with the Earthwatch experience. Perhaps I am just jaded, but a reflexive methodology is what my professors taught me 30 years ago and what I have tried to impart to the people who pay money to participate in my projects. Moreover, such reflexivity is exactly what Latour (1999) captured in his model of circulating reference. This is how science operates.

As a student of the "real Connecticut archaeologist" I was taught that I should excavate a site and make notes, maps, and records so that I could return every object from the site to its original position. The notion was that such specificity would make the data collected during an excavation perfectly available to future investigators. Thus those who followed would have complete knowledge of what was done, why it was done, and where material remains were distributed in the site. Yet such specificity is impossible. If I had held fast to the ideal, I would have spent my entire career excavating a 1 m^2 unit and would still not be able to replace every grain of sand, let alone all of the artifacts, in their original position in the unit. If all we needed was a good record of what was found and where it was found, then my kids could excavate a site. So why not let avocationalists do the hard work while we sit at our desks and propose interpretations for what they find? Archaeologists could become the equivalent of movie critics, assigning thumbs up or down in response to various retrodictions. With the emergence of reality television, the Learning Channel, the Discovery Channel, the National Geographic Channel, and Animal Planet, archaeologists have already been converted to talking heads. Furthermore, those who get the most airplay are the ones who propose the most extreme pronouncements. Space aliens get high ratings, while optimal foragers are *passé*.

It is not surprising that the Cambridge School is now promoting the detailed recording of site data, and I do agree with their goals. These data distinguish us from the wannabees. There are always new methods for recording information during fieldwork (for example, Global Positioning System [GPS] and Geographic Information Systems [GIS]), however, and we need to conduct a cost-benefit analysis with regard to research interests. Is the work cost-effective for the questions being addressed? In some situations minute details should be recorded, but sometimes we just need to know that something is there.

My emphasis on the role of the archaeologist in creating the past is an effort to recognize the choices that were made during the course of fieldwork. *Real* archaeologists cut their teeth in the field; and, especially in the 1970s, archaeological fieldwork represented the last bastion of exotic anthropology. In addition, the late 1970s were still the early days of the New Archaeology. I mention this as context for the following reminiscence.

Shaun Dorsey Sullivan

I first met Shaun Sullivan on Middle Caicos in January 1978. He was finishing his doctoral research and was preparing to return to the United States. Shaun was a student of Donald Lathrap at the University of Illinois Urbana-Champaign. He had spent time in the military and had received Special Forces training. Shaun always struck me as having a Napoleonic complex. He was short in stature but made up for it by completely dominating any space. He had a deep, thoughtful, and penetrating voice. When he spoke, people paid attention. He was larger than life. I showed up on his doorstep in Middle Caicos unannounced, and he took me in and tried to teach me what he could of Caribbean archaeology. Every night for a week we sat at the table in the main room of the house he was renting, lit only by kerosene lamps. Shaun would recount what was known of the archaeology of the region. I will be forever grateful.

Yet Shaun was cut from old cloth. His dissertation related archaeological sites to the environments that surrounded them in catchments of set size (Figure 5.1). Moreover, it struck me as strange that he used modern environmental zones to characterize past land-use practices, with no effort to re-create what might have been in the past. His strength clearly was in field methods and not in the emerging ecological theories of the day. Shaun was the consummate field archaeologist. He was far better at organizing an archaeological army and conducting field research than I will ever be. I will never forget working

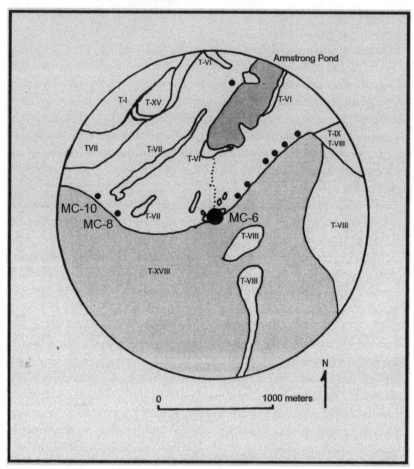

5.1. MC-6 catchment areas: T-I, *Swietenia* brushland on rockland; T-VI, mangrove; T-VII, freshwater swamp-savannah; T-VIII, coastal marl flats Bucida community; T-IX and T-VIII, mixed coastal hammock community and coastal marl flats Bucida community; T-XV, brackish pond; T-XIV, salt pond; T-XVIII, tidal flats (from Sullivan 1981: 183; courtesy of Shaun D. Sullivan).

with him for a second time on Middle Caicos in 1982. He had rented several houses in Bambarra and had arranged for us to use the local schoolhouse as our base of operations. The expedition involved more than 20 people and had to overcome major logistical obstacles, such as having no electricity, no running water, and no nearby grocery stores. At the outset, food and equipment were shipped from Miami to Providenciales and from there by ferry to Middle Caicos. The whole project almost came unglued, however, due to problems first with Customs and then with transportation en route to Middle Caicos. In sum, the preparations alone were monumental.

The plan in 1982 was to excavate MC-12 on the north coast below Bambarra and to remap portions of two sites on the south coast. I had arrived early with Shaun and Glen Freimuth to get things set up and to clear the vegetation from the sites. Shaun had brought a portable flamethrower. It was a kerosene-filled backpack attached to a pump-action handle. Pumping the handle built up pressure; when the vapor was released by pulling the trigger, a pilot light ignited the kerosene and shot a stream of fire. I will never forget running for my life as Shaun set the backside of Middle Caicos ablaze while clearing MC-6 and MC-8.

The Turks and Caicos were about as remote as a person could get in the West Indies at the time. The main settlements were on Grand Turk and South Caicos, where solar-distilled salt production had produced enormous wealth in the eighteenth century. It is said that George Washington demanded Turks Island salt for preserving meats for his army. It was considered the finest salt in the Western Hemisphere; there are reports that impostors who sold salt from other sources yet claimed it was from the Turks were prosecuted in the United States. By the 1960s, however, mechanized salt production on other islands (for example, Great Inagua) had put the Turks and Caicos out of business. Salt production ceased, and this British Crown Colony that had been too valuable to annex to either Jamaica or the Bahamas slipped into benign neglect.

When Sullivan arrived in the Turks and Caicos in 1976, Grand Turk and South Caicos were the most developed islands. In addition to the wealth accumulated from the salt trade, both had been blessed with U.S. military installations. Grand Turk was a key base on the Atlantic Missile Tracking Range and was the first station to report following Mercury, Gemini, and even Apollo launches from Cape Canaveral. John Glenn and Scott Carpenter both made their first return to dry land on Grand Turk after their successful Mercury space flights. When I first visited Grand Turk in 1978, there was a huge satellite dish next to the runway. The airport was divided into a north terminal for commercial passengers and a south terminal for personnel working at the RCA base. The RCA tracking station, the National Security Agency (NSA) listening post at the north end of the island, and the Coast Guard facility on South Caicos all closed in the 1970s. The islands, following boom and bust cycles, were once again left to their own devices.

Sullivan's military training provided an important foundation for the research he conducted. There were flights from Grand Turk to the other islands, but few amenities after reaching these islands. Middle Caicos did not get electricity until 1989, and the first asphalt road was paved in 1994. Today

Providenciales is a bustling tourist center, with Club Med and Sandals resorts. When Sullivan was working on Middle Caicos, there was a small local settlement called Blue Hills and one grocery store, BWI Trading on Provo. Even today it is considered a grave insult to call someone from Providenciales a "Blue Hills man." Shaun fed his teams peanut butter and jelly sandwiches for lunch; when the jelly and other supplies ran low, he sent Brian Riggs to the store on Providenciales to purchase more. On one occasion all that Brian could find was mint jelly, so the team had peanut butter and mint jelly sandwiches for the next week. One day when I was working with Shaun at MC-6, he had a sudden inspiration when we sat down for lunch. He reached behind the rock he was sitting on and retrieved a jar of strawberry jelly, which he offered to me. The jar was covered in ants, but how could I refuse such bounty?

I remember those days with fondness. It was the beginning of my career as an archaeologist; unfortunately it was also the end of Shaun's. His dissertation was a solid piece of work completed under difficult conditions, but there were too few jobs in the early 1980s. Archaeology had moved beyond the catchment analysis of his dissertation. After a few years of trying to establish an independent research group, Shaun left the field and went to work for the U.S. State Department as a cultural attaché. It is also unfortunate that the significance of his discoveries has not been properly appreciated in the region. This is why I have devoted a chapter to Shaun's work. It is high time that a wider audience should become familiar with his research and scholarship.

If archaeology is truly reflexive, then we need to understand the motives and abilities of those who conducted the fieldwork that we use in our analyses and syntheses. As I said earlier, Shaun was the consummate field archaeologist who used all of the methods of the day. He carried a transit and tripod to MC-6 every day in order to make a detailed topographic map. He completely surface collected the site and undertook the excavation of unusual features. Shaun was one of the first to make a systematic collection of animal bones. Although his use of ¼-inch mesh sieves for this purpose might be criticized, he later modified his collection strategy. He brought Liz Wing and Sylvia Scudder to Middle Caicos in 1982 to assist with the environmental reconstruction. At that time fine screening and new methods for calculating MNI (minimum number of individuals) were adopted.

Shaun employed a variety of techniques and collection strategies that were not common at the time, especially in the West Indies. Years later archaeologists in the West Indies would call for the creation of topographic maps of archaeological sites and the collection of faunal samples as basic requirements of fieldwork. In this regard Shaun was a pioneer. He was so concerned with accurate mapping that he even made a portable builder's level for the survey that

5.2. Shaun Sullivan in Bambarra, 1978.

Barbara Macnider and I did for him on North Caicos (Figure 5.2). Under his direction the first excavation of a Taíno structure was made at MC-12 in a unit that covered 10 by 10 meters. Ten years later the use of large-scale horizontal excavations would be considered *de rigueur*.

In addition, Shaun worked in a community that time forgot. Emanuel Hall's store had the only electric generator. We would pass evenings there playing dominoes and listening to a few well-worn reggae and calypso records. Shaun was the godfather for several children born during his stay, and he achieved a legendary status among the local people. When I returned to Middle Caicos for the first time about 10 years later, I was greeted as "Shaun." Even people who had known me for years started calling me Shaun. In 1999 a steady stream of people came to our field station in the Bambarra schoolhouse, having heard that Shaun had returned. His legacy and legend were larger than life. My return was treated as something of a second coming. I came to embody Shaun, the stranger king.

Environmental Setting

The main factors in making the case for MC-6 as Caonabó's homeland concern the environment in general and the distribution of certain resources in particular. It is not necessary to catalog the environmental characteristics of the Turks and Caicos Islands or of Middle Caicos in particular. Instead we can simply ask why anyone, let along the most prominent cacique in Hispaniola, would choose to live on Middle Caicos. The reasons put forward here are an abundance of marine resources (including fishes, lobsters, and conchs) and the ability to preserve these for export to Hispaniola. The unique feature is salt.

The Turks and Caicos Islands are the southeasternmost islands in the Bahama archipelago, about 120 km north of Hispaniola. They consist of eight main islands and numerous small cays. These limestone islands are very dry due to low rainfall and high trade winds. When Lee Newsom conducted a plant survey of Grand Turk, she found that many species did not correspond to existing plant identification keys because the vegetation was so stunted. Such hyperarid conditions provided for the efficient production of solar-distilled salt, which was the major export of these islands for centuries. In addition, these islands were located on a large, shallow marine bank that provided abundant marine resources.

The Caicos Bank covers more than 2,800 square kilometers of sand and seagrass habitats that are the favored environment of queen conchs, lobsters, and certain fishes (such as bonefishes). From the 1950s through early 1980s the islands annually exported millions of dried conchs (Doran 1958; Hesse and Hesse 1977). At one time this resource was considered limitless; but by the late 1970s there was a dramatic decline in the conch population. Yet even then it was not uncommon to see boats with pounded conchs hung from the rigging to dry, and three processing plants on South Caicos prepared the animals for market. One of the main markets at the time was Haiti. Haitian sloops would bring fresh produce and *clarín* (moonshine) to the Turks and Caicos in exchange for conch. It is likely that they were continuing an exchange pattern that had first started in pre-Columbian times.

Middle Caicos is situated above the heart of the Caicos Bank. Fishermen from Middle Caicos have long been recognized for their skills, and the conch from Middle Caicos is considered to be of the highest quality. Even today, when conch is not available in the other restaurants on Grand Turk, it can be found at Robert Hall's restaurant (the Diplomat Café), because his supply comes from his brothers who live on Middle Caicos. For the people of Middle Caicos, farming and fishing continue to be the primary occupations.

To reiterate, in Taíno times fishes were an essential part of the daily meal. As I have mentioned already, fishes were the first creatures created by the gods. When the gourd containing the remains of the son of god (Yayael) was dropped and broken, the sea and fishes spewed forth and covered the earth (Stevens-Arroyo 1988). This emphasis on fishes as a meat source is easily understood, given the limited number of land animals that were available for food. Moreover, due to overexploitation, many of the most valued foods were also the most endangered. For example, iguanas, which were prized by the Taínos, have a very fragile population structure that is easily disturbed by human predation. As a result, iguana populations can be quickly extirpated on an island (Iverson 1979). Excavations at sites that represent the initial settlement on an island (such as GT-3) show that iguanas were very common in the earliest deposits but later all but disappeared from the diet (Carlson 1999). The same is true for other prized foods, such as sea turtles, adult queen conchs, and large carnivorous fishes (Carlson and Keegan 2004).

The Taínos had individual names for a wide variety of fishes (Table 5.1). Capture techniques included the use of bows and arrows, spears, hooks and lines, basket traps, nets, and weirs. It is reported that corrals were built in some areas to keep the fish alive until they were needed. The shallow tidal flat on the south side of Middle Caicos would have been an ideal location for the construction of corrals. Given the abundant marine resources of the Caicos Bank, it is likely that MC-6 served as a source of fresh and preserved fish and shellfish for the cacicazgos of Hispaniola.

The problem of transporting fish meat before it spoils is certainly an issue. The trip from Middle Caicos to Hispaniola would have taken about 24 hours by canoe, so it was still possible for some fishes to be transported fresh, wrapped only in wet leaves. Whole fish can be left unrefrigerated for about two weeks if they are kept in a cool, wet place (Caribbean Commission 1952). The Taínos also barbecued (smoked and roasted) meats on wooden racks above fires. This technique was later adopted by Europeans, who earned the name "buccaneer" because of this practice. While roasting can provide meats for immediate consumption, the barbecue also provides a means for smoking fish that would preserve them for later consumption. As mentioned earlier, the flesh of the queen conch can be preserved by drying. After the meat is removed from the shell, the muscle is pounded to break the tough fibers (often with a *lignum vitae* baton), and the flesh is hung in the open to dry for about three days. This technique will preserve the flesh for up to six months. Finally, fishes can be "corned" or salted to preserve the flesh. Older residents of Middle Caicos recalled using this technique in the days before refrigeration. The Taínos could have developed a similar technique for salting fish to preserve the meat.

In fact, the only other resource of significance in the vicinity of MC-6 is salt. Armstrong Pond, which is connected to MC-6 by an aboriginal road, produces solar distilled salt during the summer months (Figure 5.3). Sullivan suggested that people from Hispaniola targeted this area for the harvesting of

Table 5.1. Sample of Taíno Names for Fishes

Taíno name	Scientific name	Common name
Anguila (eel)	*Anguilla anguilla* [*Anguilliformes*]	Eel
Bajonao	*Pagellus caninus* (*Calamus*)	Porgy
Balaju	*Hyporhampus unifasciatus*	Halfbeak
Bonasí	*Serranus bonaei*	Sea Bass
Buyón [esteemed]	*Scarus lineolatus*	Parrotfish
Cachicata	*Haemulon* sp.	Grunt
Cachuco	*Etelis oculatus*	Snapper
Caconeta	*Carcharhinvs limbatus*	Black-tipped Shark
Cajaya (shark)	*Cacharias glaucus* [*Carcharhinus leucas?*]	Bull Shark?
Caji	*Lutjanus apodus*	Schoolmaster (Snapper)
Carite	*Scomberomorus maculatus*	Spanish Mackerel
Carite (shark)	*Isurus tigris* [*Galeocerdo cuvier?*]	Tiger Shark?
Chibí	*Caranx ruber*	Bar Jack
Chucho	*Aetobatus narinari*	Spotted Eagle Ray
Cojinua	*Caranx crysos* (aka *fusus*)	Blue Runner (Jack)
Corocoro	*Haemulon macrostomum*	Spanish Grunt
Dajao (freshwater)	*Agonostomus monticola*	Mountain Mullet
Diahaca	*Anisotremus surinamensis*	Black Margate
Guabina (freshwater)	*Phylipnus dormitator*	Sleeper
Guaicano or Guaican	*Echeneis* [*naucrates*] or [*Remora*] *remora*	Remora
Guajil	*Mycteroperca venenosa*	Yellowfin Grouper
Guaseta or Guasa	*Serranus phoebe*	Sea Bass
Guativere	*Cephalopholis fulva*	Red Guativere
Guavina	*Doncella* or Synodontidae	Lizardfish
Guaymen	*Caranx bartholomei*	Yellow Jack
Hagueta		Small Shark
Jallao	*Haemulon album*	Margate
Jarea	*Mugil curema*	White Mullet
Jiguagua or Area	*Caranx hippos*	Crevalle Jack
Jocú	*Mesoprion jocu* or *Pargo colorado*	Mutton Snapper
Libuza	*Dasybetus torrei* [*Dasyatus americana*]	Southern Stingray
Macabí or Chiro	*Elops saurus*	Ladyfish
Macurí (see Diahaca)	*Lobotes surinamensis*	Tripletail
Manati	*Manatus americanus*	Manatee
Manjua (sardine)	*Ilisha bleckeriana* or *Anchoa pelada*	Sardine or Anchovy
Mapiro or Masaguan	*Dormitator maculatus*	Fat Sleeper
Mapo	*Cobius saporator*	Cobia
Mijúa (small)	*Jenkinsia lamprotaenia*	Dwarf Herring
Moharra	*Diplodus vulgaris*	Sea Bream
Muniama	*Pristopomoides macrophthalamus*	Lutjanidae
Muniama de afuera	*Mojarra blanquilla*	Mojarra
Oatilibi	*Bodianus ruber*	Spanish Hogfish
Paguala (has sword)	*Chaetodipterus faber*	Spadefish
Pargo	[*Lutjanus purpureus*]	Red Snapper
Patán	*Gerres brasilianus*	Mojarra
Peto (November)	*Acanthocybium solandri*	Wahoo
Sabalo	*Magalops attanticus*	Tarpon
Sesí	*Mesoprion buccanella*	Snapper
Setí	*Gobius oceanicus*	Gobiidae
Sirajo (freshwater)	*Sycidium plumieri*	Goby

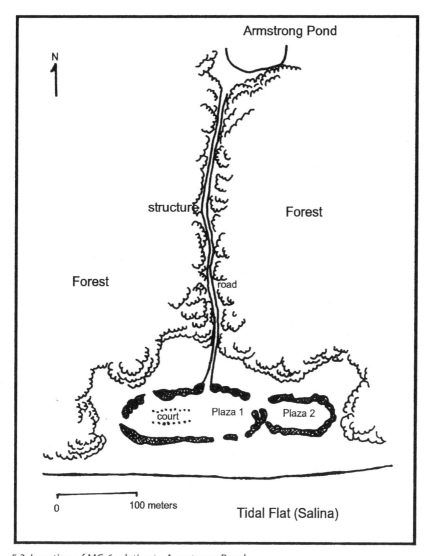

5.3. Location of MC-6 relative to Armstrong Pond.

salt. Given the importance of salt in human history (it was at one time called "white gold"), Sullivan (1981) concluded that salt was used as a nutritional supplement that was added to food to meet human electrolyte requirements in the tropics. In contrast, it is my contention that salt served the same purpose in Taíno times as it did in the eighteenth century: it was used to preserve meats. Dave D. Davis and Ken Oldfield (2003) recently suggested that access to natural salt-producing ponds was one of the main reasons why Anegada in the British Virgin Islands was settled in the late prehistoric period.

But why Middle Caicos? Why not another of these islands? The Turks Islands, including Grand Turk and Salt Cay, were among the most important during the historic period salt trade that began in the seventeenth century. People sailed all the way from Bermuda to rake salt on Grand Turk. South Caicos also figured prominently in this trade. The ancestors of the Taínos had exploited Grand Turk for fishes and turtles at the Coralie site beginning around AD 700. Later visitors from Haiti fashioned beads from *Chama sarda* shells at the Governor Beach site after AD 1100. Yet in both cases the settlements were small and temporary. Only three very small sites have been found on South Caicos, which today has the nickname "the rock." The reason that these islands did not support more permanent settlements may be that they were too dry and too barren (see Sears and Sullivan 1978). The islands average less than 500 mm of rainfall per year, and virtually no agriculture is practiced on them today.

East Caicos, the only other large island to the east of Middle Caicos, has been uninhabited for about 80 years. East Caicos was visited by Theodoor de Booy when there was a thriving sisal plantation on the island. De Booy (1912) reported "mounds" on Flamingo Hill similar to those that he observed southwest of Lorimers on Middle Caicos, as well as a cave with petroglyphs. The caves on the island were mined for guano, and a number of interesting artifacts were recovered. These mounds and the petroglyph cave have not been relocated, however, despite several recent efforts to find them. It should be noted that a systematic archaeological survey of East Caicos has not been completed. Moreover, if salt was an important site-location criterion, then East Caicos would be eliminated, because there are no natural salt-producing ponds on the island. Finally, East Caicos also may have been too arid to support permanent settlements (600–750 mm of rainfall per year).

To the west of Middle Caicos rainfall increases somewhat, but these islands had no salt ponds in historic times. To date, one small site has been found on North Caicos, and de Booy (1912) did report a cave site at the extreme western end of the island near Sandy Point. Lucayan sites may yet be found, because archaeological coverage of the island is again incomplete. Continuing to the south and west, there are sites on Parrot Cay, Pine Cay, Providenciales, and West Caicos, but none of these rival MC-6 in terms of size or complex organization. Of special note is Pine Cay, located between North Caicos and Providenciales. Pine Cay has the only freshwater ponds in the islands. It also has a large Lucayan site, but the material culture does not distinguish it from other Lucayan sites (Keegan 1981; Sullivan 1981).

Middle Caicos seems to be uniquely suited for the kind of Taíno outpost or "gateway community" that Sullivan described. It is the first island of substantial size that is relatively well watered (circa 750–830 mm of rainfall per year) and could thus support agricultural production. Yet it also is dry enough to have a large, natural salt-producing pond and is ideally situated to take advantage of the marine resources available on the Caicos Bank.

Other resources also could have been exported from (or through) Middle Caicos. First, the dry climate of all of the Bahaman Islands seems to have made them ideal for the production of cotton (Craton and Saunders 1992). When Columbus first arrived in the Bahamas, he reported that the native peoples brought him large balls of cotton ("arrobas" weighing 10 kg; Dunn and Kelley 1989). Cotton was used by the Taínos to make hammocks, nets, belts that were adorned with beads, women's skirts (*naguas*), and numerous other useful things. Middle Caicos has an ideal climate for the production of cotton.

Second, the Taínos used bird feathers and worked shell in headdresses and other adornments. These are also available on the island. In fact, a surprising variety of birds have been identified in the site, compared to other sites in the region (David Steadman, personal communication, 2005). Of the 17 taxa that Steadman identified from Unit J, 13 are residents and 4 are seasonal visitors. Most of these birds are common in the mangrove habitats around Armstrong Pond and the salina. The majority of these birds, however, are rather drab colored, which would not distinguish them as a source of feathers. The exceptions are the jet-black feathers of crows (*Corvus* sp.) and the brightly colored feathers of parrots (*Amazona* sp.), which may be evidence for trade in this commodity.

In sum, the natural resources of Middle Caicos and its neighbors made them strategic for cultural development in Hispaniola after AD 1200. The person who controlled access to the resources of the southern Bahamas would indeed be a powerful cacique. The south coast of Middle Caicos provided an ideal location for a gateway community that could transfer the resources of the Bahamas to the cacicazgos of Hispaniola (Sullivan 1981).

Cultural Setting

The first survey of archaeological sites in the Turks and Caicos was conducted by Theodoor de Booy as part of the Heye Foundation's expeditions (de Booy 1912, 1913). As was typical of the day, most of the sites that were reported for the Bahama archipelago were found in caves where bat guano was mined for fertilizer (Sears and Sullivan 1978). De Booy (1912) also noted a site on the salina to the southwest of Lorimers (Middle Caicos) that had a complex of aboriginal stone mounds or house foundations arranged in a crescent-shaped grouping of six or less. It is tempting to identify this site as MC-6. De Booy reported a surface collection of only five sherds, however, two of which have clear Meillacan design motifs.

In this case we must be mindful of the research strategies employed at the time. First, de Booy was brought to locations by people in the area who knew of aboriginal artifacts. That is why cave sites figured so prominently. Second, he was working for the Museum of the American Indian and had little interest in small and undecorated potsherds. Thus perhaps only five sherds at the mound site were sufficiently elaborate to attract his interest. Third, the archaeology of the day can be equated with the archaeology of mounds. The discovery of "mounds" in the Turks and Caicos may have been somewhat exaggerated.

Over 60 years would pass before the next archaeologist arrived. This time it was Shaun Sullivan, fresh from his survey of Eleuthera in the central Bahamas (Sullivan 1974). He arrived seeking evidence for the initial peopling of the Bahama archipelago, but he found much more (Sullivan 1981). Sullivan ended up devoting most of his efforts to Middle Caicos, where he found 35 sites in cave and open-air settings. The sites that most interested him were the 14 located on the south coast in the vicinity of Armstrong Pond. Sullivan did a seriation of pottery styles from these sites and proposed that they reflected seasonal use of Armstrong Pond prior to the establishment of MC-6. Yet most of these sites had fewer than a dozen potsherds, and a seriation based on an incomplete sample of the total ceramic population will not provide meaningful results. Thus Sullivan's attempt to use these sites was misplaced. It is more likely that the sites represent individual pot drops, which may have been associated with farmsteads located away from the main settlement(s) (Keegan 1995b). In other words, these isolates do not reflect permanent settlements and therefore are of interest only by virtue of the activities that they represent in the vicinity of Armstrong Pond.

Sullivan did locate several larger sites. The most important of these for the present study are MC-6, MC-8, and MC-10 on the south coast and MC-12 and MC-32 on the north coast. The results of Sullivan's investigations at these sites are presented below (chapter 6 discusses how Shaun's research influenced future work at these sites).

MC-8 and MC-10

MC-8 and MC-10 are located about 2 km to the west of MC-6 on the first permanently dry land above the salina on the south coast (see Figure 6.1). The sites are only about 70 m apart. Sullivan conducted extensive surface collections and test excavations. Based on the surface scatters he estimated that MC-8 measured 110 by 160 m and MC-10 measured 160 by 80 m. Of the 1,140 sherds collected from MC-8, 93 percent were imported from Hispaniola (as indicated by their noncarbonate tempers). In all, 1,466 sherds were collected from MC-10, with 96 percent of Hispaniolan origin (Sullivan 1981). These sherds were later restudied by Mark Tromans (1986).

The preponderance of imported pottery at these sites is exactly the pattern we expect to observe at the initial settlement of an island in the Bahama archipelago. The initial settlers would have had to bring everything with them that they needed. Moreover, all of the decorated sherds had Meillacan motifs, which predate the use of Chican decorations on the north coast of Hispaniola (Rouse 1992). The high frequency of imported sherds and the style in which designs were executed led Sullivan to suggest that these sites represented the initial settlement of the island between AD 750 and 950. Moreover, the test excavations indicated that the sites lacked any substantial subsurface components. In other words, they were surface scatters that seemed to reflect a seasonal or short-term use of the area.

Sullivan (1981) also reported that there was a stone alignment at MC-8 similar to that observed at MC-6. He suggested that this alignment represented a map from Middle Caicos to Île de Tortue off the north coast of Haiti. Being the careful scientist that he was, he revisited the site in 1982 in order to make a more accurate map of the alignment using a transit. I assisted him with this effort. It became clear that the stone alignment was not as straight as it originally appeared and that it did not trace the course that he originally proposed (Figure 5.4).

At MC-10 Sullivan identified a small rectangular plaza. A main factor in this identification was that trees similar to those growing on the court at MC-6 were also growing in a restricted area at this site. Associated with the plaza was a roughly square arrangement of limestone rocks. This was interpreted as the foundations for a structure.

No faunal remains were recovered, and no additional work was conducted at the sites until we returned in 2000. These sites are discussed in greater detail in chapter 6.

MC-12

There can be true beauty in science. In this regard, I have always found Sullivan's (1981: 237) map of the guinea grass densities on MC-12 to be one of those beautiful insights. He observed that the concentration of guinea grass on the site reflected an oval pattern that probably corresponded to the original ar-

5.4. Stone alignment at MC-8 in 1982.

rangement of the settlement. Sullivan also noted that surface concentrations of artifacts corresponded to guinea grass densities. The site was estimated (by pace and compass) to measure about 115 m east to west by 50 m north to south and was associated with a small freshwater pond on the south side. Initially, a 1-square-meter test pit was dug in the eastern side of the site. The deposit was at least 65 cm deep, with the main concentration of materials between 10 and 60 cmbs (centimeters below surface). Sullivan had one radiocarbon date run by the Illinois State Geological Survey (ISGS 1098), which yielded a 2σ range of cal AD 1142 to 1422.

Table 5.2. Vertebrate Remains from MC-12

Taxon	MNI	Biomass (g)
TERRESTRIAL		
Canis	1	11,052
Laridae	1	435
Cyclura	2	1,224
Iguanidae	1	612
Total Terrestrial	5	13,323
FISHES		
Sparisoma	60	45,720
Serranidae	6	19,674
Albula vulpes	·10	11,190
Haemulon	7	13,839
Lutjanidae	3	6,474
Halichoeres	6	5,478
Lactophrys	1	913
Scarus	10	10,910
Sphyraena	1	913
Carangidae	2	1,404
Balistes sp.	4	3,652
Acanthurus	4	1,712
Diodon	6	5,478
Dasyatis	1	913
Total Fish	121	128,270
Cheloniidae	[1]	210

Source: Wing 2001: table 4.

Surface collections recovered 172 sherds, of which 50 were from imported vessels (29 percent). The test excavation recovered 201 sherds, however, of which only 4.9 percent were imports (Sullivan 1981: 232). Discounting collector's bias, it is apparent that 95 percent of the pottery was Palmetto ware. The predominance of Palmetto ware identifies MC-12 as a Lucayan site. The deposits reflect cultural adaptation to the Bahama Islands. The imported sherds had both Meillacan and Chican motifs, which may indicate that the site was occupied for an extended period covering the transition from Meillacan to Chican subseries pottery on the north coast of Hispaniola. This conclusion is consistent with the radiocarbon dates for the site.

Faunal remains were collected using ¼-inch mesh sieves (Table 5.2). They were analyzed by Wing (2001; originally reported in Sullivan 1981), who concluded that 97 percent of the identified vertebrate and invertebrate flesh came from within the site's 5 km catchment area (Wing and Scudder 1983). Fishes account for 96 percent of the faunal sample, and iguanas constitute another 3 percent. Reef fishes were the most common, accounting for 53 percent of the sample. The dominant species is parrotfish (*Sparisoma* sp.), which is seven times more abundant in terms of meat yield than any of the other fishes. The high incidence of parrotfish is typical of Lucayan sites, as is the rest of the species list, which includes porcupinefish, jack, wrasse, bonefish, grouper, grunt, and surgeonfish. The mollusks in the deposit also are typical of those found in Lucayan sites and include queen conchs, West Indian top shells, cockles, tellins, tiger lucines, and other venus clams.

Sullivan returned to MC-12 in 1981 and 1982. I participated in the 1982 project, during which we excavated the remains of a structure. The structure had five post stains 10 cm in diameter arranged in a semicircular pattern at 3 m intervals. We excavated a 10-m by 10-m area over the structure but did not cover its entire space. The floor of the structure was hard-packed sand, like cement, and the only artifacts were very small potsherds and very small fish bones that were compacted into the floor. This area gave the appearance of a clean-swept surface. Dense midden deposits with a darker soil, larger sherds, animal bones, and complete mollusk shells were discovered around the margins of this floor.

Unfortunately, the results of this research have never been reported. All of the artifacts from these excavations have been lost, but the field notes are curated at the Turks and Caicos National Museum. Moreover, a housing development in the area has destroyed the north part of the site. We met the developer in 1994 while conducting an archaeological impact assessment for the site. He regaled us with stories of how he had excavated the rich, humic topsoil for the gardens surrounding the houses he was building as part of a tourist development. He even mentioned finding a greenstone celt beneath a palm tree that he had removed to landscape the property. In addition, the south side of the site now has a paved road built across it. In sum, MC-12 is gone. It was certainly a contemporary of MC-6, but there is no longer any possibility of gaining useful information from the site.

MC-32

Sullivan estimated this site to be 150 by 100 m. It is located on the north coast about 1 km east of Bambarra landing. He made both a surface collection and one 1-m by 1-m test excavation. Of the 286 sherds collected from the surface, 67 were imports (23 percent). Again, imported sherds were overrepresented in the surface collection. In his test excavation Sullivan recovered 180 sherds, of which only 14 were imports (8 percent). It is not possible to attribute the imported sherds to a particular style, because Sullivan did not describe the

Table 5.3. Vertebrate Remains from MC-32

Taxon	MNI	Flesh weight (g)
TERRESTRIAL		
Cyclura	1	5
Total Terrestrial	1	5
FISHES		
Sparisoma	3	145
Serranidae	3	40
Albula vulpes	2	40
Haemulon	2	30
Halichoeres	2	24
Lactophrys	2	22
Scarus	1	18
Caranx	1	17
Balistes	1	8
Acanthurus	1	8
Diodon	1	6
Unidentified	NA	109
Total Fish	19	467

Source: Sullivan 1981: 301–302.

motifs that he observed. MC-32 was a contemporary of MC-6 and MC-12 and in fact shows a higher frequency of imported pottery than do other sites in area.

With the exception of a single iguana bone (1 percent by meat weight), the remainder of the faunal sample was fishes (Table 5.3). Parrotfish was the dominant species, although Wing (in Sullivan 1981: 302) detected a somewhat higher frequency of fishes from flats and tidal inlets. The proximity of Farm Creek Pond probably accounts for this (Wing and Scudder 1983). Other fishes included porcupinefish, jack, wrasse, bonefish, grouper, grunt, and surgeon-fish. The site contains the typical mollusks observed on Lucayan sites. In addition, Sullivan noted a high incidence of "Indian opened" conchs (with a round hole in the spire) to the northeast of the site, which he interpreted as evidence for a "conch meat extraction activity" (Sullivan 1981: 294).

The site was of special significance because here again a salt pond was associated with a Lucayan settlement. As Sullivan (1981: 296–297) noted: "A portion of the barrier ridge that separates the salt pond . . . from the main body of the brackish pond, called Farm Creek Pond, may be an aboriginal construction for the production of salt." He also noted some residents of Bambarra at the time were still raking salt in the pond for personal use. This feature also may have been used as a corral to hold fishes and conchs prior to processing.

Sullivan observed a modern fish pen made from tree branches in the pond during his investigation of the area.

Sullivan's MC-6

To reiterate, MC-6 is a large Lucayan site on the south coast of Middle Caicos. It may first have been reported by Theodoor de Booy in 1912 and was the focus of Sullivan's Ph.D. dissertation and subsequent research in the late 1970s and early 1980s (Sullivan 1981). The site is located on the first permanently dry land above a salina 6 km wide. The salina, a seasonally flooded marl flat, is today only 25 cm above mean sea level. Recent geological studies suggest that sea level may have been up to 50 cm higher in 1492 (Valdés 1994). If this is correct, then canoes could have been paddled right up to the site when it was occupied.

Sullivan's work at MC-6 was remarkable. The site is a 3.5-km trek from the town of Bambarra over a series of ridges covered with dense vegetation. Sullivan and his crews spent nearly seven months working at the site. All of the vegetation was cleared, which was an enormous undertaking. MC-6 is the equivalent of three football fields in area, yet the entire site was cleared by hand! The major ground cover is "guinea grass," which was imported by Europeans as animal fodder. Guinea grass has tough, fibrous stems and a dense root mat. It can grow as tall as 5 feet, and I have been at the site when we were in danger of losing people in the grass. To make matters worse, Sullivan (1981: 141) noted that the "guinea grass grew back about as quickly as it was cleared."

During his investigations Sullivan made a detailed topographic map and surface collected almost 100 percent of the site. At first, surface collections were made in standard square collection units, but it was quickly realized that circular ("dog-leash") collection units were faster and more efficient. Surface collections were made in a 10-m radius with a maximum time of 20 minutes allowed, in a 5-m radius in 10 minutes, and in 5-m by 5-m units in 45 minutes. Sullivan noted that small Palmetto ware sherds and abraded coral might be underrepresented in these samples. In addition, surface collections tended to emphasize the collection of olive shell beads and pendants, rough igneous rock and stone tools, cemí lugs and adornos from pottery vessels, and elaborately decorated and rare types of imported pottery.

The one, uncalibrated radiocarbon date for the site is AD 1437 ± 70 (courtesy of the Caribbean Research Foundation). The archaeological deposits are relatively shallow, so the site does not appear to have been occupied for a long time. Sullivan collected almost 30,000 potsherds from the surface of the site.

More than 90 percent of the sherds were locally made, shell-tempered Palmetto ware. The others were predominantly imports in the Chican Ostionoid subseries, which postdates AD 1300 on the north coast of Hispaniola (Rouse 1992; compare Keegan 2000b).

Finally, although the site is located in an area that is little used by the present inhabitants of Middle Caicos, it was once part of a Loyalist land grant. Even today "Loyalist" cotton grows on the margins of the site. A stonewall leading to Armstrong Pond and stone piles to the north of the site attest to historic activities in the area. A number of metal objects also were found scattered on the surface. Because the pre-Columbian deposits are so shallow, it is highly probable that the deposits have been disturbed by historic cultivations. Yet there is no evidence that anyone actually lived in this area, and cotton is far less destructive than sugarcane.

Community Plan

Sullivan had a military sensibility when it came to details. Every day he would carry a transit 3.5 km to the site and then back to Bambarra over the rough trail. Based on his investigations he concluded that MC-6 had a two-plaza community plan. By his calculations, the site measured 270 by 70 m, with the margins defined by midden ridges. The western plaza, called Plaza I, was larger. The midden ridges were punctuated by pit features with low limerock walls, which Sullivan interpreted as semi-pit houses (Figure 5.5). Eight stone-lined pit features were identified around the central court. Four structures were on the north side, three on the south side, and one on the east side at the juncture of the two plazas. Although most of the site was covered in guinea grass, Sullivan noticed that hardwoods covered a large area in the middle of Plaza I. After he cleared these trees, he realized that this was a court defined by a double row of undressed limestone rocks. In addition, an aboriginal road originated between structures III and VI and connected the north side of Plaza I to Armstrong Pond. The eastern plaza, Plaza II, was smaller and less distinctive.

The quality of the artifacts found on the two plazas varied in ways that seemed to reflect the hierarchical organization of Taíno society. Plaza I had far more imported potsherds and jewelry than did Plaza II. In fact the deposits around Plaza I contained far more materials of all kinds. Sullivan concluded that Plaza I was an elite compound and that commoners were living around Plaza II. The structure at the east end of Plaza I was interpreted as a cacique's house due to its larger size, its two-chamber floor plan, and its position at the juncture of the two plazas. Moreover, despite its central location, an embankment of materials physically connected this structure to the south side of the

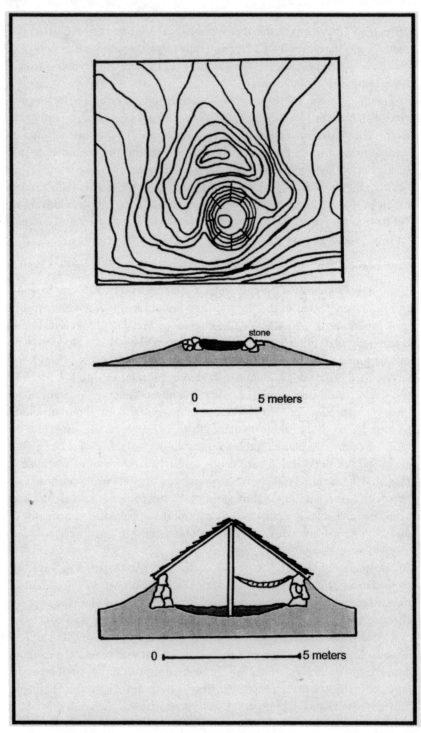

5.5. House mounds and house reconstruction (Sullivan 1981: 168; courtesy of Shaun D. Sullivan).

plaza. Artifacts from the south side were superior in quality to those on the north. This arrangement fits Harris's (1994) observation that south was superior to north in the cacicazgos of Hispaniola. Thus the community plan and distribution of artifacts seemed to reflect a division of the community into elite and commoner precincts, with a further distinction between elites living on the north and south sides of Plaza I.

The stone-lined court at the center of Plaza I is a remarkable piece of engineering. It is virtually flat, exhibiting only 10 cm of grade despite 500 years of weathering. The northern and southern margins of the court are flanked by double rows of undressed limestone that are incorporated into earthen ridges. These ridges appeared to be in part the by-product of leveling the court. The long east to west axis measures about 31 m. Where the stones stop at the eastern and western ends, the court is about 15 m wide. Those edge markers, combined with the discovery of a stone at the center of the court with a ball-sized depression, led Sullivan to propose initially that this was a ball court (*batey*). When it was first discovered, it was assumed that the rows of stones were parallel; but the detailed topographic map showed that the double rows of stones bow proportionately along their course. At its widest the court measures 19 m.

The rest of the settlement is organized around the court. Sullivan found that when a transit was positioned over the central stone and then pointed at a structure mound on the periphery of the plaza, a complementary structure on the other side of the plaza was intersected by turning the transit 180°. In addition, two structures were precisely reciprocal in a special sense. Both had prominent high points on the side toward the plaza. When the transit was centered on the midpoint of one of the structural prominences and then flipped, it precisely bisected the central stone and the prominence of the reciprocal structure. The prominences are composed primarily of stone and were not functionally integral to the structures to which they were attached. Although their original function is not clear, they seem to have been used for sight alignment, because they are aligned with the rising position of the Pleiades.

As mentioned, Shaun thought that the stone-lined plaza might be a *batey*. To place the site in the context of the day, in the late 1970s everyone was finding ball courts (for example, Olsen 1974 for Antigua). Ball courts were cool! For this reason Sullivan brought Irving Rouse to the site in December 1977 to get his opinion. Rouse told Sullivan that not all courts were ball courts but that the stone alignments at MC-6 were very similar to those observed at stone-lined courts in Hispaniola and Puerto Rico. Furthermore, the evidence that Sullivan brought to bear was sufficient to convince Ricardo E. Alegría (1983: 27–28) to include MC-6 in his review of Taíno ceremonial plazas and ball courts. Those of us who saw MC-6 when the site was cleared of vegetation have no doubt that the site was laid out with astronomical alignments in mind. This conclusion is patently clear to anyone who has visited similar sites in Hispaniola and Puerto Rico (Rodríguez Álvarez 2003).

Rituals, games, and dances may have been enacted on this court. In addition, the court served as a direct link to the heavens as an observatory that marked important astrological/cosmological events. The main alignment through the center of the court conforms to the rising and setting sun on the summer solstice, an event that Sullivan observed firsthand in 1981. He also identified a number of other alignments with the rising and setting of stars that are significant in Native American astronomical calendars. Of special note are alignments with the rising and setting positions of Betelgeuse, one of the principal stars in the constellation Orion. Orion had a central place in Taíno mythology (Robiou-Lamarche 2002; Stevens-Arroyo 1988). Sullivan also identified alignments with the rising positions of Altair, Procyon, Vega, and the Pleiades and the setting position of Fomalhaut. The significance of these alignments is discussed in greater detail in chapter 7.

Two additional factors indicate that this was a plaza and not a ball court. First, the stone alignments are like those that characterize ceremonial plazas elsewhere in Hispaniola (Alegría 1983). They are not like the ball courts of Puerto Rico, which have parallel sides. Second, another stone alignment crosses the eastern side of the plaza. This alignment bends at the middle and points first to the south and then to the southwest. Sullivan proposed that this was a map depicting a canoe trip first to Bush Cay on the southern edge of the Caicos Bank and then to the north coast of Haiti near Île de Tortue. Whether or not this alignment represents navigational instructions, it is not the kind of feature that would be found crossing a ball field.

The other significant feature of MC-6 is a road that leads from the center of the north side of Plaza I to Armstrong Pond, a distance of about 1 km. The road is about 2 m wide, with a stone and earthen ridge along both sides. As noted earlier, such roads are common at other ceremonial plazas in Hispaniola (Alegría 1983). About halfway between the site and the pond is a two-chambered, low, limerock-walled foundation. This feature is on the west side of the road, and the road's earthwork forms one wall. Sullivan did not find any artifacts associated with this feature. Although the structure may not have been of Taíno construction, it also does not appear to be of modern construction or use. Whatever its origins are, it is very similar in appearance to the semi-pit features on the site.

Plaza II

Plaza II had no structures, no stone alignments, and far fewer artifacts. Surface collections on the southern midden of Plaza II yielded 1,152 potsherds, of which 3.2 percent were imports. There were also three specimens of igneous/metamorphic rock on the south midden and five such specimens on the north. A sandstone artifact found on the northern midden has reversed comma–shaped lines incised on opposite sides. This *cemí* originally measured 8 cm by 8 cm by 4 cm, although about one-third was missing. Finally, only 199 sherds (0.35 percent imports) were recovered from the center of Plaza II.

Sullivan did not excavate any part of Plaza II, although the midden ridge that seemed to surround this plaza was mapped. Based on the material remains recovered from surface collections, he concluded that Plaza II was the temporary residence for commoners who were conscripted to work for the elites who lived on Plaza I. Given what was known of Taíno social organization, and the unique character of Plaza I and its court, Sullivan's diagnosis was compelling. The main problem was that other explanations could be devised, and more research was needed to investigate them.

Material Culture

Given what was known of archaeology in the Turks and Caicos, combined with the difficulty of working on the back side of Middle Caicos, Sullivan focused his efforts on surface collections. Furthermore, the deposits at MC-6 are very shallow, so surface collections provide a more accurate picture of activities on the site than do surface collections made at sites that have deeper strata (see Versteeg et al. 1993). Sullivan surface collected nearly 100 percent of MC-6. The main materials recovered were potsherds, mollusk shells, and coral.

Of the almost 30,000 sherds collected, the vast majority (93 percent) were Palmetto ware. Palmetto ware is known only from the Bahama archipelago and is considered to be characteristic of the Lucayans. This ware was tempered with burnt and crushed conch shell, because the islands lack the igneous and metamorphic sands that served as the tempering agents for pottery in the Greater Antilles (Mann 1986). The paste is an iron-rich eolianite that was transported on wind currents from the deserts of North Africa. These soils are not true clays, although they have the most plastic qualities of any soils available in the archipelago. Thus, despite a community plan that is more reminiscent and more typical of Taíno settlements in Hispaniola, the pottery indicates that this was a Lucayan site. Some of the pottery at the site was imported, but the vast majority was locally made Palmetto ware.

The imported pottery is of interest because decorations were executed primarily in the Chican style. Chican Ostionoid pottery is associated with the ethnohistoric Taínos. Rouse (1992) suggests that this pottery was the main style on the north coast of Hispaniola by AD 1200, but it is possible that Meillacan and Chican styles coexisted until at least AD 1300 (Rainey and Ortíz Aguilú 1983). Whatever the case, MC-6 shows a clear trading relationship with Taíno settlements on Hispaniola. It should be mentioned that Sullivan also found a white-paste pottery with red slip that he attributed to the Ostionan Ostionoid series. It is not clear what style this pottery reflects, but it is unlikely that the site was occupied during the time when Ostionan pottery was still being made in Hispaniola. Sullivan suggested that this pottery might be "Ostionoid" because this style included the use of red slips and because there were no other styles to which it could be assigned. In other words, this was simply an exercise in classification. If the pottery was not Meillacoid or Chicoid (the terms used at the time), then by default it had to be Ostionoid. This pottery does not look like Ostionan Ostionoid pottery from Hispaniola, however, and more recent studies have shown considerable variability in Meillacoid and Chicoid series pottery.

The other main component of the site was mollusk shells (Table 5.4). Unfortunately, there is a problem in how Sullivan quantified these data. His tables record shells in terms of MNI (minimum number of individuals). The idea behind MNI is that one unique character of a species is counted, yet Sullivan counted MNI by excavation unit and not by unique character. He looked at each excavation unit and estimated how many individuals were represented in that unit based on the range of shells encountered. As a result, his counts for *Strombus gigas* are overestimated, and he concluded that about 95 percent of the meat weight represented by shellfish came from *Strombus*. But is this a big problem?

It would be easier to evaluate mollusk remains at the site if NISP (number of identified specimens) and/or weights also were provided, but these numbers were not recorded. Nevertheless, recent investigations indicate that there was no reason to transport the large, heavy shells of adult *Strombus gigas* to the site unless some further use was anticipated (such as making shell temper or tools). Thus it always will be impossible to determine the total *Strombus gigas* catch, because many large shells probably were discarded away from habitation sites (O'Day and Keegan 2001). The pile of Indian opened shells observed at MC-32 is an example of this practice, which also was observed on Pine Cay (Keegan 1981). Fragments of *Strombus gigas* shells at the site are important for what they tell us about tool making and are not a reliable measure of food procurement.

Table 5.4. Mollusks Identified at MC-6

Taxon	Plaza I MNI	Plaza II MNI
Strombus sp.	311	48
Strombus gigas	262	12
Strombus pugilis	12	3
Codakia orbicularis	139	12
Tellina listeri	78	6
Cittarium pica	14	1
Charonia variegata	14	0
Oliva sayana	8	0
Tellina radiata	5	3
Cassis sp.	3	0
Nerita versicolor	2	0
Lucina pennsylvanica	2	0
Chiton	1	1
Tectarius muricatus	1	0
Anondontia alba	1	0
Pteria colymbus	1	0
Barbatia candida	1	0
Polinices lactus	1	0
Chione cancellata	1	0
Tonna sp.	1	0
Totals	858	86

Source: Sullivan 1981.

The molluscan data that Sullivan reports are surprising. At no other site in the region are mollusk counts so low (see Carlson and Keegan 2004). Moreover, the diversity of identified species is also extremely low. These data indicate that conchs were the main focus of procurement activities, even if their contributions were overestimated in terms of MNI. I have presented the mollusk data as part of material culture because the relatively small sample size can be interpreted as reflecting tool manufacture more than it does diet. *Strombus* shells were modified to provide a variety of expedient tools, including hoes for digging soil on the salina to build the site, picks for peeling cassava and chiseling wood, hammers for driving wedges to split wood, knippers to fashion shell bead blanks, and gouges to exhume charred wood from basins of sizes ranging from cassava troughs to canoes. Clam shells (*Codakia orbicularis* and/or *Tellina* sp.) were used for scraping and peeling yuca tubers (called *cuguará* by the Taínos) and for cutting hair. Olive shells (*Oliva sayana*) were made into beads and pendants, and one incised olive shell pendant was recovered. Beyond these species there are very few others of significance on Sullivan's list.

Table 5.5. Corals Identified at MC-6

Taxon	Plaza I Weight (g)	Plaza II Weight (g)
Monastrea anularis	69,882	4,683
Siderastrea siderea	42,792	141
Diploria clivosa	13,077	70
Diploria strigosa	1,150	0
Acropora cervicornis	4,849	166
Acropora palmata	1,077	15
Favia fagnum	155	0
Myceta ferox	1,460	0
Solenastrea hyodes	14	0
Colpophyllis natans	41	0
Unidentified	9,619	199
Totals	144,116	5,274

Source: Sullivan 1981.

Sullivan also recovered a wide variety of corals from the site, the most common of which was star coral (*Monastrea* sp.) (Table 5.5). Some of these were available on the Caicos Bank, especially during expeditions that crossed the southern reef system. It is also possible that corals were imported from reefs on the north coast. Corals were used for a variety of purposes in which a rough, sharp surface was needed (for example, rasps, drills, and abraders).

The most unique artifact was a small semicircular nose ornament called a *caracol*. An elemental analysis of the artifact showed that it was made from brass, which indicates that the raw material came from a European source. It is important as evidence that the site continued to be occupied after Europeans arrived in the Americas. As discussed earlier, *caracoli* are associated with *guanín* and a heavenly origin (*turey*). In the mythology they are associated with the culture hero Deminán (see chapter 2).

Economy

If MC-6 was a gateway community then we would expect to find material evidence for the production of goods for export. Two components of the economy reflect this practice. The first is the collection of salt as a dietary supplement or to preserve fish flesh; the second is the capture of vertebrates. These are discussed in turn.

MC-6 is situated in a position to control access to Armstrong Pond. Armstrong Pond is important because it produces substantial quantities of crystalline salt during the summer months. The site is connected to the pond by an aboriginal road, along which there is an enigmatic two-chambered structure.

In addition, along the western side of the pond, Sullivan found at least 20 remnants of stone alignments in "J," "V," and half-moon shapes. Many of these were under water during the rainy season. Two of these were excavated, but no aboriginal artifacts were found. Nevertheless, the closed portions of these shapes are all on the downhill side, and it is possible that they were used to drain the water from the salt slurry when it was collected (Sullivan 1981: 178). To gain a sense of how much salt could be harvested, Sullivan had his 16 crew members collect salt for 15 minutes during the height of the dry season in July 1977. Their labors produced 480 liters of salt, weighing more than half a ton (542 kg).

In an effort to identify and quantify the use of vertebrate species, several of the structures at the site were excavated. The soil from these excavations was sieved through ¼-inch mesh hardware cloth. The animal bones recovered from structures I, II, and III were identified by Elizabeth Wing at the Florida Museum of Natural History. Wing's identifications were reported in Sullivan's dissertation and have been discussed in other publications (for example, Wing and Scudder 1983; Wing 2001) (Table 5.6). The vast majority of the animal bones in the site came from fishes (about 90 percent by meat weight). A total of 429 MNI from about 25 taxa (most identified to the level of genus) were identified. In contrast to MC-12 and MC-32, the majority of the fishes came from tidal flats, which is to be expected given the site's location on the edge of the shallow Caicos Bank. The most important species in terms of meat yields was bonefish (*Albula vulpes*). Snappers, groupers, wrasses, jacks, grunts, porgies, barracudas, porcupinefishes, and sharks also were identified. Parrotfishes are present in significant quantities, but the genus *Sparisoma* does not dominate the sample as it does at other Lucayan sites, probably because the inhabitants of the site relied less on reef habitats.

Of special note is the identification of sea turtles (Cheloniidae). Sea turtles are not common in Lucayan sites, because their numbers were depleted by the earliest inhabitants of the islands (Carlson 1999). In the case of MC-6, the turtles in the sample were the size of dinner plates and likely were captured in the tidal inlets on the south side of the island near the site. Small turtles were observed in this area during a population census conducted in the late 1970s. Finally, a few iguanas (less than 4 percent), a few birds (less than 1 percent), one hutia (*Geocapromys* sp.), and one porpoise (Delphinidae) round out the sample.

Wing reported (in Sullivan 1981) that less than 5 percent of the fauna was captured within the site's 5-km catchment area. This percentage reflects only the availability of terrestrial species, however, because the now-dry salina extends to the south beyond the boundary of the catchment (thus no marine

Table 5.6. Vertebrate Remains from MC-6

Taxon	MNI	Biomass (g)
TERRESTRIAL		
Geocapromys	1	1,666
Ardeidae	1	877
Pandion	1	1,000
Cyclura	11	6,732
Anolis	1	8
Total Terrestrial	15	10,283
FISHES		
Sparisoma	7	5,061
Lutjanus	12	10,188
Epinephelus	5	4,670
Albula vulpes	37	45,103
Calamus	2	918
Haemulon	10	2,330
Gerreidae	4	620
Halichoeres	1	459
Lactophrys	1	459
Scarus	9	5,238
Sphyraena	3	2,547
Caranx	3	2,961
Balistes	1	459
Acanthurus	2	1,062
Diodon	1	459
Ginglymostoma	1	459
Carcharhinus	1	459
Gymnothorax	1	459
Belonidae	3	570
Centropomus	1	459
Selene	1	459
Eucinostomus	10	610
Sciaenidae	1	459
Sphoeroides	1	459
Total Fish	118	86,927
Cheloniidae	[4]	896

Source: Wing 2001: table 4.

species live within the catchment). Yet it has been suggested that this salina was flooded when the site was occupied. If this was the case, then most of the fishes (about 60 percent, with another 30 percent unidentified as to habitat preference) and mollusks in the sample would have been available within the catchment. Even if the salina was not flooded, the marine habitats that are closest to the site are those inhabited by the identified taxa.

Sullivan's Conclusions

The major focus of Sullivan's research, above and beyond his concern with the environmental setting of sites, was on the initial colonization of the Bahama archipelago. Based on his investigations in the Turks and Caicos, he proposed two cultural periods. The first was called the Antillean Period, which he dated to between AD 750 and 950, and the second was a Lucayan Period, which he dated to between AD 950 and 1500.

Sullivan characterized Antillean Period sites as small (less than 0.25 ha) and as having pottery that predominantly was imported from the Greater Antilles. Most of the Antillean period sites had fewer than 50 potsherds. The largest of the sites were MC-8, MC-10, and MC-33, which are all located on the south coast near Armstrong Pond. These sites had no polished igneous rock tools (although a few fragments of rough imported stone were collected), no shell tools, no decorated shell or jewelry, and no midden accumulations. Thus they were known more for what they lacked than for what they had. The pottery in these sites had strong affiliations with Meillacan motifs. According to Rouse (1939, 1941), who along with Froelich Rainey had conducted the most recent investigations in Haiti (40 years earlier), the comparative data that Sullivan had at his disposal indicated that there was a pre-Meillacan phase between AD 750 to 800, a Meillacan phase from AD 800 to 900, and a Chican phase from AD 900/950 to 1500 (Rouse 1964).

Sullivan tried to fit his data to Rouse's time-space scenario. The main problems were that he did not recover pottery that was executed in the pre-Meillacan "Ostionan" style (red painted), he had no radiocarbon dates for the Antillean Period sites, and he assumed that the earliest settlements should reflect an "inland" versus "coastal" settlement pattern (Sears and Sullivan 1978). In sum, he pushed his data to fit a model of settlement that has since been shown to be inadequate. To his credit, he did recognize that there was a period of exploration during which the peoples of Hispaniola familiarized themselves with the Turks and Caicos Islands. It would take 15 years, and a voice from the Pacific (Irwin 1992), before Caribbean archaeologists would acknowledge the significance of such voyages of exploration in the colonization of the Bahamas (Berman and Gnivecki 1995).

With the benefit of hindsight, today it is possible to assert that Sullivan was wrong in the details of his culture history. The very small sites that he identified as dating to the Antillean phase are mostly pot drops that are probably associated with temporary farmsteads. As such they cannot be used to characterize a period of settlement, because they do not represent the full range of ceramic diversity or cultural activities (Keegan 1995b). Sites on Grand Turk, however, do show that Sullivan was essentially correct in identifying a period of exploration in the islands that began about AD 700 and witnessed a second wave at about AD 1000, when the first settlements were established on Middle Caicos.

For his Lucayan Period (AD 950 to 1500) Sullivan again used dates drawn from Rouse's (1964) general outline of West Indian prehistory. In contrast to Antillean period sites, the main pottery style was locally made Palmetto ware, a variety of stone and shell tools were recovered, faunal remains were abundant, and evidence for house and other structural remains indicated permanent habitations. The most important of these village sites were MC-6, MC-12, and MC-32. Finally, Sullivan concluded that M-6 was a gateway community through which goods from the Bahamas were exported to the Greater Antilles. It is possible that entrepreneurs from Hispaniola who sought to control trade through the southern Bahamas founded the site. Among the possible items exported were cotton balls, parrot feathers, marine animals (such as fishes, conchs, and turtles), and shell ornaments. Yet the main export from MC-6 would have been solar-distilled salt, either in its raw form or as a preservative for exported meats.

Conclusions

Shaun Sullivan was a true pioneer. He recognized a significant question—the initial colonization of the Bahama archipelago—and went to the place where he was most likely to find the answer. In doing so he had to overcome substantial obstacles, yet he succeeded in making discoveries that he never could have anticipated. Moreover, he was the consummate field archaeologist. He introduced field methods that were not in common practice in the West Indies at the time. Without the attention to detail that Sullivan brought to his work, the significance of sites like MC-6 might never have been realized. Although his conclusions were influenced by the conventional wisdom of the day, his study provided a solid foundation upon which future investigations were built.

6

There and Back Again

During the 1980s most of the field research that I conducted involved archaeological surveys. My research was modeled on the work of Kent Flannery (1976) and William Sanders (Sanders et al. 1979), who had described the importance of complete archaeological coverage of a region. Why conduct a stratified random sample when we can obtain complete coverage? With this in mind my assistants and I set out with camping gear to walk the entire coastline of the Bahama archipelago. Although we never did achieve complete coverage, we did survey most of the southern Bahamas, including the Turks and Caicos Islands, and we identified more than 150 open-air sites (Keegan 1992, 1997).

The most surprising thing about sites in the Bahama archipelago is that over 90 percent of the open-air sites occur in pairs. Settlement pairs were defined as two sites that occur with overlapping 5-km catchments. This distance was set by Sullivan's work on Middle Caicos and by Wing's interpretation of resource use at these sites (Keegan 1985; Wing and Scudder 1983). While investigating the possible reasons for settlement pairs, Morgan Maclachlan and I decided that social factors were the most likely cause; based on an extended review of Taíno ethnohistory, we proposed that the pairs reflected the practice of localizing males in a society that practiced matrilineal descent and matrilocal residence (Keegan and Maclachlan 1989). Moreover, we proposed that the localization of males reflected a shift to avunculocal residence among the Taíno elites (see chapter 4). The main criticism of the avunculocal model was that we had no independent confirmation that the settlement pairs were contemporaneous. There are very few radiocarbon dates for Lucayan sites, and the local pottery style is not varied enough to allow for temporal distinctions. Thus it still remains a possibility that these settlement pairs represent sequential settlements in the same area.

MC-6 was viewed as especially important in this regard because it seemed to be the exception that proved the rule. Based on Sullivan's work, the site was interpreted as a settlement pair at which the commoner and elite segments of the society had joined. Furthermore, Sullivan observed differences in the quality of artifacts between the northern and southern halves of Plaza I and suggested that these represented a separate elite moiety at the site.

By 1990 I was looking for an island on which site contemporaneity could be established. A year earlier I had returned to the Turks and Caicos in anticipation of the Columbus Quincentenary. At the time San Salvador, Samana Cay, and Grand Turk were all claiming to have been Columbus's first landfall, the island the Lucayans called Guanahaní. The main problem with Grand Turk was that it lacked any evidence of pre-Columbian settlement. Charles A. Hoffman Jr. failed to find any pre- Columbian sites during his visit to Grand Turk in the 1970s, and Sullivan also failed to find any sites in the Turks group. For this reason he and Bill Sears concluded that these islands were too dry to have supported permanent habitation (Sears and Sullivan 1978).

The main protagonist for Grand Turk, the late Robert Power, was undeterred. He invited me and an assistant, Maurice Williams, to conduct an archaeological survey that would determine once and for all whether the claim for Grand Turk was credible or not. Although we did find two sites during our survey, and two others have been found since, all of the sites predate Columbus by at least two centuries. Nevertheless, Power claimed that our discovery proved that Grand Turk could have been Columbus's first landfall. Columbus sealed my fate as well. I would spend the next ten years directing projects on Grand Turk. And still, as always, the sirens of Middle Caicos called to me.

I returned to Middle Caicos in 1991 with funding from the National Geographic Society to pursue a more complete survey of the Turks and Caicos. What attracted me to Middle Caicos was the fact that several sites seemed to be contemporaneous and to reflect the pattern of settlement expected from the avunculocal model (MC-12 and MC-32). The following year we did the archaeological impact assessment for the first paved road on the island. The road was built across the south side of MC-12. During these projects we identified a large site near the modern settlement of Conch Bar (MC-36), and we did further testing at MC-12 and MC-32. We also obtained radiocarbon dates for these sites that showed they were all occupied after AD 1200 and that MC-12 had been settled by AD 1000. The pieces of the puzzle were falling into place. The importance of Middle Caicos could not be ignored. If the avunculocal model was correct, then sites on Middle Caicos seemed to hold the key.

Then and Now

I have never been one for coincidences. Being an archaeologist does not preclude being observant of modern social conditions and pondering how these may be related to the past. I find it striking that the pre-Columbian and post-Columbian settlements on the island followed each other with remarkable similarity. Middle Caicos today has three main postemancipation settlements:

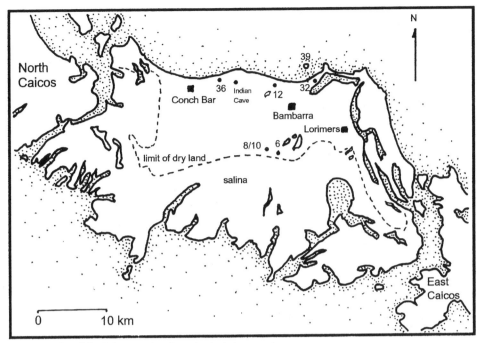

6.1. Map of Middle Caicos and archaeological sites.

Conch Bar in the west, Lorimers in the southeast, and Bambarra near the middle of the island (Figure 6.1). I mention postemancipation because during the plantation period the settlement pattern was more dispersed, as landholders controlled and farmed particular parcels that were spread across the island. With the breakdown in this system of enslavement and human exploitation, the now Afro-Caicosians congregated in the three modern settlements. I am not sure why, and neither are they. Yet the modern settlements correspond to the main Lucayan villages at MC-36 (Conch Bar), MC-12 and MC-32 (Bambarra), and MC-6 (Lorimers). The settlements are not located in exactly the same places. Conch Bar is to the west of MC-36. Lorimers is to the east of MC-6 and is situated to take advantage of the deep-water passage between Middle and East Caicos. Bambarra is also located on the ridge, although older residents claim that before several devastating hurricanes people lived closer to the beach where the Lucayan sites are located.

I find it interesting that the major villages from these two very different periods have such similar settlement patterns. Moreover, the competition between the modern communities raises important issues about community relations. There have never been more than about 500 people living on the island, yet the sense of community identity seems to me to be exceptionally strong. The people of Conch Bar feel superior to those living in Bambarra and Lorimers because the airport is located in their community. In addition, Lorimers is about as remote as possible in the Turks and Caicos, so the people in this community are viewed as backward, out-of-touch, and what we might call hillbillies.

I have mentioned already what an insult it is to call someone from Providenciales a "Blue Hills man," but people are known by their places of birth. Years ago I heard the story of a man who was born on Salt Cay but whose family moved to Grand Turk when he was four years old. Despite living on Grand Turk well into his sixties he was always regarded with some suspicion by the people of Grand Turk because he was a "Salt Cay man." I repeat these stories not to disparage the people of the Turks and Caicos but to recognize a common human behavior. We all mark our territory in the same way other animals do. Ask the people who fly to Nantucket so their baby will be born there.

Let us take one more example from Middle Caicos today. Conch Bar and Bambarra are both located on the north coast and have access to different resources. Conch Bar, by plane or boat, provides more immediate access to Providenciales, where today people can buy virtually anything. In addition, the sea is much rougher near Conch Bar, and marine access focuses on windward reefs. Bambarra provides more immediate access to more protected fishing grounds that are not subject to intense human predation. These include the waters near East Caicos and the highly productive Caicos Bank. Some people in Conch Bar have a second boat that they keep near Bambarra landing, and some people from Bambarra have a boat that they keep near Conch Bar. Yet the boats in both places are kept apart. The three or four boats from Conch Bar are not mixed with the local boats at Bambarra landing, and the same is true for Conch Bar. Why not? Why do people from these small communities maintain, or defend, their separate identities? Social relations in even small-scale societies (perhaps especially so) are exceedingly complex. It is my contention that we cannot understand what was happening on Middle Caicos more than 500 years ago if we do not recognize the complexity of social identities in small-scale societies today.

I am trying to understand the relationships between several communities on a small island. We might assume that small groups on a small island would reflect common goals, shared relations (for example, intermarriage), and a sense of harmony. The time I spent living on Middle Caicos, however, led me to recognize that even 10 km can represent a huge gap in terms of social identity. Thus while I am tempted to link all of the sites on Middle Caicos to a single cooperative whose main node (market, export center, port of trade, and so forth) was located at MC-6, I wonder how cooperative such relations actually were. Was it necessary for a cacique on Hispaniola physically to impose control over Middle Caicos and perhaps all of the Turks and Caicos? Moreover, why have we failed to find archaeological sites on North and East Caicos? Was there a demilitarized zone, an uninhabited buffer-land, surrounding Middle Caicos? The social dynamics of Middle Caicos today are complex and chaotic. It is important to keep this in mind when looking at social dynamics on the island in the fifteenth century.

Middle Caicos Encore

In the years following Sullivan's work at MC-12 the coastal zone, including the site, was sold to foreigners ("strangers") as part of a housing development. Although very few houses were actually built, the impact on the site was substantial. I have mentioned meeting the developer who bragged that his son had found a greenstone celt under a palm tree that they had removed by bulldozer to landscape the property. Moreover, the gardens around the houses contain the midden soils that were removed from the site due to their organic enrichment. As a result, shells and potsherds surround these houses. MC-12 is a total loss.

To make matters worse, the material remains from Sullivan's work at the site disappeared. Because there was no central repository for artifacts in the Turks and Caicos prior to the founding of the Turks and Caicos National Museum in 1992, there were no adequate arrangements for the curation of artifacts. In addition, Sullivan's display of "exotic" materials from MC-6 disappeared from the library on Grand Turk in 1984 along with a wooden *duho* that also was displayed there. More mundane artifacts from MC-6 were later found in the police storeroom on Grand Turk in 1992 under cast-iron cannons removed from shipwrecks during the Peter Benchley and Teddy Tucker expedition of 1977 (see Benchley's book *The Island*, 1978). The artifacts from Sullivan's work at MC-12 have never been found, although copies of the field notes are on file in the Turks and Caicos National Museum.

I finally took the opportunity to return to Middle Caicos for four weeks in 1999. This research was followed by a second season in 2000, and future work was planned until local logistical problems intervened. My accomplishments during this time need to be evaluated with that in mind, as well as the composition of the crews that were brought to the island. Volunteers from the Earthwatch Institute conducted the work. Although they were warned of the difficult conditions that this research would entail, I still tried to make their experience a positive one. Because MC-12 had been destroyed, I decided that the teams would work first at MC-32, which was a relatively easy one-mile walk from our field station, and then move on to MC-6. I felt that this would give them time to get acclimated and to learn the techniques of archaeological excavation. I must admit that my interest in MC-32 came more from my efforts to deal with my labor pool than from any special interest in the site. The work at the site proved to be highly informative, however.

I returned to Middle Caicos with several research questions in mind. First, the sites on the south coast were of special interest because Sullivan had used them to develop a chronology for the islands (Sears and Sullivan 1978). MC-8 and MC-10 were of special interest because Sullivan proposed these as the first settlements in the Turks and Caicos. Second, MC-6 was unique in the entire Bahama archipelago. Third, I was interested in how similar the material culture would be between the major sites that were occupied at contact (MC-12, MC-32, and MC-36). Unfortunately, we never got to work at MC-36 near Conch Bar, so the focus of this review is on the sites near Bambarra where we did work.

In addition to the main project, Pete Sinelli (2001) conducted his master's research at MC-8 and MC-10. Pete also led the team that discovered a new site on Pelican Cay (MC-39). Lee Roth (2002) undertook soils analysis of MC-6 and MC-32 as part of his master's research. Sharyn Jones O'Day (2002) analyzed some of the faunal sample from MC-6. Finally, in 1997 I organized an expedition with David Steadman (curator of Ornithology, Florida Museum of Natural History), Dick Franz (herpetologist at the Florida Museum of Natural History), and several volunteers during which we excavated Indian Cave near Conch Bar. Only six imported potsherds were recovered from the uppermost strata, and all of these had a paste that is most similar to Meillacan pottery (Ann Cordell, personal communication, 1997). Steadman has continued working at the site; his research promises to provide a clearer picture of animal life on the island before and after the arrival of humans. Already the work has recovered the bones of the extinct tortoise first identified on Grand Turk at site GT-3 (Carlson 1999; Dick Franz, personal communication, 1997) and 38 bird taxa, of which 21 no longer live on Middle Caicos (David Steadman, personal communication, 2004). These sites are plotted in Figure 6.1.

On the one hand I am tempted to write this chapter chronologically, following the sequence of my research. This would be useful because it would provide insights into my thinking and how it changed over time (that is, be reflexive). On the other hand I am tempted to go straight to the heart of the matter and describe my work at MC-6. I feel that the work at MC-6 is the product of intellectual growth achieved by working at different sites in the islands, however, and maybe this other work needs to be addressed first. I have settled on a third hand: treating MC-6 as a core and moving toward that core through peripheral sites located elsewhere on the island. We start with Pelican Cay.

MC-39

Pelican Cay is connected to the north coast of Middle Caicos by a tombola (sand bar) that originates near Bambarra landing. Although the sand bar is submerged, it is possible to walk out to the cay at low tide without having to swim. The site is fascinating for several reasons. First, the cay is little more than a rock, with virtually no soil; permanent settlement, even one house, would not be possible on it. In fact, it would be easy to throw a rock from one side of the cay to the other. There is a small beach on the Middle Caicos side, but a rock ledge (2 m high) forms the outer perimeter. With the exception of its relative isolation in the bay near Bambarra, today there is nothing of interest or use on this cay. Yet the modern name suggests one possible reason for using the cay. It is likely that it served as a rookery or nesting area for pelicans and other shorebirds (such as the red footed booby, *Sula sula*, which was extirpated by the Lucayans; Carlson 1999). The bay contains two other small cays—inner cay and outer cay—that cannot be reached on foot. These cays were surveyed, but no artifacts were found.

The artifacts recovered from Pelican Cay were very interesting. There was a high incidence of pottery imported from Hispaniola, including one sherd with a bat adorno. A few shallow test pits were dug on the island, and a shell inlay was recovered in one of these. The inlay is made from conch shell and is cut to represent teeth; it would have been fitted in the mouth of a wooden idol.

Archeological surveys throughout the Bahamas have found evidence for pre-Columbian activities on a substantial number of small, offshore cays (Keegan 1997). In the Turks and Caicos, similar finds were made on Middleton Cay near South Caicos, another small cay that could not support long-term occupation, on which a substantial number of imported and finely crafted artifacts were recovered. When Bob Gascoine took me to Middleton Cay in 1998, I found that the island was literally crawling with iguanas (*Cyclura carinata*), despite its proximity to South Caicos. Iguanas are no longer found on most of the Turks and Caicos due to human and animal (for example, dogs and cats) predation. Other small cays in the Turks and Caicos with archaeological sites are Gibbs Cay, Cotton Cay, Long Cay, Iguana Cay, and Ambergris Cay.

Pelican Cay and similar tiny cays in the archipelago indicate that ceremonial activities were conducted offshore and that valuables were discarded during these activities. It may be that these cays were the last refuge for species that were extirpated from the larger and more densely settled islands; or perhaps they represented seasonal aggregations such as those associated with nesting among birds. In any case, Pelican Cay is close to both MC-12 and MC-32 and seems to have attracted people for special purposes.

MC-12

I worked with Sullivan at MC-12 in 1982 and had the opportunity to return to the site in 1991 when we conducted the archaeological impact assessment for the first asphalt road on the island. We cut a series of five 1-m by 6-m transects, oriented to the north, across the proposed roadbed. It was immediately clear that we were in an area with few archaeological deposits, clearly at the limits of the south edge of the site. No additional information came from this work. The road has been paved since that time.

Although it was established earlier, it is important to remember that MC-12 was occupied at the same time as MC-6 and MC-32. The oval arrangement of midden soils and the presence of at least one large structure attest to this as a planned community of substantial size. Certainly the people at MC-12 had some relationship with the people who were living in other villages on the island. Unfortunately, the site has been destroyed and we are limited to the information collected by Sullivan during his investigations of the site.

MC-32

MC-32 is located about 1.2 km to the east of MC-12 on the north coast (see Figure 6.1). Like MC-12 it is situated on a broad shallow bay that provides access to excellent fishing grounds. Simon Forbes told me that the area of the site was called "snapper grass" ("snapper" refers to the Lutjanidae family of fishes). Moreover, Simon and his family have farmed the site repeatedly. The organic enrichment from the archaeological deposits made this land far more productive than other areas. In comparison, most of the soil along the north coast is oolitic limestone and contains few nutrients. Simon claims title to the property. I did promise to tell people that the land is for sale, and I do so here. Unfortunately, land titles are often complicated in the Turks and Caicos; plats in the government survey office list this area as government-owned "Crown Land."

The site is located on a relatively high sand dune and is virtually surrounded by Farm Creek Pond, a large tidal creek. A tidal creek is the Bahamian equivalent of a lagoon or estuary (see Sealey 1985). Unlike a lagoon, however, it is not particularly deep and is not located at the center of the island; unlike an estuary, it has no freshwater input. Tidal creeks typically are large, shallow coastal ponds that are influenced by the tide and at some time had a marine outlet. They can be categorized as shallow bays that have been closed by sand bars and filled by aeolian deposits.

Sullivan associated tidal creeks with the collection of salt. He suggested that MC-32 was established to take advantage of salt production in Farm Creek Pond. Geological survey work conducted in the Bahamas suggests a different and more complex association. During the 1980s I had the good fortune to work with Steven Mitchell, a geology professor at California State University, Bakersfield. He was interested in how coastlines in the Bahamas develop and was studying the transition from open bays to restricted tidal creeks to coastal ponds (Mitchell 1984). Mitchell found that every coastal pond that had a marine outlet between about 500 and 1,000 years ago also had at least one Lucayan site associated with it. His dating of pond sediments was inexact; the dates were based on an estimated rate of sedimentation. The objective, however, was to distinguish ponds that had been closed to the sea prior to Lucayan settlement from those that were tidal creeks when people first settled in the area. The timing of initial settlement dates roughly to around 1,000 years ago. Prior to Mitchell's research, very few archaeological sites had been identified along the windward coasts of the Bahamas (Sears and Sullivan 1978). As a result of his work, it was realized that tidal creeks should be considered an extension of the coastline. Surveys conducted around present-day and former tidal creeks revealed a substantial number of windward sites (Keegan 1992).

In sum, Mitchell found that ponds that existed more than 1,000 years ago did not have Lucayan sites associated with them, while ponds that were tidal creeks did have sites. His conclusions indicate that an active marine outlet was an important consideration in the decision to establish a settlement. The advantages of tidal creeks are that they provide access in shallow water to a wide variety of marine resources and provide protected areas for canoe landings, especially along windward coasts. An open marine outlet is essential for maintaining the productivity of the tidal creek by introducing oxygenated water, nutrients, and new animals and also for canoe access to open water. Once a tidal creek has closed to form a pond, the marine environment becomes stagnant; animal populations are first stressed and then extirpated.

Today the tidal creek at MC-32 is not open to the sea. Yet older residents of Bambarra told me that Farm Creek had only become a pond in their lifetimes.

When they were young, the creek had a sand bar across its mouth that was underwater at high tide. During extreme low tides the creek would dry out, and people walked all the way from Conch Bar (about 12 km away) and literally picked up fishes from the dry creek bed. Although Sullivan (1981) reported that people still raked salt for personal use when he lived in Bambarra, I was told that Farm Creek Pond was never used as a source of salt (but memories fade).

The point to all this is that Farm Creek Pond has been used for multiple purposes. The feature that Sullivan identified in the pond may have been constructed by the Lucayans to facilitate salt production or as a place to corral fishes. The pond also provided an important fishing area, however, and could have been used as a place to store live fishes and conchs in pens prior to processing. Protected fishing grounds are especially important when the open bay is unsuited for fishing. When I lived in Bambarra, we were able to purchase fresh fish on only a few days, although several fishermen lived in the community. On day after day of beautiful, calm, sunny weather I was told that they were not going fishing because "the bottom is walking." By this they meant that sediments suspended in the water column limited the likelihood for success. It was not worth the effort to go fishing. Tidal creeks would have provided an alternative fishing ground on days when other marine habitats were deemed unproductive. This conclusion is supported by the high frequency of fish species that inhabit tidal-flat environments in the deposits at MC-32 (Sullivan 1981: 302).

Lee Roth (2002) did a soils analysis of the site and produced a series of maps based on topography and other characteristics. Our excavation units at the site are identified on Figure 6.2. His analyses indicate that the site is smaller than Sullivan proposed based on the surface scatter of artifacts (150 by 100 m). Roth defined an area of 70 m by 40 m as reflecting the subsurface distribution of archaeological materials. The site deposits extend to a maximum depth of 1 m but are only this deep along the northern edge, which has been covered by aeolian sand deposits. The site has a dense central midden and a more "ephemeral" southern midden (Figure 6.3). In this regard it would seem that houses were located along the beach ridge with midden deposits behind them (Roth 2002: 135).

During test excavations at the site in 1993 we obtained a radiocarbon date from the deepest strata of cal AD 1290 ± 50. The date comes from the 1 m^2 unit near the center of the map (Figure 6.2). In addition, there was an imported Chican style adorno sitting on bedrock at the bottom of this 1 m^2 unit. This is not unusual given the date for this stratum, but it is unusual for Meillacan and Chican sherds to co-occur. The site dates to a century after the Meillacan

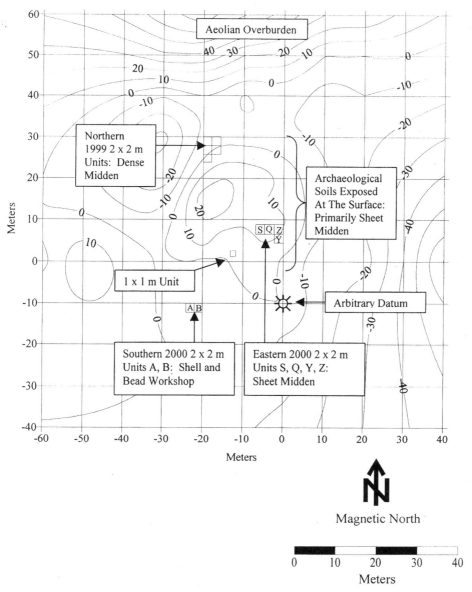

6.2. Map of MC-32 (courtesy of Lee Roth).

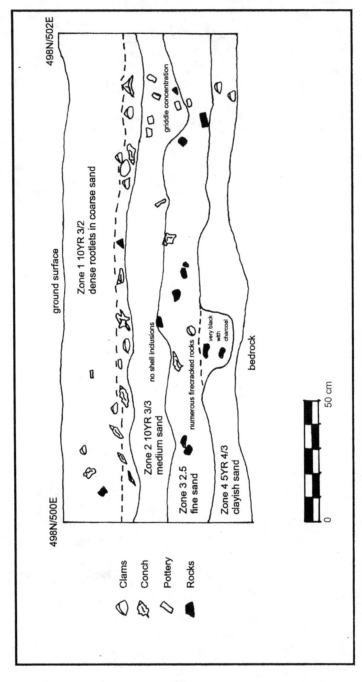

6.3. Stratigraphy of the south wall of Units 498N/500–502E at MC-32.

style is supposed to have disappeared on the north coast of Hispaniola. In contrast, the data point to multiple interactions (or down-the-line exchanges) with people who made and used both Meillacan pottery and Chican pottery. In sum, cultural relations were far more chaotic than they have been portrayed (compare Rouse 1992).

Our excavations in 1999 focused on the central midden, where we excavated 17 m^2 (Figure 6.3). The units were excavated in 10 cm levels. The base of the deposit was encountered at bedrock at 80 cm below ground surface. The deposits seem to be relatively undisturbed. There are a few crab burrows in the area, and farming has been limited to slash-and-burn cultivations accomplished with a machete, which limits the depth to which the subsoil was disturbed. The best evidence for limited disturbance is several concentrations of bones from a single fish. The nearly complete assemblages of bones from a large barracuda, a large grouper, and a porcupinefish indicate that they remained intact where they originally were deposited. The site also contains much larger potsherds than are typically found in Lucayan sites. If the deposits had been disturbed substantially, then the bones and other cultural materials would have been more fragmented and widely dispersed.

Our excavations in 2000 were located at the southern and eastern margins of the site. In both locations we recovered far less material than we did in the central excavation area. This result fits Roth's (2002) soils analysis, in which he found that these units were on the outer margins of the site. Of special note in the southern units was a cache of five coral drills (*Acropora cervicornis*). These cylindrical coral pieces have a pattern of wear in which the outside of one end is completely abraded around its circumference. This use-wear pattern is created when the end of the drill is rotated into a piece of wood.

Overall, during the 1993 transect survey we recovered 1,957 sherds, of which 264 (13 percent) were imports. In our 2000 excavations we recovered a total of 320 sherds, of which 79 were Palmetto ware vessels (25 percent), 35 were Palmetto ware griddles (11 percent), and 206 were imports (64 percent). The imported sherds had both Meillacan and Chican motifs. Although the former were concentrated in the deeper levels, there was still a mixing of styles.

What was most unusual about the site was the relatively high incidence of decorated Palmetto ware. There is no reason why Palmetto ware could not have been decorated, yet the vast majority of sherds are plain (Sears and Sullivan 1978). At MC-32 we recovered about a dozen large Palmetto ware sherds with punctations, incised designs, and in some cases both. Moreover, a large number of griddles had matt-marking, which Charlene D. Hutcheson (1999) views as a decorative versus functional feature. We also recovered bowls with matt-impressions along the lower part of the vessel, representing several different kinds of basketry weaves. In particular, one vessel had matt-marking along the lower portion of this hemispherical vessel that was subsumed by three 30-mm-wide coils whose juncture was not completely smoothed, above which there is a 70-mm smoothed surface that ends at the rim. Although there was not enough of the vessel's circumference to make an exact measurement, it was very large and of the size expected for a pepper pot. If the people at MC-32 were making their pottery, they were doing so with designs derived from both Meillacan and Chican styles. MC-32 shows the strongest affinities to Hispaniola of any Lucayan site, especially with regard to the decoration of pottery.

The central deposit contained a very high incidence of fire-cracked limestone from cooking hearths, charcoal, and lots of animal bones. There were also a substantial number of griddle sherds, which seem to be associated with a greater emphasis on cassava bread during the terminal periods of settlement in the West Indies. The relatively high incidence of iguanas and sea turtles is noteworthy, because Oviedo y Valdés (1959) reported that these were reserved for feasts that were hosted by the caciques. It is possible that the remains observed at MC-32 represent ceremonial feasting; however, the site itself is too small to have been the village of an important cacique. Alternatively, the people who lived at the site may have been involved in capturing and processing foods that were used in local feasts or were exported to Hispaniola. Columbus described specialized fishing villages along the south coast of Cuba. When he entered Guantanamo Bay in April 1494, he encountered men who were barbecuing fishes and iguanas in preparation for a feast that their cacique was hosting for a visiting "potentate" (Morison 1942).

There currently is no evidence for structures at the site. As mentioned above, Roth (2002) concluded that the structures would have been located on the dune ridge next to the beach. To date, this area has received limited attention. In the main midden area we also recovered the vault of a human cranium. Given the absence of other bones in the area, this may reflect a curated specimen: the skull of an ancestor initially preserved in an adjacent structure.

Betsy Carlson analyzed the faunal remains from our excavations (Table 6.1). As noted above, the site contains the remains of a number of large fishes, which shows that the local fishing grounds had not been significantly depleted at this time. The bones of Old World rats (*Rattus rattus*) indicate that the site was still occupied after Europeans arrived. Finally, the site contains a very high incidence of very small, bait-sized fish. These fish likely were captured with fine-gauge nets and may have been added to the pepper pot or used as bait for capturing prized carnivorous fishes (such as barracudas, groupers, and snappers) on hook and line.

Table 6.1. Vertebrate Remains from MC-32

Taxon	MNI
TERRESTRIAL	
Rattus rattus	3
Cyclura carinata	26
Iguanidae	3
Trachemys	1
Tropidophis greenwayi	8
Leiocephalus psammodromus	1
Epicrates chryosogaster	1
Aves	2
Ardeidae	2
Columbidae	1
Total Terrestrial	48
FISHES	
Sparisoma viride	104
Atherinomorus stipes	47
Lutjanus	41
Lutjanus analis	1
Epinephelus	38
Albula vulpes	25
Calamus	15
Haemulon	64
Gerreidae	11
Gerres	8
Halichoeres	29
Elops saurus	13
Lactophrys	8
Scarus	23
Sphyraena barracuda	8
Caranx	11
Caranx ruber	6
Caranx crysos	1
Balistes	10
Balistes vetula	3
Acanthurus	35
Diodon hystrix	18
Mulloidichtyyes	16
Gecarcinidae	1
Opsanus	3
Serranidae	2
Centropomus undecimalis	3
Labridae	2
Negaprion brevirostris	1
Eucinostomus	10
Sphoeroides	27
Mycteroperca	1
Muraenidae	1
Trachinotus	1
Sciaenidae/Sparidae	1
Total Fish	588
Panulirus argus (lobster)	7
Cheloniidae	2
Caretta caretta	1

Source: Carlson 1999.

MC-32 is an unusual site. It is small relative to other villages. Using my criteria of one house for every 30 m (Keegan 1985), then the site had no more than 2 houses and perhaps 60 inhabitants (of which half would have been children). We would not expect a site of this size to be so concerned with demonstrating its connection to villages in Hispaniola, as reflected in locally made pottery decorations that reflect allegiances to both Meillac and Carrier styles. Nor would we expect the relatively high frequency of imported pottery. Finally, the site had a high incidence of *Strombus* beads, olive shell beads and pendants, and a perfect mother-of-pearl shell inlay about 20 mm wide in the form of an eye. It is oval and pointed at the ends; a slit down the center indicates that the eye was closed.

There is something special about MC-32. One interpretation, first suggested by Sullivan, is that the site operated in concert with MC-6. In this regard resources from the north coast may have been recovered and then brought to MC-6, where some were used at the site (for example, corals) and others were sent on to Hispaniola. Moreover, the people who lived at MC-32 may have supplied at least some of the labor that went into building the ceremonial court and surrounding midden at MC-6. We can view this arrangement at several levels. First, marriage alliances could compel people from MC-32 to contribute to ceremonial feasting at MC-6. Given their access to high-ranked resources (such as iguanas and sea turtles) the people at MC-32 enjoyed a better potential diet than the people at MC-6 and many of the people living in Hispaniola (Carlson and Keegan 2004). Thus we do not need to conceive of their relationship as one of corvée labor in which people from MC-32 were conscripted to rake salt and build raised earthworks. They may have been full partners who invested in extracting export commodities from the north coast that could be exchanged for exotic imports from Hispaniola.

MC-8 and MC-10

The earliest sites on Middle Caicos date to the eleventh century AD. They are located on the north coast at MC-12 and on the south coast. Of the 14 early sites identified along the south-coast salina only two were of a size that would indicate long-term occupation. Two of these sites, MC-8 and MC-10, are located about 2 km west of MC-6. Sullivan's main conclusion (discussed in chapter 5) is that these sites represent an initial Antillean Period of settlement.

Pete Sinelli (2001) conducted master's research at these sites, further evaluating the possibility that they were among the earliest sites on the island. He employed two excavation strategies. The first involved the excavation of small (50 cm²), regularly spaced shovel tests along transects. The second was more judgmental: mounded areas were targeted, and larger excavation units (1 m^2) were used. Neither site contained an abundance of materials or very deep deposits. It is likely that the sites either were occupied for a short period or were seasonal camps. Sinelli did obtain one radiocarbon date on charcoal from the deepest strata at MC-10, cal AD 1130 ± 50.

Only a tidal inlet (140 m wide) separates the sites. For this reason Sinelli (2001) concluded that they may actually be components of a single site or may reflect repeated short-term camps in the same area. Both MC-8 and MC-10 contain primarily Meillacan pottery, which predates the Chican and Palmetto ware pottery styles that are predominant at MC-6 (Sullivan 1981; Rouse 1992). In addition, a petrographic analysis of the pottery suggests that the main ties were with the Fort Liberté area of Hispaniola, not with peoples living farther to the west (see Cordell 1998 for the background to this study). Sinelli concluded that these sites do indeed reflect an early phase of settlement on the island, although the one radiocarbon date is later than the date associated with Sullivan's Antillean Period.

The sites contain evidence for bead production, an activity viewed as the main impetus for the seasonally occupied Governor Beach site on Grand Turk. The Governor Beach site also contains only Meillacan pottery and is radiocarbon dated to the same period. Access to salt does not appear to have been the main consideration in locating these sites. In fact, seasonality data from the Governor Beach site suggest that the site was visited in early spring at the beginning of the dry period.

If MC-8 and MC-10 also were seasonal occupations, then there would not have been salt on Armstrong Pond during the Spring when the sites were in use. Furthermore, many locations much closer to Armstrong Pond could have been settled (for example, MC-6). So it would seem that the primary reason for their locations was to take full advantage of the marine resources on the Caicos Bank, including the thorny jewelbox shells (*Chama sarda*) that were made into disk-shaped beads. In addition to making beads, the people who used these sites probably captured fishes and other animals that were brought back to Hispaniola when they returned. At the Governor Beach site the majority of the faunal remains come from the head parts of the grunt (*Haemulon striatus*), which has been interpreted as evidence for processing prior to export (Carlson 1993). In sum, MC-8 and MC-10 were short-lived and likely seasonal camps that reflect an early episode of resource extraction. They also would have been instrumental in the discovery of Armstrong Pond and the recognition of its value as a source of salt.

These sites are significant in providing another example of the people who made Meillacan pottery striking out on their own. These colonies or camps on

Middle Caicos and Grand Turk seem to have been focused on the manufacture of shell beads. At the time of European contact, such beads were an important component of woven belts and other objects associated with caciques (Taylor et al. 1997). Finally, these data point to the distinct cultural identities of Meillacan and Chican peoples (Veloz Maggiolo 1993). Although the Chicans may have overrun the territories of the Meillacans, this certainly involved more than a simple change in the way pottery vessels were decorated.

MC-6

When Sullivan found the site, he followed a trail that was being maintained by Simon Forbes, who at the time burned charcoal near Armstrong Pond. It took six full days to recut the trail using machetes when we returned to work at the site in 1999. I remember sitting with Brian Riggs at midday in a hollow below the third ridge, sharpening our machetes. What came to mind was the final scene of *Butch Cassidy and the Sundance Kid*, as they reloaded their weapons before taking on the entire Bolivian army. We were still kilometers from MC-6, and the whole enterprise seemed hopeless. I realize that I am romanticizing this work, but that is part of the attraction of archaeology.

The walk to MC-6 took at least 50 minutes each way. The conditions limited what Shaun and I were able to accomplish at the site. Still, my daughter Lindsay (then 10 years old) and two octogenarians worked at the site, so it was not in any way impossible. When I visited MC-6 at the end of Sullivan's research in 1978, the entire site was cleared of vegetation, although guinea grass had begun to reestablish itself. I visited the site again in 1991 and waded through guinea grass almost 2 m tall. By the time we began our new phase of research at the site in 1999, hardwoods had replaced most of the guinea grass.

Sullivan had done an excellent job of mapping and surface collecting at MC-6, but he had conducted very limited excavations. For this reason I was left wondering about the function of the structures ("houses") that he had identified, the settlement organization of Plaza II (where the commoners were supposed to have lived), and structure VIII, which Shaun had identified as the cacique's house. I returned to MC-6 in 1999 and 2000 with several questions in mind. Where did the people live? What was the function of the semi-pit features around Plaza I? What were the characteristics of settlement on Plaza II? What was the cacique's house? And, finally, what food remains, pottery, and tools were associated with the structures in stratigraphic context? Furthermore, Sullivan used only ¼-inch hardware cloth sieves to recover faunal samples. We collected fine-screen voucher samples from all of our excavation units to obtain a more comprehensive faunal sample.

Lee Roth's Soils Analysis

Although most of my work focused on relatively localized excavations, we did attempt to gain a better overview of the site through the soils analysis conducted by Lee Roth as part of his master's research. With the help of Earth-watch volunteers, Lee cut a series of transects across Plaza I and then made a systematic collection of auger samples. The soils from these samples were analyzed for phosphorus and carbon. He used the center stone at the site for his datum and was thus able to tie directly into Sullivan's grid.

Roth (2002) made two very important contributions. First, he showed that the central court was not natural. It was made by people who transported soil from the salina and purposely placed rocks in a double row. The court clearly was not some random arrangement of stones that had been given structure by an imaginative archaeologist. Roth's (2002: 201) map of total phosphorus clearly shows that the surrounding earthwork is distinct from the central court. Second, Roth (2002) recognized that Sullivan had assumed that people lived on their middens. He noted that in most documented cases the middens were located behind the houses and that people did not live on their garbage. Because the structures were in the midden, Roth suggested that the stone-lined pits were special-use structures for the storage of goods prior to export. As Sullivan himself noted (1981: 179), "once dried thoroughly, it is desirable to move the salt under shelter so that individual crystals are not fused by rainfall into large blocks."

In this regard, Roth amplified my concerns regarding the identification of these semi-pit structures as houses. First, they seemed too small. Second, during Sullivan's excavations of the structures he encountered a substantial amount of trash. In comparison, other Taíno houses appear to have had clean-swept floors, such as the one I described for MC-12. Thus the accumulated refuse in the structures also was not typical of a residence.

With regard to structures, Roth also questioned whether structure VIII was a cacique's house. Sullivan's (1981) interpretation was based on the structure's location at the juncture of Plaza I and Plaza II, which mirrored the Taíno prac-tice of locating the cacique's residence at the center of the village (for example, Guacanagarí's village at En Bas Saline). In addition, the structure seemed to have two chambers. It was common for caciques to have a separate chamber attached to their houses in which the village's *cemíes* were stored. Roth (2002) noted that some ethnohistoric sources indicated that the cacique's residence was located on one side of the central plaza and usually was adjacent to a road (see Rouse 1948). He concluded that structures III and VI on the north side of the plaza on opposite sides of the beginning of the road to Armstrong Pond might have been the location of the cacique's residence. Sullivan excavated structure III, however, and did not find anything of significance. Moreover, although the faunal remains from structure III are consistent with those from other parts of the site (see below), the sample size is too small (only 13 MNI) to draw any substantive conclusions.

At the outset it is also worth noting that excavating at MC-6 is an exercise in rock removal. The soil is relatively shallow, and our progress was slowed by having to work around rocks of various sizes. There is other evidence that the midden ridge surrounding Plaza I was a purposely constructed earthwork and is not simply the product of refuse disposal. Large rocks were repeatedly brought to the ridge to augment its height, and sand from the nearby salina was brought in as fill. In our excavations near structure II we repeatedly encountered large rocks that had been set down on a pavement of potsherds. In this regard MC-6 is like other Taíno sites in Hispaniola with a raised enclosure of human manufacture (see Alegría 1983).

Along the northern side of the site is a series of piles composed of limestone blocks. Based on his chemical analyses, Roth (2002) concluded that this might have been an area in which agricultural fields were located. During research at the site in 2000, Dennis Kendrick had the notion that these limestone piles might be burial cairns. He excavated one of the piles but found no cultural remains beneath the rocks. It is more likely that these reflect the historic clearance of rocks from an area on which cotton was planted. These are common features created by determining a central place and then walking around it while throwing large rocks into the middle. The result is a field that is relatively clear of large rocks, with a series of stone piles distributed across the field. The area has not been cultivated for many years and is today overgrown by low scrub vegetation and cactus.

Plaza II

Based on the community plan of Plaza I, I selected an area on Plaza II that should have produced evidence for the hypothesized habitation area of the commoners. Four units (2 m by 2 m) were excavated from the southern edge of the "midden" ridge toward the center of the plaza. They were excavated to limestone bedrock. The area has a dark, rich soil that covers bedrock by only about 25 cm along the southern edge and by 10 cm or less toward the center of the plaza. Virtually no artifacts or animal remains were found in these excavations. The one exception is a feature that looks like a firepit in the bedrock at the base of Unit O.

The results suggest that this was never a habitation area and, by extension, that there was not a commoner precinct at MC-6. If this area was used at all, it was more likely used for house gardens. If the second plaza is excluded from the total site dimensions, then the site actually measures 190 by 70 m. This really is not a significant change in size, especially if we accept the possibility that people living elsewhere on the island worked seasonally at MC-6. As Sullivan and I have shown, it was no more than an hour's walk from sites on the north coast of Middle Caicos (MC-12 and MC-32).

Structure II Excavations

As discussed in chapter 5, Sullivan concluded that the stone-lined pit features around Plaza I were houses. Yet these features were so small (circa 5 m in diameter) that I found it hard to accept his conclusion. Ethnohistoric descriptions and archaeological research indicated that pre-Columbian houses in the region were much larger. Las Casas described houses that could hold 40 to 60 heads of households in Cuba, the post stains at MC-12 were indicative of a large structure, the structure in the center of the village at En Bas Saline was large (Deagan 1989), and large houses were identified at the Golden Rock site on St. Eustatius (Versteeg and Schinkel 1992). In sum, I was thinking in terms of large houses. The other issue was that houses with semi-pit, stone-lined foundations had not been described elsewhere in the Caribbean.

In 1999 I initiated excavations to the west of structure II in the hope of finding evidence for a larger structure made of perishable materials. If the houses were located between the earthwork and the court, I believed that we had a good chance of intercepting postholes in this area. In addition, my decision to excavate here also was influenced by the notion that this area represented the place where the highest-status individuals lived at the site, because Sullivan's surface collections recovered a higher incidence of exotic, high-status goods along the south side of Plaza I. We did not find any evidence for a perishable structure in this area. Moreover, only 10 m separate the earthwork from the court, so it would be nearly impossible to fit a large house there that did not spill over onto the court.

In the end, I came to accept Sullivan's conclusion that these features—these "structures"—were indeed houses. Support for this conclusion also came from Antonio Curet's review of house remains in archaeological sites on Puerto Rico. Curet (1992b: 166–168) describes three structures from the El Bronce site that are all about 5 m in diameter (though slightly larger) and that date to the late prehistoric period. Moreover, he views the reduction in house size in Puerto Rico as reflecting changes in household composition. In other words, the initial emphasis on extended family households was replaced by an emphasis on the nuclear family as the domestic unit of production.

Curet's notion of smaller domestic units during the later prehistory of the islands was consistent with the special-purpose functions of MC-6. These structures may have housed small groups of related individuals who assisted the cacique in the procurement of resources for export to Haiti. This behavior can be illustrated with a modern parallel, albeit one that does not involve living spaces. Today in Haiti small groups of men cooperate in breaking rocks into manageable-sized pieces for use in construction. These rocks are piled on the side of the road, where they are picked up by large dump trucks. Every group has its own separate pile, and each is compensated accordingly. This example is comparable to the Trobriand Islands, where each family displays its annual agricultural output in specially built yam houses (Malinowski 1978).

The use of small houses may also involve a stronger social component. If Plaza I was the precinct of a cacique, then the small structures may have been houses that were occupied by the cacique's allies. Taíno caciques had many wives from arranged marriages that served to cement alliances between the caciques' lineage and those of their allies. If MC-6 was the settlement of a cacique who controlled access to goods from the Bahamas, then evidence for marriage alliances with other communities in the southern Bahamas should be present at the site. It is possible that in-marrying wives and their offspring were long-term residents at the site and that men and women from allied villages came to MC-6 periodically to engage in activities related to the procurement of local resources and their export to Hispaniola. Alternatively, the small houses may reflect a shift to production by nuclear families (Curet 1992b).

There also is evidence around structure II for the specialized production of nacreous objects for use as tools or jewelry. Although there are only a few shells with a mother-of-pearl (rainbow-looking) surface, it is not always possible to tell which shell the finished objects came from. The two main sources were Caribbean oyster (*Pinctada radiata*) and West Indian top shell (*Cittarium pica*). It has been suggested that mother-of-pearl was used mainly for inlays in statues or for jewelry, and we did recover a nacreous eye inlay from MC-32. It is equally likely, however, that at least some of these objects were used as fishing lures—"spinners" in the modern parlance—to attract fishes like the barracuda to a hook and line.

One unusual discovery near structure II was a large rock that appears to have a petroglyph carved on it. Quite by accident I had a petroglyph specialist on site (see Marquet 2002). Although she originally agreed that the rock was purposely carved, she later changed her mind. Nevertheless, to my eye the markings on the rock look like the outline of a frog. This "frog" petroglyph was on a large rock on the ground surface and was positioned to look out at an angle of 280°. This orientation happens to coincide with the setting position of Betelgeuse, which is one of the principal stars in the constellation Orion and one of the astronomical alignments that Sullivan noted for the court. The possible association of Orion and the frog is developed further in the next chapter.

"Cacique's House" Excavations

Eleven units (1 m^2)were excavated in the area that Sullivan identified as the cacique's house. When we began the excavations, I expected to find a substantial quantity of imported pottery and other elite goods such as carved shell, shell beads and pendants, imported stone beads, inlays from wooden statues, stone *cemíes*, and other objects that would distinguish this area as the residence of a high-status individual. In addition, it was anticipated that the caciques would have a higher quality of food remains (or none at all if their meals were prepared elsewhere and then brought to them) than those found in other areas of the site.

That is not what we found. Only 6 percent of the pottery from these excavations was imported from the Greater Antilles, and none of the sherds were from particularly elaborate vessels. Although we found a few stone beads, a small piece of conch shell carved in the shape of a plummet, and a few shell beads and olive shell pendants, there were not substantial quantities of what I would call high-status goods. We also found a variety of shell tools, which reflect either agricultural work or the construction of the midden on which the structure was built. If this was indeed the cacique's residence, then it appears that the cacique was no better off than the other people who were living at the site. Our finds (or lack thereof) do not necessarily prove that this was not the house of a chief. In his restudy of materials from the site of En Bas Saline (Guacanagarí's village) in Haiti, Brad Ensor (personal communication, 2000) found that members of the cacique's household were involved in the same production activities as other members of the community. Apparently chiefly status did not carry with it exemption from basic production activities.

Food remains present an equally difficult interpretive problem. Faunal samples were collected using fine-mesh (2.2 mm) screens in order to evaluate the degree to which Wing's analysis of Sullivan's ¼-inch mesh samples accurately reflected the size range of species deposited in the site. At some sites (such as MC-32) a substantial number of small bones were recovered from the fine-screen samples, while at other sites (such as GT-3 and Wes-15a in Jamaica) we found that fine-mesh samples do not significantly change the species list or size range generated from ¼-inch mesh samples (Carlson and Keegan 2004). In addition, I wanted to see if the presence and/or absence of particular bones would provide evidence for the processing of fishes by salting or smoking prior to export (see Zohar et al. 2001). For example, if fish were being exported to Hispaniola we might expect that the bulky and relatively meatless heads would be removed prior to shipment. To date, only Unit J (2 m by 2 m) from this area of the site has been analyzed, and neither of these objectives was addressed directly in the published report (O'Day 2002). Moreover, it is possible that the analyzed sample came from a disturbed context. Nevertheless, the analysis provides some interesting insights.

The faunal lists compiled by Wing and O'Day are not exactly comparable. Wing focused on the identification of animal bones to the taxonomic level of genus while O'Day identified bones to the species level whenever possible, so comparisons have had to be made at the higher taxonomic level. Yet the high degree of conformity between the samples is striking. Bonefish (*Albula vulpes*) is far and away the most important species in terms of biomass (consumable flesh). When the estimated biomass contributions of unidentified fishes (Osteichthyes) are eliminated from consideration, bonefish constituted 51 percent of biomass for Wing's sample and 34 percent of the Unit J sample. Bonefishes would be very common on the shallow seagrass flats adjacent to the site and could have been captured in large quantities by driving them into corrals or nets set in the shallows.

The remainder of the 53 taxa from Unit J each contributed very little to total biomass (less than 5 percent); the only exception is the porcupinefish, which contributed about 10 percent. I already have mentioned that this species may have been targeted because it contains a toxin that could have been used for medicinal or hallucinogenic purposes. It is also very common in other Lucayan sites.

In all, 11 taxa that do not appear on Wing's list were identified in the sample from Unit J, while there are 4 additional taxa in Wing's analysis (2 puffers, a moray eel, and a jack). One of the taxa unique to Unit J is a stingray (*Dasyatis* spp.). Stingray bones do not preserve well in archaeological sites, because most are composed of cartilage (shark bones present the same problem). Although the element(s) identified by O'Day are not reported, we can speculate that her two MNI were tail spines. Spines tell us more about tool use on the site than about diet, because the spine was used to tip spears (see Siegel 1992). Oviedo y Valdés (1959) also reported that the placoid scales that run along the back of the southern stingray were used to process manioc for the finest cassava bread (called *jaojao*). The absence of stingrays from Wing's list is not surprising, given their relative rarity in Lucayan sites and the small size of the sample that was analyzed.

The other animals missing from Wing's list represent only 20 of the total 343 MNI and contributed only 5 percent of the total identified biomass. What is significant about these differences is that the bones are not from small fishes. All but one of these taxa reach a maximum length of 30 cm (Randall 1968), and all of them have been identified in ¼-inch mesh samples from other sites (Wing and Reitz 1982). The one exception is the herring (*Harengula* spp.), which is represented by 1 MNI and contributed 0 percent to total biomass. Therefore the fine-screen sample from Unit J did not add a significant contribution to our understanding of faunal remains at MC-6. This is an extremely important contribution, because it means that Wing's analysis provides an accurate portrait of the fauna.

Other fauna from Unit J were iguanas (6 MNI, 6.4 percent of biomass), other small reptiles, 12 NISP of freshwater turtles (0 MNI, 0.6 percent of biomass), and sea turtles (1 MNI, 3.7 percent of biomass), but no hutia (O'Day 2002: 7). These represent a very small contribution to the diet. The relatively high frequency and diversity of birds is noteworthy. As mentioned, David Steadman identified 17 different taxa in Unit J. These probably reflect dietary practices, because the identified birds for the most part lack beautiful plumage. Yet bird bones are very rare in Lucayan sites, and the reasons for this unusual concentration are unclear.

Based her analysis, O'Day (2002) concludes that Unit J did not contain the types of animals that we would expect to find associated with a chief's residence. She notes that prestige foods such as hutia and iguana were not common in the deposit, but their relative rarity is in part a function of her sample size. O'Day seems to assume that caciques were eating only hutia and iguanas. As a result she undervalues the nonfish contributions to the diet. Reptiles, birds, and sea turtles contributed 15.5 percent of the total biomass, which is a very high percentage for Lucayan sites (Carlson 1999).

Furthermore, O'Day's conclusion is based on two critical assumptions. The first is that the comment by Oviedo y Valdés (1959) that prestige foods were "reserved" for caciques means that only caciques consumed these foods. Although such dietary restrictions may have been true for Hawaii (O'Day 2000), the ethnohistory of the Taínos suggests that the caciques used these foods in ceremonial feasts. In this regard, prestige was derived from the control and (re)distribution of such foods and not from their exclusive consumption. Second, she assumes that the meals consumed by the cacique were prepared at the cacique's house and that the remnants of these meals were deposited just outside the residence. Given a cacique's exalted status, we could argue that the meals were prepared elsewhere, that the leftovers were shared with other members of the community, and that the remnants were disposed of at a distance from the house to avoid the stench of rotting garbage. In sum, this is a far more complicated situation than it appears at first glance.

The comparison of faunal remains from MC-6 with those from Guacanagarí's village at En Bas Saline is illuminating, but complex. Using numbers for MNI alone, the fauna from MC-6 appears to be superior to the fauna for En Bas Saline. Only three mammals (one *Brotomys* and two *Isolobodon*, both small rodents), one iguana, one freshwater turtle, and one sea turtle were identified at En Bas Saline. Given differences in the sample sizes, biomass is a better category for comparison. In this regard, 23 percent of the biomass at En Bas Saline came from nonfish species, compared to 15.5 percent for Unit J and 11 percent for Wing's samples from MC-6. The differences do not seem very great, especially if we accept that the cacique at MC-6 was of lower status than Guacanagarí.

Comparisons are again complicated, because biomass was estimated differently in the three studies. For example, the most common species in the samples from MC-6 is the bonefish. These were given individual biomass values of 184 g (in Sullivan 1981: 187), 1,219 g (Wing 2001: 487), and 910 g (O'Day 2002: 6). It is hard to explain these differences, especially given the fact that Wing is using the same sample. The reporting of zooarchaeological data from the site is inconsistent, which creates more confusion than clarity.

To me, the relatively high frequency of nonfish species in MC-6 is consistent with what we would expect at the village of a cacique. The people who lived at MC-6 had a diet superior to the diet identified in Hispaniolan sites at the same time with regard to fishes and some nonfish species. For example, En Bas Saline has a much higher frequency of very small fishes. The exploitation of small fishes indicates that near-shore resources had already been depleted (Carlson and Keegan 2004). Such resource depletion would have encouraged the establishment of colonies like MC-6 to extract more abundant resources in a system of staple finance.

In addition to the faunal sample from Unit J, other evidence suggests that this area may not have been where the proposed cacique lived in the village. As mentioned earlier, Roth (2002) pointed out that the cacique's house was sometimes located along the road to control access into and out of the village (Rouse 1948). Thus the cacique's residence may actually have been along the north side of the village, where the road from Armstrong Pond is located, and in the area identified as structures III and VI (Sullivan 1981).

A comparison of the faunal assemblages recovered from structures I and II (on the south side of Plaza I) and structure III on the north side is illuminating. I have mentioned that the sample size from structure III is too small to draw credible conclusions, so my focus here is on structure I. Structure I is about 35 m to the southwest of the cacique's house and is connected to it by a raised earthwork. It is directly across the plaza from the road that leads to Armstrong Pond. If we conceive of the road as crossing the site, then its southern terminus is between structures I and II. Thus structures I and II would guard the southern entrance and form the portal to MC-6.

In this regard, Roth's (2002) suggestion that the cacique's house should be located on the road to control access to the village is reinforced. In fact it may have been more important to control access to the site from the south, where foreign visitors would arrive by canoe. This location would also fit Harris's (1994) suggestion that the south side of the site was superior to the north and Sullivan's (1981) conclusion that the quality of artifacts was superior along the southern midden ridge. Such superiority is also expressed by the structure being to the east of the proposed extension of the road across the site.

The faunal sample from structure I is four times the size of the analyzed sample from Unit J. In terms of MNI, Wing identified 4 mammals (including a hutia), 32 iguanas, 22 birds, and 4 sea turtles. Yet there is still another problem with the reporting of data. Sullivan includes a table for structure I in which he lists MNI. This turns out to be the table used by Wing and Scudder (1983) to report measurements of vertebral centra. The problem is that Sullivan lists 26 sea turtles and 1 Delphinidae in his table, but these are missing from the table reported in Wing and Scudder. At my request, Scudder looked at the data sheets from MC-6 and found evidence for only 4 sea turtles. To complicate matters, Wing and Scudder did not report the cetacean bone from the site, but Wing and Reitz (1982) did. Sullivan must have gotten a report that there were 26 sea turtles and 1 cetacean from Wing. It is unclear why these numbers do not agree with what was later reported.

These numbers look far more impressive with regard to prestigious foods, although these nonfish taxa account for only 11 percent of the total biomass. Furthermore, in addition to the dominant fish species (bonefish), the sample records a much higher incidence of the most favored fish species. At sites throughout the northern West Indies large and mostly carnivorous fishes were targeted first (Lutjanidae, Serranidae, Scaridae, and barracudas). The presence of these fishes in site samples tends to decline in frequency over time, so their relatively high frequency at MC-6 reflects access to a superior diet (Carlson and Keegan 2004). In sum, the residents of the site were able to exert significant control over the capture and distribution of favored fishes.

Turks and Caicos Islands: A Taíno Outpost?

The data assembled by Sullivan and myself illustrate a clear developmental sequence in the colonization of the Turks and Caicos Islands. This sequence was based on strong ties to Hispaniola and the export of materials from the southern Bahamas to the growing cacicazgos in Haiti.

Beginning in the eighth century AD, Ostionan peoples from Haiti established a seasonal base on Grand Turk where they exploited abundant, and previously unexploited, marine and terrestrial resources. This short-term occupation at the Coralie site fits the exploration phase proposed for island colonization (Berman and Gnivecki 1995; Irwin 1992).

In the eleventh and twelfth centuries Meillacan peoples from Hispaniola established seasonal camps on Grand Turk (Governor Beach site) and Middle Caicos (MC-8 and MC-10), where their efforts focused on the production of shell beads from the thorny jewelbox shell. This shell was of special significance because it retains its bright red color for centuries, unlike most shells, whose color rapidly fades. These beads and other resources would have been brought back to Haiti. In both cases, my specific identification of Haiti as the point of contact is based on Cordell's (1998) petrographic analysis of potsherds with noncarbonate tempers from sites in the Turks and Caicos and the north coast of Hispaniola.

During that period a permanent colony was also established on the north coast of Middle Caicos at MC-12. This community seems to have grown through time and had a circular arrangement of structures (as inferred from the surrounding midden) around an open plaza. In this regard it mirrors the community plan of contemporaneous settlements in the Greater Antilles. By the beginning of the fourteenth century, additional sites had been established on the north coast at MC-32 and MC-36, and MC-12 continued to be occupied. The pottery at MC-32 exhibits strong ties to Hispaniola, and it may have been a partner with MC-6 in extracting resources for export to Haiti. The advantages of MC-32 are that it provided access to a different set of marine resources, especially coral reef habitats, and was located on a pond that could have been used to corral fishes and extract salt. Finally, the site on Pelican Cay (MC-39), which is located in the bay on which both MC-12 and MC-32 are situated, provided a focus for ceremonial activities that were perhaps associated with seasonal aggregations of nesting birds. Other sites in the Turks and Caicos could be included in this sequence. They are peripheral to the main issues, however, and would add little to the sequence described here.

It is not clear when MC-6 was first established. The exclusive presence of Chican decorated imports suggests that it was no earlier than AD 1300, when this style of decoration displaced previous styles along most of the north coast of Hispaniola. Sullivan's radiocarbon date for the site has a mean of AD 1430, and the discovery of a brass *caracol* indicates that the site was occupied until after the arrival of the Spanish. The site deposits are very shallow (circa 25 cm), which suggests that the site was not occupied for a long time.

Such shallow deposits could indicate that this was a seasonal settlement that was occupied during the period when salt was available on Armstrong Pond. In this regard, Gary Vescelius has suggested that similar ceremonial centers on Puerto Rico were not residential communities but rather the sites of ritual combat as expressed through the ball game (*batey*). This suggestion is still being scrutinized, however, and may not be correct. It is evident that the site was occupied year-round: two birds identified in Unit J (the cacique's house) are winter visitors to the island. These are the lesser scaup (*Aythya affinis*) and the ring-billed gull (*Larus delawarensis*), which typically arrive in the Bahamas in mid-December and depart in late March or early April, with extreme dates of November 6 to April 17 (Brudenell-Bruce 1975). Thus the presence of winter birds in the site would be indicative of year-round occupation.

The layout of MC-6 is unique. It is unlike any other site in the rest of the Bahama archipelago and is more typical of chiefly villages in the Greater Antilles. An earthwork constructed of rocks and soil that were moved there from surrounding areas defines the circumference of the site. The court at the center of the plaza was built using soils collected from the salina on the south side of the site. A double row of undressed limestone rocks was aligned on the margins of the court to record specific astrological and cosmological events. The most notable of these alignments are with the summer solstice and the rising and setting of the constellation Orion. In sum, the community plan was based on well-established notions of cosmology.

Around the earthwork is a series of eight structures. These roughly circular, semi-pit features are lined with undressed limestone blocks to form a foundation. They measure about 5 m in diameter. Although I was initially reluctant to accept Sullivan's conclusion that these were houses, I now agree with him. There is too little room between the earthwork and court to erect larger structures of perishable materials. Although the construction of semi-pit houses with stone foundations has not been found elsewhere in the islands, these may reflect the special needs of a community that was assembling perishable foods in a tropical climate for later export. Such "fish cellars" would be the equivalent of the modern wine cellar. Finally, Curet (1992b) has suggested that the size of houses decreased through time as production shifted from extended to nuclear family domestic units. The houses at MC-6 are similar in size to the ones he described for the El Bronce site in Puerto Rico. Thus the nature of activities involving the social relations (organization) of production may have limited the need for larger structures.

If this was the village of a cacique, some question as to the location of the cacique's house remains. Structure VIII is certainly a candidate, given its location at the eastern margin of the site and the two-chambered plan that Sullivan identified. At present we have insufficient evidence to distinguish this structure from the others that surround the central plaza. One conclusion is clear. Structure VIII is not at the juncture of two plazas. There is too little evidence to support the conclusion that Plaza II was a residential area, which also means that it may not have been a commoner barrio. A second candidate for the cacique's house is structure I, which is located at the southern entrance to the site and contains the bones of the most-prized vertebrate species.

The material remains from the site are not particularly spectacular: stone and shell beads, inlay for statues, carved shell, a brass *caracol*, and imported vessels with large adornos. Yet the vast majority of the pottery (94 percent) is undecorated and locally made Palmetto ware. Although we might expect to find more imported vessels in the village of a cacique, this need not be the case. Some Chican vessels are elaborately decorated; but, unlike other societies (Helms 2000), the Taínos did not use pottery vessels as a primary medium for expressing supernatural relations (Roe 1995b, 1997). If pottery was primarily functional, then the use of locally made vessels makes perfect sense. In fact, the first transition in the material culture of the Spanish colonists was the shift to locally made pottery (Cusick 1989, 1991). Pottery is too fragile to rely on foreign sources to meet daily requirements.

The faunal remains are difficult to interpret, given the ways in which they have been reported. Nevertheless, the site contains a high frequency on non-fish taxa that is comparable to the frequency identified for En Bas Saline. Although mammals are underrepresented (a common feature of Lucayan sites), there are substantial quantities of iguanas, birds, sea turtles, and even a sea mammal. In addition, the fishes represented at MC-6 can be considered superior to those at En Bas Saline in terms of size and preference. In addition, so few small fish are found in the site that the collection of faunal samples using ¼-inch mesh screens provided a nearly complete inventory of the sizes and taxa that were consumed.

MC-6 is cosmologically charged. It was of relatively short duration due to the arrival of the Spanish in 1492. It reflects a high degree of integration with the cacicazgos of Hispaniola. It was a gateway community through which resources from the southern Bahama archipelago were shipped to Hispaniola. The people of MC-6 were entrepreneurs who enhanced their status by supplying the Taínos of Hispaniola with foods and other goods, some of which were no longer readily available in their territories. Yet all of the material culture points to its identification as a Lucayan settlement. Las Casas clearly identified Caonabó as a Lucayan, and this site offers the best candidate for his homeland. It is exactly this situation from which a stranger king might be expected to emerge.

Under the Rainbow

In the industrialized world nature is an adversary against whom we do battle. We shade ourselves from the sun, block the rain with umbrellas, and climate-control our houses, cars, and workplaces. This view of nature is markedly different from the view in traditional societies. For them the human experience is not only enmeshed in the (super)natural world but is reproduced and made comprehensible by it.[1] For us mythology means legends, fables, and parables; the "just so" stories of Rudyard Kipling or the fantasies of Lewis Carroll and Roald Dahl. Although we plead innocent to unfounded beliefs, we buy more checkout counter tabloids than we do "newspapers." For the Taínos, the supernatural world was officially a part of their daily existence.

Take sunrise, one of two crepuscular skirmishes between day and night. With dawn the sun has won the battle and the daily cycle of activity begins. But this is only one of many cycles and many conflicts. The circle of culture radiating from the village's central plaza extends less and less influence into the surrounding forest or sea, until it disappears like the ripples on a pond. Men and women, parents and children, lineage and lineage, village and village are all locked in a friend:foe or close:remote interaction as the cycle of seasons traces the orbit of the earth through the cosmos. Individuals are born, mature, and die. The world is continuously changing, yet culture acts to moderate the changes and to maintain continuity (Amodio 1999). How do we explain what we cannot comprehend? How do we build consensus from competition? These are the lessons that are found in myths.

Taíno mythology is accessible because the Jeronymite friar Ramón Pané was sent by Columbus to study and record the beliefs of the Macorix. E. Gaylord Bourne (1906) may have been correct when he called Pané a "simpleton" who only recorded what he was told and was incapable of making (reproducing) any grand theological schema out of what he heard. Bourne's conclusion is partly supported by the phantasmagoric stories that Pané recounted. Still, there is a nagging sense of Catholicism in the 12 *cemíes* that Pané reported, although the emphasis on twins does not easily fit Catholic dogma. The issue at hand is how to relate Taíno myth to Taíno practice as filtered through the writings of Spanish chroniclers and present-day archaeologists.

More general frames of reference can also be brought to bear (for example, Roe 1982). As Mary Helms (2000: 9) expressed this situation, "individual mythologies and cosmologies of diverse tribal peoples of tropical America reflect aspects of a generalized, logically consistent, and ultimately very abstract cosmology common in its broadest concepts to an extensive region of native America." In this regard, the physical manifestations of Taíno worldviews can be informed by more detailed studies from other parts of tropical America. We must always be mindful, however, that these generalized cosmological understandings do not conform exactly to particular people living at specific times.

Rainbows as Landscapes

The Taíno symbol for the cacique was the rainbow. As an aside, rainbows are very common in the Turks and Caicos despite the lack of rainfall. The rainbow represented the bridge between the heavens and the earth, and the cacique was the only individual who could cross that bridge. It appears that at one time the shaman or *behique* also was able to cross over to the supernatural realm, but by the time of European contact the caciques had appropriated the sacerdotal status of the *behiques* and left them as mere healers or medicine men (Roe 1997). Moreover, it was the double rainbow, the virtually complete circle, that symbolized the cacique (Stevens-Arroyo 1988: 191). This is the mirror image of the double rainbow reflected in a calm sea. The reflected double rainbow joined sky to earth and water to earth to create a complete cosmos. As a symbol for the cacique, these twin, but opposite, forms represented the fullness of authority.

Yet rainbows are ephemeral in the same way that the cacique's hallucinogenic communication with the spirits through the use of *cohoba* was short-lived. It is worth investigating how the Taínos produced more permanent representations of cacical authority and the double rainbow on physical objects. One artifact that has been identified as representing the double rainbow is a "belt buckle" made from a human cranium (Figure 7.1). (The Taínos also made flutes from human leg bones.) The center of the object has a depression representing the navel of the universe, the cave from which the Taínos emerged, and is surrounded by the incised representation of a double rainbow and its mirror image (Stevens-Arroyo 1988: 192). Around the outside of this circular object are nine perforations. The Taínos were certainly capable of placing these holes so that they reflected a mirror image, yet the holes form a pattern that is not a simple reflection of top and bottom. If we assume that the pattern of holes was made on purpose, then we need to investigate what they represent. Moreover, because they are placed beyond the bounds of the double rainbow,

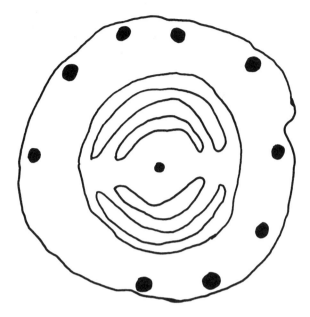

7.1. Ornament made from a human cranium representing the double rainbow.

it is possible that they represent an aspect of the cosmos that we might identify as a constellation.

When we compare the layout of MC-6 to this ornament, we see a remarkable conformity in the arrangement of lines and semi-pit structures (Figure 7.2). Although MC-6 is somewhat flattened relative to the "belt buckle," it nonetheless represents a series of structures around a central court that has a keystone (navel) and a double row of stone alignments that define the interior court. Is it a coincidence that the object interpreted as representing cacical authority and the complete universe and is associated with *guanín* is virtually a perfect map of MC-6? Is it also a coincidence that I have proposed that Caonabó, whose name means golden house or golden most, was associated with this site? I think not.

Let us do some accounting. First, the ornament was made from a human cranium and thus symbolizes a direct link to the ancestors. Second, the perforations are not symmetrical, which suggests that the person who made the artifact had a particular arrangement in mind. Third, it has too many holes to serve a strictly functional purpose. If the object was worn on a belt or headband, then it would need at most two holes on either end for attachment. Thus the holes are not strictly functional. The ornament is telling us something about Taíno beliefs.

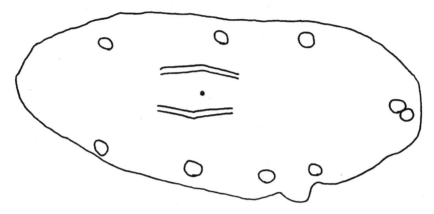

7.2. Schematic plan of MC-6.

The site has similar issues. First, the structures around the central court of Plaza I have been identified as marking particular star alignments. Second, the arrangement of these structures is asymmetrical, which suggests that some other spatial concept was represented. Third, the alignment of stones marking the edges of the court did not have to be executed in a double row. A single row of stones would certainly have served the purpose of aligning the site with the summer solstice. Furthermore, the stone alignments bow at the center. MC-6 clearly represented more than a simple outpost or gateway community in the southern Bahamas. I propose that it was constructed to represent Taíno cosmology, the image of *guanín*, the double rainbow, and the power of a paramount cacique. As is typical of Hispaniolan courts, the primary alignment conforms to the seasonal passage of the sun, with the baseline established by the summer solstice (Rodríguez Álvarez 2003).

The court has other alignments as well. The principal star (Betelgeuse or Alpha Orionis) that Sullivan (1981) identified for the court's alignments is found in the constellation Orion. The stars of Orion are exceptional even in a night sky diminished by modern light pollution.[2] Orion is located on the celestial equator and has three of the 25 brightest stars in the night sky (Betelgeuse, Bellatrix, and Rigel). Because the belt of Orion is aligned with the equator at the center of the tropical sky, it has served as an important constellation in many native South American cosmologies (Robiou-Lamarche 2002; Stevens-Arroyo 1988: 181–184).

Moreover, Orion follows a cycle that coincides with tropical seasons. It arrives, being chased by the sun, in early July; reaches its zenith in mid-December; and begins to depart, this time chasing the sun, around the ides of March. In this way Orion marks with surprising accuracy the summer solstice, win-

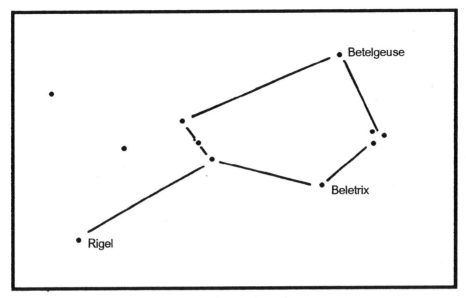

7.3. Map of the constellation Orion as the one-legged man.

ter solstice, and vernal equinox. Orion provides an obvious means for telling time. It marks the main rainy season and is associated with fertility and fishing (Robiou-Lamarche 2002). In addition, early July is the beginning of the summer dry season on Middle Caicos, when solar distilled salt first becomes available at Armstrong Pond.

Aside from the proposed astronomical alignments marking the rising position of Orion, it is worth asking whether the constellation had additional meaning for the people who built MC-6. If we take the modern constellation and turn it so the "head" is to the east (the cardinal direction that the Taínos perceived as up), the arrangement of stars is remarkably similar to the layout of structures at MC-6 and to the double-rainbow belt buckle (Figure 7.3). In fact, it provides a better match with the flattened (elongate) arrangement of structures at the site. This concordance extends to the identification of a slightly off-center stone at the site and to the representation of the plaza with more structures on the south side. The asymmetry of structures around the plaza fits the representation of Orion in native cosmologies as the one-legged man (Robiou-Lamarche 2002; Rodríguez Álvarez 2003). More than just marking the summer solstice and the rising position of Orion, it would appear that Plaza I is a map of Orion.

If we next turn to the mythical identity of Orion we find that this constellation was associated with Anacacuya (Stevens-Arroyo 1988). According to the myth recorded by Ramón Pané, Guahayona took all of the women, including those of his cacique Anacacuya, who was his brother-in-law. Guahayona then drowned Anacacuya by tricking him into looking at a beautiful *cobo* (seashell) in the water. Guahayona took the women to the mythical island of Matininó and went himself to the mythical island called Guanín.

This part of the myth reifies a form of social organization based on matrilineal descent and matrilocal/avunculocal residence. In a society practicing patrilocal residence a man is surrounded by his brothers, but in a matrilocal society he is living with his wife and her unmarried brothers (his brothers-in-law). Moreover, the cacique is different. By virtue of avunculocal residence he can live with his clansmen in the village of his sister, into which her husband would move and again live with his brothers-in-law. The myth serves to define the rules of marriage (Stevens-Arroyo 1988: 177). In addition, male leaders in avunculocal societies control the marital arrangements for their daughters and nieces. Thus Guahayona's mythical capture of all women mirrors the cacique's control over the marriage arrangements for all of the women in his clan.

Furthermore, the myth emphasizes the importance of mythical islands to the east, where Guanín is the central focus. We return again to *guanín* as the justification for cacical authority. For Guahayona not only stole the women but also took his cacique's emblem of power. Anacacuya is cast into the sea, and it is through the sea that he enters the sky as Orion. The calm sea is the mirror image of the sky, the source of a double rainbow that is reflected by the sea. The story would make no sense if Anacacuya had been cast into the sky; the only human recourse for entering the sky is through the water.

It is possible to reduce the myth to a simple structuralist dichotomy of close:remote. Yet the myth includes far more chaos and complexity. "Here the Taínos have used cosmology, sociology, geography, and alimentary discretion" to justify agency and practice (Stevens-Arroyo 1988: 186). So Anacacuya entered the sky by being cast into the sea. He was the first cacique and controlled the destiny of women until he was overthrown by his brother-in-law, Guahayona. Alliances are tenuous,[3] and every leader must marshal sufficient support to retain a position at the top of the political hierarchy. Unless the cacique's followers are strong and supportive, the lineage might lose its position of authority. This is a call to action. Our ability to accumulate wealth for the purpose of ceremonial feasting must exceed that of our allies, or else we will lose control of our women. The control of women is of great significance in matrilineal groups, because women are centralized while men are dispersed.

In contrast, Sebastián Robiou-Lamarche (2002) proposed that Anacacuya was associated with Ursa Major (the Big Dipper) and that Orion is a rep-

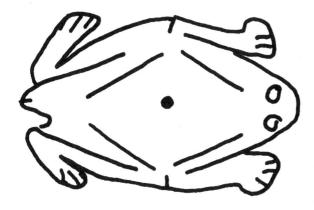

7.4. The Taíno frog motif.

resentation of Yayael. This association provides a second perspective on the physical layout of MC-6. In the origin myth, Deminán and his brothers were instrumental in taking culture from the principal deity, Yaya. In doing so they captured the fishes that were the transformed bones of Yayael. By the process of transference, MC-6 represents Yayael in his cosmological guise, as Orion. The capture of fishes in the waters surrounding MC-6 (and their export to the cacicazgos of Hispaniola) takes on a mythical status. This is not simply the transfer of foodstuffs from one island to another; it is the reproduction of myth in which humans, represented by Deminán (Caonabó), capture the food of the gods for their people.

To this point I have tried to show how one physical representation of the double rainbow, the community plan of MC-6, and the Orion constellation all share features that would make them indistinguishable. In other words, the structure of Taíno society was reinforced at the level of cosmology, mythology, village organization, and personal artifacts. Yet the layering of meanings went even further. As Stevens-Arroyo (1988: 162) also concludes with regard to the myth of Guahayona and Anacacuya: "The logic of the natural and mythological categories of rainfall and the mythic islands is held together by the symbol of the frog, whose characteristics had both seasonal and sexual meaning for the Taínos."

If we take a Taíno amulet that represents the frog and turn it so the head is facing east (the principal direction), then the same pattern emerges. The frog is the double rainbow, the double row of stones outlining the court at MC-6. Frogs are associated with rainfall and fertility. They represent seduction, which led Guahayona to steal the women from his cacique, and they denote periodicity with regard to the seasons (wet:dry) and women (fertile:infertile). Orion and the frog are complements. Orion is constricted at the middle, while the frog bows outward (Figure 7.4). These symbols of male and female fertility represent a complete cosmos in the layout of MC-6. In addition, the possible petroglyph near structure II appears to be a frog that is facing the setting position of Betelgeuse in Orion. This conjoining of male and female symbols mirrors the use of stone collars and three-pointed stones in Taíno ceremonialism (Walker 1997).

MC-6

MC-6 is supercharged. It contains multiple layers of reference to mythology and cosmology and reifies the most basic structures of Taíno social organization. Why then is it located in an obscure place on the periphery of the Taíno political sphere of influence? Was it a cathedral established to civilize the Lucayans?[4] These questions get to the heart of the matter: Does myth determine practice, or is practice justified by myth?

Given the careful layout and specific attention to detail in the construction of MC-6, it is clear that this was much more than a simple village or even gateway community. It would have been possible to extract resources from the southern Bahamas without such reference to cosmology. The people who made and used MC-6 as a base for extracting salt and other resources certainly did not need the physical representation of a calendar in order to determine when such activities should be conducted. Yet, as Sullivan (1981) recognized, the site was laid out with a specific plan in mind, and the central court was constructed with soils brought to the site from the adjacent salina.

One question that immediately comes to mind is whether or not anyone actually lived at the site. Other ceremonial centers, such as Caguana in Puerto Rico, contain little evidence for permanent residence (Oliver 1998). Yet Caguana was the site of multiple ball courts, while plaza sites in Hispaniola typically are associated with the villages of caciques. Permanent residence is a difficult question to address, because MC-6 is unique. The structures at the site are very different from those observed at other Taíno sites. We could argue that they were not used as houses, and Roth (2002) has suggested that residences more likely were erected between the midden ridge and court. In my opinion, however, there is not enough space to build a house in this zone.

If the availability of salt on Armstrong Pond was the main factor in establishing this site, then it is possible that MC-6 was only occupied on a seasonal basis. Yet many potsherds and lots of animal bones are distributed across the site. Among these are the bones of birds that are seasonal residents of the island. For example, the lesser scaup and ring-billed gull are resident between November 6 and April 17, and the sandpiper (*Tringa flavipes*) is not resident in the winter months (Brudenell-Bruce 1975: 36; David Steadman, personal communication, 2004). The bird remains are one indicator that the site was used throughout the year.

The pottery at the site reflects a full range of domestic activities. Unlike the Governor Beach site on Grand Turk (where fish bones and the virtually absence of pottery represent a restricted range of activities associated with the seasonal procurement of shells for beads), the animal remains and potsherds from large vessels and griddles at MC-6 attest to the preparation of complete meals, including pepper pots and cassava bread. This evidence suggests not only males but also females were living in the area. Moreover, Roth (2002) interprets the soil chemistry as indicating the presence of agricultural fields to the north and east of the site. Such fields require an annual commitment in terms of clearing, burning, weeding, and harvesting.

If we start with culture and work toward practical reason, then the site is first and foremost a representation of the cosmos. The structures are enigmatic and seem smaller than we would expect for permanent residences. Yet their uniqueness may have been dictated by the need to store goods in a cool place prior to export. Even though they were designed to serve as storage facilities in addition to their use as houses, they were aligned specifically to map the cosmos. Furthermore, the unique design of the "cacique's house," with its two chambers, does not necessarily mean that it was the residence of a chief. Its two-chambered construction may actually have been dictated by the need to represent the eyes of the frog and stars in Orion rather than being a living chamber and antechamber for the storage of idols (although the antechamber could also have served this purpose). Roth's (2002) suggestion that the cacique's house would have been located closer to the road has been considered with regard to the superior subsistence remains and high-status goods recovered from structure I and from along the south side of the site (see also Harris 1994). The south side is also where canoes would first arrive at the end of their voyage from Hispaniola.

Material evidence for the presence of a cacique is equivocal. Aside from the community plan, most of the material remains are mundane. The vast majority of the pottery is Palmetto ware, which identifies this as a Lucayan site. There is no evidence for a high incidence of imported materials, and the focus would seem to be more external than internal. This situation may speak to the practical reason for the site. One aspect that distinguishes it from the villages of caciques in Hispaniola is that the people at MC-6 enjoyed a superior diet. There are far more iguanas, birds, and sea turtles (high-ranked foods) at MC-6 than have been identified at En Bas Saline, for example (see Wing 2001).

It is also worth considering alliances among the villages on Middle Caicos. Unfortunately, too much of MC-12 was lost before its relation to MC-6 could be evaluated. Yet Sullivan's (1981) vegetation map suggests that it had an oval settlement plan with middens surrounding a central plaza. This community plan is more typical of Hispaniolan settlements than it is of Lucayan settlements. In contrast, MC-32 has a community plan that is dominated by a large central midden. Such middens are associated with the villages of caciques, who occupied the middle of the plaza. Although MC-32 is much smaller than most villages in Hispaniola, it has a very high frequency of locally made Palmetto ware with incised Meillacan and Chican motifs. Decorated Palmetto ware is very unusual in Lucayan sites. Thus it is likely that MC-32 had strong ties with relatives living in Hispaniola and may have been one of the principal allies contributing labor to the work at MC-6.

Caonabó

Just as MC-6 was imbued with cosmological significance, Caonabó was imbued with mythical significance. The two would seem to go hand in hand, especially given Las Casas's conviction that Caonabó was from the Lucayan Islands. Only one of the archaeological sites throughout the Bahama archipelago that have been described has the characteristics that would fit the ethnohistoric record. In sum, MC-6 is the only site that has all the characteristics expected for the homeland of a great chief.

Taíno social organization makes it possible that Caonabó's mother was married to the Lucayan cacique who ruled MC-6. In fact, her husband may have been sent from Hispaniola to control trade with the southern Bahamas. Following avunculocal rules of residence, Caonabó would have grown up on the frontier and later returned to the village of his mother's brother in Hispaniola. Given his hard-scrabble early years in the Lucayan Islands, it is not surprising that Caonabó exhibited the political entrepreneurship required to succeed his uncle and become the cacique of Maguana. His experience on the periphery would have given him skills that exceeded those of his cousins from Hispaniola who also sought to succeed their uncle.

It is also possible that the story of the stranger king is just that, a story. In this regard, we can look to Hawaii and Fiji, where the stranger king had arrived generations earlier, and his descendants were now the "king" (Sahlins 1985). Yet Las Casas specifically and adamantly identified Caonabó as a Lucayan. Moreover, if all caciques were stranger kings, then why were the other principal caciques of the island not identified as coming from other lands? And why were the Lucayan Islands identified as Caonabó's homeland and not Cuba, Jamaica, Puerto Rico, or other neighboring islands? If we accept MC-6 as the only village worthy of a stranger king, then its short period of occupation further supports the conclusion that Caonabó came from Middle Caicos. Caonabó was an "old" man by the time the Spanish arrived; if MC-6 was only occupied for several human generations, he either came from the site or was only a generation removed. I would favor the former.

In sum, everything points to Caonabó as being a Lucayan, a stranger king, and to Middle Caicos and MC-6 as his homeland. This exercise in tracing one individual through the maze of circulating reference seems to confirm the writings of the Spanish chroniclers. Moreover, whether or not Caonabó grew up on Middle Caicos, his story tells us of the meanings attributed to a stranger king in the Taíno culture.

Cultural Archaeology

It may seem that I have neglected the task that I set for myself in the first chapter. What can be learned from an archaeological perspective that focuses on the notion of culture, and how does this relate to the story of Caonabó and the archaeology of the Bahamas? What I am suggesting is that we look for points of articulation and disarticulation. Every tale, every myth, every legend makes sense, even if—especially if—they make sense in counterintuitive ways (see Lévi-Strauss 1963). The task is to accumulate weights of evidence in which different data sets support the same premise and also to look for data sets that contradict conventional wisdom. In sum, I have tried to give equal footing to all of the categories mentioned in Tylor's definition of culture (chapter 1).

I recognize that most of my presentation of the archaeological materials is the same discussion that has been presented for decades. In my opinion this is normal. In other words, the data have not really changed; it is the meanings we ascribe to the data that has changed. Every society sloughs off a residue that is unique to its time and place. As archaeologists we attempt to use what is available, and to interpolate the missing data, in order to develop a portrait of life in the past. Although this life was lived by self-interested agents, the remnants of their actions typically are aggregated in sediments that encompass hundreds of years and dozens of human generations.

When we are lucky we encounter an individual like Caonabó, who offers the hope of tracing the actions of a single individual. Even the story of Caonabó is not straightforward, however. The Taínos clearly imbued him with mythical characteristics, and the Spanish added another mythical dimension in the portrait of him that they created. Even when individuals and their actions seem normal and appropriate, we need to deconstruct these stories to identify the ascribed contributions to oral and written histories.

Anthony Giddens (1976) proposed a theory of structuration to describe the behavior of individuals in a society. I would argue that what often passes as structuration is actually *ascribed* agency based on oral and written histories of the events. In other words, the actions of one individual, one agent, are not significant in human history. What is important is the meaning(s) ascribed to that agent. I suggest that we adopt a theory of ascription (a theory of meaning) to replace the theory of structuration. Individuals do not create structure; structure is a consensual framework based on shared notions of cultural meaning.

Furthermore, there is no reason to slide down the slippery slope of a hermeneutic spiral. Although human existence may be described by language, language does not structure our daily lives. We live by actions, not by words. Our visual senses are far more important than our tactile or aural senses. We use language to communicate and to describe our actions, senses, and feelings to others. In this regard language is only necessary as a means for conveying information to extended social groups. Moreover, based on the evidence for repeated failures to communicate a message, I would contend that language is a lousy way to express meaning. In the present case, the Taínos used space extensively to express meaning. There are multiple ways of expressing beliefs, and language may in fact be the worst. In this regard I side with the physicists: harmonics, the songs of the universe, convey more than mere words can.

We also need not fear descending into relativism. Although we can be open minded and allow every culture to adopt its own set of meanings, we can also recognize that particular realities are more efficient for describing anticipated outcomes. When I put a kettle of water on an electric burner, I expect the water to boil eventually (I could also use a gas burner or other heat source). And when I put this water in a tray and set it in a box cooled to below $0°$ C, I can reasonably expect that the water will turn into a solid ice cube. In sum, behaviors that we reenact every day produce expected consequences, and in most cases we do not even worry about the outcome (compare Shanks and Tilley 1987).

Yet in a chaotic world anything can happen, even if the probability is extremely low.[5] We live our lives with shorthand, seat-of-the-pants, back-of-the-envelop, rule-of-thumb expectations about what reactions will be elicited by our actions. All people do so, and those who preceded us have done so as well. We do not need to apologize to the philosophers for our expectations. The world is structured by our experiences and the meanings that we attribute to it.

So here we are, trapped in written American English. I know what I mean, but do you? To complicate matters further I have attempted to resurrect the concept of "culture," a word first defined by Sir Edward Burnett Tylor that has since been expanded to more than 200 definitions (Kroeber and Kluckhohn 1952). I do not seek obscurantism, *mais je peut écrire en français parce que je voudrais faire le point que le langue est crucial pour compréhension.* But what good would this do?

One final spin on the Tilt-a-Whirl: life is chaotic, multidimensional, code-termined, correlated, infused with meaning, structured by structure, driven by needs, directed by goals, responsive to causes and effects, elevated by supernatural aspirations . . . We are not simply self-interested agents who navigate and negotiate the structures imposed by our society; nor are we simply selfish genes striving to survive for one more generation through the slavish devotion to caloric need and sexual reproduction (our most basic animal instincts). Both culture and practical reason exist. To deny one is to deny the other.

The Stranger Archaeologist

I first went to Middle Caicos as a bachelor of arts student in anthropology from the University of Connecticut. I was totally wet behind the ears. I returned to Middle Caicos with a master's degree from Florida Atlantic University, where I studied under Shaun Sullivan's mentor, Bill Sears. I returned again with a Ph.D. from UCLA and then again as a museum curator from the Florida Museum of Natural History. My attitude has been that I need to keep doing it until I can do it right!

What do I call us: scientists, scholars, researchers, investigators? We go to places with a personal history; we try to adapt to a local history; and we try to write a (pre)history. I returned to a community that 20 years later still awaited the return of Shaun. In some ways this bruises my ego, because I am not convinced that 20 years from now people on Middle Caicos will await the return of Bill. Mine was a different time, a different context. We swept into town for a month or so, took over the place, and then disappeared, and we have repeated this cycle at intervals for the past 15 years. Yet life is lived through daily choices based on the opportunities that present themselves. Chaos has a funny way of defining reality. In many ways my life has been enriched by the people I lived and worked with on Middle Caicos. I am forever grateful to the many people who made this personal experience possible. They have strongly influenced how I interpret the world.

Notes

Chapter 2. The Legend of Caonabó

1. Even these seemingly straightforward names are inaccurate. Two of Columbus's ships actually were named *Santa Clara* and *La Gallega*. Columbus was aboard *La Gallega*, the largest of the three vessels. Originally named for Galicia, the town in which it was built, the ship was known to its sailors as "Marigalante" (literally, "dirty Mary"). As a devout Catholic Columbus could not sail on a ship by that nickname, so he rechristened it *Santa María*. The others were also given nicknames. The *Santa Clara* was known as *Niña* ("little girl") a play on the name of its owner, Juan Niño. Although we do not know the original name of the *Pinta* (again a play on the owner's name, Pinzón), the nickname glosses as "painted one." The names that we use today are all allusions to prostitutes, which fits well with our stereotype of sailors. With regard to *bohio*, Carl Sauer (1966: 73) suggests that the Taínos actually said *cibao* (meaning "stony mountain") and that Columbus confused these words. Cibao is the region in the Dominican Republic where gold deposits were found.

2. Sauer (1966) has questioned whether Guacanagarí and Caonabó were truly powerful chiefs or whether their status was due to their interactions with the Spanish. The high status attributed to Guacanagarí does seem to reflect his alliance with Columbus. Nothing in Columbus's descriptions of the many caciques who tried to entice him to their village would distinguish Guacanagarí from the others. Caonabó, however, is a different story.

3. Morison (1942) criticized Columbus for selecting the site of La Isabela. Yet the criticism is based solely on an evaluation of the physical geography, without regard for political and human factors. It is likely that Columbus's colony would have been overrun by the Taínos or Macorix if he had selected a settlement location in which a particular cacique held sway. In other words, Columbus was successful because he selected a less than optimal physical location, but one that was not controlled by a particular Taíno cacicazgo.

4. Sahlins (1985: 136–140) notes that King Kaneoneo of Hawaii also began by ignoring the European intruders. It was only because the common people were circumventing their rulers and trading directly with the Europeans that the Hawaiian rulers finally stepped in and became the intermediaries in all trade with the Europeans.

5. It is worth recognizing that the Spanish had developed a hierarchical category of punishments based on the nature of an offense. In some cases ears, noses, or hands would be cut off; in others the prisoner would be decapitated, burned to death, or hanged. The formality of feudal punishments was brought to the Americas.

6. It was suggested as early as 1520 that the name "Cannibal" derived from *canis*, the Latin word for dog.

7. Although the verbs "eat" and "consume" are synonyms, they can have very different connotations. The Taíno association of Caribes with the world of the dead can be interpreted as meaning that they consumed the spirit of the dead and thereby took the person away from the land of the living. It need not mean that they ate human flesh.

8. Shipworms are not really worms at all; they are mollusks (*Teredo* spp.). Shipworms bore into wood, creating holes and leaks and weakening the ship's structure. They are most active in warm tropical waters and were a major problem for European ships sailing for extended lengths of time in the Caribbean Sea.

Chapter 3. Caonabó's Homeland

1. The terminology used in this classification scheme can get very confusing. The names were chosen based on the time when the characteristic modes were first described, so the named site is not a "type site." Thus the site assemblage need not reflect the earliest or even the most representative expression of the style, subseries, or series. For example, the Meillac site in Haiti, which gave its name to the style and subseries (Meillacan), is not representative of either and in fact contains only a small Meillac component beneath a much larger assemblage of Chican Ostionoid pottery.

2. In a draft of his compelling paper "Storytelling in Prehistory," John Terrell (1990) devoted an extended and highly critical section to Rouse's (1986) account of the peopling of the Pacific. John sent the draft to me for comment, and I advised him to delete all reference to Rouse, which he did. I made my recommendation based on the fact that Rouse's opinions on the region were peripheral to Oceanic archaeology; they were the comments of an outside observer. I was concerned that if John focused on someone perceived as an outsider, then the validity of his argument would be weakened. In other words, "insiders" might claim that Rouse's views did not reflect the conventional view for the region. After all, only Rouse has classified early Polynesian pottery as "Lapitaoid." Yet Terrell's insightful view of storytelling as it relates to Pacific Island archaeology is equally relevant to West Indian archaeology. The careful reader will see the parallels. I apologize to John for mentioning an early draft of his published work but am confident he will forgive me.

3. Froelich Rainey and Juan José Ortíz Aguilú (1983) did excavate the large Taíno site of Bois Neuf, but all that has been presented is a preliminary report that remains unpublished.

4. Curet and Oliver (1998) have reported that Taíno houses on Puerto Rico were much smaller and were the residences of nuclear families.

5. At the risk of weakening my argument, it is worth noting the similarity of the names "Mayaguana" and "Maguana."

Chapter 4. Kinship and Kingship

1. The whole notion of nature versus nurture seems bizarre to me, having raised three children to puberty. The kids all had a unique and well-developed personality

before my wife and I had much influence on them. Hence DNA would seem to be the key to behavior. Yet recent experiments with cloning (actually it was already known from studies of twins) showed that even an exact replica of DNA will not produce identical individuals. Thus nurture would seem to hold the answer. Individuals are chaotic; although there is an underlying structure of genes woven in a double helix, there are so many dimensions that all individuals are unique no matter how many genes they share.

2. I use the term "surfeit" to recognize that an autonomous household must overproduce in order to ensure subsistence security. In any given year some natural or cultural disaster could severely challenge the household's ability to survive the subsistence cycle. What I call a surfeit is sometimes erroneously called a surplus. In economic terms, a surplus is the conversion of excess production to a useful end. In other words, in good years produce that cannot be stored for the future is a surfeit that may rot in the fields; yet that same produce when mobilized by a leader could be employed as a surplus to free some individuals from their reliance on the household production of staples.

3. A compelling example of proper behavior comes from the ways in which the Spanish punished and executed the Taínos. A European sense of hierarchy was evident in the punishment of crimes, with removal of extremities (ears, noses, hands), followed by burning, and finally hanging. Anacaona was hanged, as was appropriate for someone of her exalted position.

4. Hernández Aquino's dictionary includes words from outside the Taíno area. Thus we must pay careful attention to the source of a word before accepting it as being of Taíno origin.

5. This conclusion is based on the absence of large villages in the vicinity of these sites. It must be recognized, however, that additional research is necessary to determine whether or not settlements were located in these areas, and further refinements of prehistoric political boundaries are needed.

Chapter 7. Under the Rainbow

1. I am tempted to go off on a tangent in which the cultural world is recognized as creating the natural world, which in turn reifies the cultural world, which also structures and is structured by the supernatural world. Suffice it to say that humans live in a chaotic world inhabited by us, them, other(s), ancestors, gods, spirits, nature, and so forth. All of these are melded to create a worldview, a cosmology, a legitimated, negotiated, and logical world in which we operate as self-interested agents.

2. In Greek mythology Orion was the hunter, the son of Poseidon, who was king of the sea.

3. I do not want to disrupt the narrative do but want to make certain my language is clear. The relationship between brothers-in-law is one of alliance based on marriage. For example, Caonabó and Behecchio were brothers-in-law.

4. I do not mean to overemphasize the religious connotation of "cathedral." A second definition is a place where people come to pay the gods through the representatives of those gods (for example, the bell of *turey* at La Isabela).

5. I remember hearing years ago of a study attributed to a major university that listed the probabilities for pregnancy based on various forms of birth control. One possibility that it listed was "immaculate conception," even though the probability of getting pregnant in this way is extremely low.

Glossary of Taíno Words

Abawana Taíno name for Grand Turk Island.

Anacacuya The cacique from whom women were taken. He was tricked into looking at a seashell and was drowned. Through his drowning he entered the sky and is associated with the constellation Orion.

Anacaona The sister of Behecchio and the wife of Caonabó. She became the ruler of Xaragua following the death of her brother.

Aniyana Taíno name for Middle Caicos Island.

Behecchio One of the most powerful caciques on Hispaniola when the Spanish arrived. His village was near present-day Port-au-Prince. He was allied with Caonabó by marriage.

Behique Taíno word for shaman or healer.

Bohio Word that glosses as "home," used as one name for Taíno houses and also used by Lucayans from the Bahamas as the name for Hispaniola.

Cacicazgo The region or province ruled by the most important caciques on the island.

Cacique Term referring to several levels of leadership, translated by the Spanish as lord, ruler, and king. At the lowest level were village headmen, followed by district caciques, and finally paramount caciques, who ruled large territories called cacicazgos.

Caney The typical Taíno house with a round to oval shape and a high-pitched thatch roof.

Caniba Columbus's name for the "people of the Grand Khan."

Caníbales Mythical beings associated with transporting the dead to the afterlife. The name has come to be associated with anthropophagy, because these spirits "consumed" the life of the dead.

Caonabó One of the principal caciques of Hispaniola, whose cacicazgo was called Maguana. He was the first cacique deposed by the Spanish, because he attacked and destroyed La Navidad.

Caracoli Crescent-shaped ear or nose ornaments made from *guanín*.

Carib One of the three mythical islands for the Taínos, the one associated with men. The Spanish confused this term with their notion of geopolitics and identified the Caribs as real people who were the enemy of the Taínos and were the subjects of the Grand Khan. The Spanish use of the term eventually was expanded to include all native peoples who opposed their rule and who were characterized as the consumers of human flesh.

Caribe One of several Taino words used in reference to mythical beings who came from the otherworld and carried the spirits of the dead to the afterlife. Columbus was at first identified as a Caribe by the Taínos.

Casiripe Cooking technique in which meats and vegetables are slowly stewed in a large pot. The name comes from the practice of using chili peppers in the stew (pepper pot).

Cemíes Taíno name for their spirits (gods) and for the objects they made to represent them.

Cobo A seashell, usually associated with the queen conch (*Strombus gigas*).

Deminán One of the culture heroes in the Taíno origin myth. He and his three brothers took the basic elements of culture from the chief god, Yaya.

Guacanagarí The cacique whose village was located on the north coast of Hispaniola to the east of Cap Haïtien. Columbus established Fort La Navidad in this village and remained a life-long friend.

Guacayarima The southwestern peninsula of Haiti. Translated as place of anus or filth.

Guahayona A symbol of social unity in Taino mythology. He stole the women from his brother-in-law, the cacique Anacacuya, and left them in Matininó. Guahayona went on to live on the mythical island of Guanín.

Guanahaní The name for the first island that Christopher Columbus reached in the Americas (today known as San Salvador).

Guanín Term with two meanings: (1) one of the mythical islands, associated with pleasure, fulfilment, and sexual union; (2) objects made from a gold-copper alloy that were imported from South America.

Guarionex The cacique of Magua. He was the principal cacique involved in dealings with the Spanish. When he realized that the Spanish could not be ousted, he went into exile in the cacicazgo of Mayabonex but was hunted down and captured by the Spanish.

Macorix Word that glosses as "foreign tongue." In the two provinces Macorix de Arriba and Macorix de Abajo a different language than Taíno was spoken. Ramón Pané collected his information on Taíno religion in Macorix de Arriba.

Magdalena The principal village of the province Macorix de Arriba.

Magua The cacicazgo ruled by Guarionex. It was located near Concepción de la Vega in the Dominican Republic.

Maguana The cacicazgo ruled by Caonabó. The main village was located near San Juan de Maguana in the Dominican Republic.

Marien The cacicazgo ruled by Guacanagarí, located on the north coast of Hispaniola to the east of Cap Haïtien.

Mayabonex The cacique of Magdalena in the territory of the Macorix.

Naborias Term translated as "personal slave," referring to people who were indentured to caciques following warfare among cacicazgos. There apparently was no notion of ownership associated with these servants, unlike European slaves.

Nitaínos The noble or elite class in Taíno society.

Samaot Term that Columbus understood to mean the island or village where the gold is. If such a place existed it was to the south of the central Bahamas.

Turey Literally, "from the heavens." *Turey* is often associated with *guanín* and other rare objects that were gifts from the gods.

Yaya The principal deity in the origin myth. He is associated with Yucahuguamá, the giver of manioc.

Yayael The son of Yaya in the origin myth.

Yucahuguamá The principal *cemí* in the Taíno pantheon. He was the male god of fertility and the giver of manioc.

Bibliography

Aberle, D. F. 1961. Matrilineal Descent in Cross-Cultural Perspective. In *Matrilineal Kinship*, ed. D. M. Schneider and K. Gough, 655–727. Berkeley: University of California Press.

Adams, J. 1973. *The Gitksan Potlach*. Toronto: University of Toronto Press.

Alcina Franch, J. 1983. La cultura Taína como sociedad de transición entre los niveles tribal y de jefaturas. In *La Cultura Taína*, 69–80. Madrid: Biblioteca del V Centenario.

Alegría, R. E. 1979. Apuntes para el estudio de los caciques de Puerto Rico. *Revista del Instituto de Cultura Puertorriqueña* 85: 25–41.

———. 1983. *Ball Courts and Ceremonial Plazas in the West Indies*. Yale University Publications in Anthropology No. 79. New Haven: Yale University Press.

Allaire, L. 1977. Later Prehistory in Martinique and the Island Carib: Problems in Ethnic Identification. Ph.D. dissertation, Yale University. Ann Arbor: University Microfilms.

———. 1981. The Saurian Pineal Eye in Antillean Art and Mythology, *Journal of Latin American Lore* 7: 3–22.

———. 1987. Some Comments on the Ethnic Identity of the Taino-Carib Frontier. In *Ethnicity and Culture*, ed. Reginald Auger, Margaret F. Glass, Scott MacEachern, and Peter H. McCartney, 127–133. Calgary: Archaeological Association, University of Calgary.

———. 1996. Visions of Cannibals: Distant Islands and Distant Lands in Taino World Image. In *The Lesser Antilles in the Age of European Expansion*, ed. R. Paquette and S. Engerman. Gainesville: University Press of Florida.

———. 2003. Agricultural Societies in the Caribbean: The Lesser Antilles. In *General History of the Caribbean, Volume I: Autochthonous Societies*, ed. J. Sued-Badillo, 195–227. Paris: UNESCO Publications.

Amodio, E. 1999. Los Caníbales mutantes: Etapas de la transformación étnica de los caribes durante la época colonial. *Boletín Américas* 49: 9–29.

Arrom, J. J. (ed.) 1974. *Fray Ramón Pané, "Relación acerca de las antigüedades de los Indios": El primer tratado escrito en América*. Mexico City: Siglo XXI Editores.

———. 1975. *Mitología y artes prehispánicas de las Antillas*. Mexico City: Siglo XXI Editores.

———. 1980. *Estudios de lexicología Antillana*. Havana: Centro de Estudios del Caribe Casa de las Américas.

Ashman, K. M., and P. S. Baringer (eds.). 2001. *After the Science Wars*. New York: Routledge.

Bell, J. A. 1994. *Reconstructing Prehistory: Scientific Method in Archaeology*. Philadelphia: Temple University Press.

Benzoni, G. 1857. *History of the New World.* Translated by W. H. Smyth. London: Printed for Hakluyt Society.

Berman, M. J., and P. L. Gnivecki. 1995. The Colonization of the Bahama Archipelago: A Reappraisal. *World Archaeology* 26: 421–441.

Berman, M. J., A. K. Sievert, and T. R. Whyte. 1999. Form and Function of Bipolar Lithic Artifacts from the Three Dog Site, San Salvador, Bahamas. *Latin American Antiquity* 10: 415–432.

Binford, L. R. 1972. *An Archaeological Perspective.* New York: Academic Press.

Blanton, R. E., G. M. Feinman, S. A. Kowalewski, and P. N. Peregrine. 1996. A Dual-Processual Theory for the Evolution of Mesoamerican Civilization. *Current Anthropology* 37: 1–14.

Boomert, A. 1986. The Cayo Complex of St. Vincent: Ethnohistorical and Archaeological Aspects of the Island Carib Problem. *Antropológica* 66: 3–68.

———. 1987. Gifts of the Amazons: "Green Stone" Pendants and Beads as Items of Ceremonial Exchange in Amazonia and the Caribbean. *Antropológica* 67: 33–54.

Boucher, P. P. 1992. *Cannibal Encounters: Europeans and Island Caribs, 1492–1764.* Baltimore: Johns Hopkins University Press.

Bourne, E. G. 1906. Columbus, Ramón Pané and the Beginnings of American Anthropology. *Proceedings of the American Antiquarian Society* 17: 310–348.

Bradford, M. A. C. 2001. Caribbean Perspectives on Settlement Patterns: The Windward Island Study. Ph.D. dissertation. Department of Anthropology, University of Iowa.

Braudel, F. 1997. *Les Ambitions de l'histoire.* Edited by R. de Ayala and P. Braudel. Les Écrits de Fernand Braudel 2. Paris: Fallois.

Brinton, D. 1871. The Arawack Language of Guiana and Its Linguistic and Ethnological Relations. *Transactions of the American Philosophical Society* 14: 427–444.

Brudenell-Bruce, P. G. C. 1975. *The Collins Guide to the Birds of New Providence and the Bahama Islands.* Lexington, Mass.: Stephen Greene Press.

Budinoff, L. 1991. An Osteological Analysis of the Human Burials Recovered from an Early Ceramic Site on the North Coast of Puerto Rico. In *Proceedings of the 12th Congress of the International Association for Caribbean Archaeology,* edited by L. S. Robinson, 117–134. Martinique: IACA.

Byrne, B. 1991. Toward the Integration of Kinship Terminology Theory into Ethnoarchaeological Middle-Range Research. Unpublished manuscript in possession of the author.

Callaghan, R. T. 2003. Comments on the Mainland Origins of the Preceramic Cultures of the Greater Antilles. *Latin American Antiquity* 14: 323–338.

Capote, T. 1966. *In Cold Blood: A True Account of Multiple Murder and Its Consequences.* New York: Random House.

———. 1987a. *Answered Prayers: The Unfinished Novel.* New York: Random House.

———. 1987b. *A Capote Reader.* New York: Random House.

Caribbean Commission. 1952. *Fisheries of the Caribbean.* Port-of-Spain, Trinidad: Central Secretariat, Kent House.

Carlson, L. A. 1993. Strings of Command: Manufacture and Utilization of Shell Beads among the Taino Indians of the West Indies. M.A. thesis. Department of Anthropology, University of Florida, Gainesville.

———. 1999. Aftermath of a Feast: Human Colonization of the Southern Bahamian Archipelago and Its Effects on the Indigenous Fauna. Ph.D. dissertation. Department of Anthropology, University of Florida, Gainesville.

Carlson, L. A., and W. F. Keegan. 2004. Prehistoric Resource Depletion in the Prehistoric Northern West Indies. In *Voyages of Discovery: The Archaeology of Islands*, edited by S. M. Fitzpatrick, 85–107. Westport, Conn.: Praeger Publishers.

Carneiro, R. L. 1970. A Theory of the Origin of the State. *Science* 169: 733–738.

Cassá, R. 1992. *Los indios de las Antillas*. Madrid: Editorial MAPFRE.

Castellanos, R. 1981. La Plaza de Chacuey: Un instrumento astronómico megalítico. *Boletín del Museo del Hombre Dominicano* 16: 31–40.

Chanlatte Baik, L. 1981. *La Hueca y Sorce (Vieques, Puerto Rico): Primeras migraciones agroalfareras antillanas*. Santo Domingo: Taller.

———. 2003. Agricultural Societies in the Caribbean: The Greater Antilles and the Bahamas. In *General History of the Caribbean, Volume I: Autochthonous Societies*, edited by J. Sued-Badillo, 228–258. Paris: UNESCO Publishing.

Charlevoix, P., and J. de Francisco. 1977. *Historia de las Isla Española o de Santo Domingo* (1730). 2 vols. Santo Domingo: Editorial de Santo Domingo.

Cobb, C. R. 2000. *From Quarry to Cornfield*. Tuscaloosa: University of Alabama Press.

Conrad, G. W., J. W. Foster, and C. D. Beeker. 2001. Organic Artifacts from Mantanial de la Aleta, Dominican Republic: Preliminary Observations and Interpretations. *Journal of Caribbean Archaeology* 2: 1–20.

Cook, S. F., and W. Borah. 1971. The Aboriginal Population of Hispaniola. In *Essays in Population History. Vol. 1: Mexico and the Caribbean*, edited by S. F. Cook and W. Borah, 376–410. Berkeley: University of California Press.

Coppa, A., A. Cucina, B. Chiarelli, F. Luna Calderón, and D. Mancinelli. 1995. Dental Anthropology and Paleodemography of the Precolumbian Populations of Hispaniola from the Third Millennium B.C. to the Spanish Contact. *Human Evolution* 10: 153–167.

Cordell, A. 1998. Possible Manufacturing Origins of Ostionoid Pottery from the Bahamas. Paper presented at the 55th annual meeting of the Southeastern Archaeological Conference, Greenville, S.C.

Craton, M., and G. Saunders. 1992. *Islanders in the Stream: A History of the Bahamian People, Volume One: From Aboriginal Times to the End of Slavery*. Athens: University of Georgia Press.

Curet, L. A. 1992a. The Development of Chiefdoms in the Greater Antilles: A Regional Study of the Valley of Maunabo, Puerto Rico. Ph.D. dissertation. Department of Anthropology, Arizona State University, Tempe.

———. 1992b. House Structure and Cultural Change in the Caribbean: Three Case Studies from Puerto Rico. *Latin American Antiquity* 3: 160–174.

———. 1996. Ideology, Chiefly Power, and Material Culture: An Example from the Greater Antilles. *Latin American Antiquity* 7: 114–131.

————. 1998. New Formulae for Estimating Prehistoric Populations for Lowland South America and the Caribbean. *Antiquity* 72: 359–375.

————. 2002. The Chief Is Dead, Long Live . . . Who? Descent and Succession in the Protohistoric Chiefdoms of the Greater Antilles. *Ethnohistory* 49: 259–280.

————. 2003. Issues on the Diversity and Emergence of Middle-Range Societies of the Ancient Caribbean: A Critique. *Journal of Archaeological Research* 11: 1–42.

————. 2004. Island Archaeology and Units of Analysis in the Study of Ancient Caribbean Societies. In *Voyages of Discovery: The Archaeology of Islands*, edited by S. M. Fitzpatrick, 187–202. Westport, CT: Praeger.

Curet, L. A., and J. R. Oliver. 1998. Mortuary Practices, Social Development, and Ideology in Precolumbian Puerto Rico. *Latin American Antiquity* 9: 217–239.

Cusick, J. G. 1989. Change in Pottery as a Reflection of Social Change: A Study of Taino Pottery before and after Contact at the Site of En Bas Saline, Haiti. Master's paper. University of Florida, Gainesville.

————. 1991. Culture Change and Pottery Change in a Taino Village. In *Proceedings of the 13th International Congress for Caribbean Archaeology*, 446–461, Curaçao: IACA.

Dacal Moure, R., and M. Rivero de la Calle. 1984. *Arqueología aborigen de Cuba*. Havana: Editorial Gente Nueva.

D'Altroy, T., and T. Earle. 1985. Staple Finance, Wealth Finance, and Storage in the Inca Political Economy. *Current Anthropology* 26: 187–206.

Davis, D. D. 1992. Rumor of Cannibals. *Archaeology* (January/February): 49.

Davis, D. D., and R. C. Goodwin. 1990. Island Carib Origins: Evidence and Non-evidence. *American Antiquity* 55: 37–48.

Davis, D. D., and K. Oldfield. 2003. Archaeological Reconnaissance of Anegada, British Virgin Islands. *Journal of Caribbean Archaeology* 4: 1–11.

Davis, W. 1985. *The Serpent and the Rainbow*. New York: Simon and Schuster.

Deagan, K. 1987. Initial Encounters: Arawak Responses to European Contact at the En Bas Saline Site, Haiti. In *Proceedings of the First San Salvador Conference*, edited by D. Gerace, 341–359. San Salvador: College Center of the Finger Lakes.

————. 1988. The Archaeology of the Spanish Contact Period in the Caribbean. *Journal of World Prehistory* 2: 187–233.

————. 1989. The Search for La Navidad, Columbus's 1492 Settlement. In *First Encounters*, edited by J. T. Milanich and S. Milbrath, 41–54. Gainesville: University Press of Florida.

————. 2004. Reconsidering Taíno Social Dynamics after Spanish Conquest: Gender and Class in Culture Contact Studies. *American Antiquity* 69: 597–626.

Deagan, K., and J. M. Cruxent. 2002. *Archaeology at La Isabela: America's First European Town*. New Haven: Yale University Press.

de Booy, T. 1912. Lucayan Remains in the Caicos Islands. *American Anthropologist* 14: 81–105.

————. 1913. Lucayan Artifacts from the Bahamas. *American Anthropologist* 15: 1–7.

Deetz, J. 1968. The Inference of Residence and Descent Rules from Archaeological Data. In *New Perspectives in Archaeology*, edited by S. R. Binford and L. R. Binford, 41–48. Chicago: Aldine.

De France, S. D., W. F. Keegan, and L. A. Newsom. 1996. The Archaeobotanical, Bone

Isotope, and Zooarchaeological Records from Caribbean Sites in Comparative Perspective. In *Case Studies in Environmental Archaeology*, edited by E. J. Reitz, L. A. Newsom, and S. J. Scudder, 289–304. New York: Plenum Press.

Delpuech, A. and C. L. Hofman (eds.). 2004. *The Late Ceramic Age in the Eastern Caribbean*. BAR International Series. Oxford: BAR.

Divale, W. 1974. Migration, External Warfare and Matrilocal Residence. *Behavior Science Research* 9: 75–133.

Doran, E., Jr. 1958. The Caicos Conch Trade. *Geographical Review* 48: 388–401.

Dreyfus, S. 1992. Indian America: Island Caribs. In *The Christopher Columbus Encyclopedia*, edited by S. A. Bedini, 349–351. New York: Simon & Schuster.

Dunn, O., and J. E. Kelley, Jr. (eds.). 1989. *The Diario of Christopher Columbus's First Voyage to America 1492–1493* (abstracted by Bartolomé de las Casas). Norman: University of Oklahoma Press.

Earle, T. K. 1978. *Economic and Social Organization of a Complex Chiefdom: The Halelea District, Kauai, Hawaii*. Anthropological Research Paper 63. Ann Arbor: University of Michigan, the Museum of Anthropology.

———. 1987. Chiefdoms in Archaeological and Ethnohistorical Perspective. *Annual Review of Anthropology* 16: 279–308.

———. 1997. *How Chiefs Come to Power: The Political Economy in Prehistory*. Stanford: Stanford University Press.

Earle, T. K., and R. W. Preucel. 1987. Processual Archaeology and the Radical Critique. *Current Anthropology* 28: 501–538.

Ember, M. 1974. The Conditions That May Favor Avunculocal Residence. *Behavior Science Review* 9: 203–209.

Ensor, B. E. 2000. Social Formations, Modo de Vida, and Conflict in Archaeology. *American Antiquity* 65: 15–42.

———. 2003. Crow-Omaha Marital Alliances and Social Transformations: Archaeological Case Studies on the Taino, Hohokam, and Archaic Lower Mississippi Valley. Ph.D. dissertation. University of Florida, Gainesville.

Espenshade, C. T. 2000. Reconstructing Household Vessel Assemblages and Site Duration at an Early Ostionoid Site from South-Central Puerto Rico. *Journal of Caribbean Archaeology* 1: 1–22.

Fewkes, J. W. 1907. The Aborigines of Porto Rico and Neighboring Islands. In *Twenty-fifth Annual Report of the U.S. Bureau of American Ethnology, 1903–1904*, 35–281. Washington, D.C.

Flannery, K. V. (ed.). 1976. *The Early Mesoamerican Village*. New York: Academic Press.

———. 1982. The Golden Marshalltown: A Parable for the Archaeology of the 1980s. *American Anthropologist* 84: 265–278.

———. 1986. A Visit to the Master. In *Guilá Naquitz, Archaic Foraging and Early Agriculture in Oaxaca, Mexico*, edited by K. V. Flannery, 511–519. Orlando: Academic Press.

Fox, R. 1967. *Kinship and Marriage*. New York: Cambridge University Press.

Frazer, Sir J. G. 1911–1915. *The Golden Bough*. 3rd ed. 13 vol. London: Macmillan.

Fuson, R. H. 1987. *The Log of Christopher Columbus*. Camden, Maine: International Marine Publishing.

Gero, J. 1990. Facts and Values in the Archaeological Eye: Discussion of "Powers of Observation." In *Powers of Observation: Alternative Views of Archaeology*, edited by S. M. Nelson and A. B. Kehoe, 113–119. Archaeology Papers of the American Anthropological Association No. 2. Washington, D.C.

Giddens, A. 1976. *New Rules of Sociological Method: A Positive Critique of Interpretive Sociologies*. London: Hutchinson.

Gillespie, S. D. 2000a. Introduction. In *Beyond Kinship: Social and Material Reproduction in House Societies*, edited by R. A. Joyce and S. D. Gillespie, 1–21. Philadelphia: University of Pennsylvania Press.

———. 2000b. Lévi-Strauss: *Maison* and *Société à Maisons*. In *Beyond Kinship: Social and Material Reproduction in House Societies*, edited by R. A. Joyce and S. D. Gillespie, 22–51. Philadelphia: University of Pennsylvania Press.

Goldman, I. 1970. *Ancient Polynesian Society*. Chicago: University of Chicago Press.

Goodenough, W. H. 1955. Residence Rules. *Southwestern Journal of Anthropology* 12: 22–37.

Granberry, J. 1979–1981. Spanish Slave Trade in the Bahamas, 1509–1530: An Aspect of the Caribbean Pearl Industry (3 parts). *Journal of the Bahamas Historical Society*. Vols. 1, 2, and 3.

———. 1991. Lucayan Toponyms. *Journal of the Bahamas Historical Society* 13: 3–12.

Granberry, J., and J. Winter. 1995. Bahamian Ceramics. In *Proceedings of the 15th International Congress for Caribbean Archaeology*, edited by R. E. Alegría and M. Rodríguez, 3–14. San Juan: Centro de Estudios Avanzados de Puerto Rico y el Caribe.

Greene, B. 1999. *The Elegant Universe*. London: Vintage Books.

Grouard, S., W. F. Keegan, and L. A. Carlson. n.d. Captures animales et pratiques alimentaires d'une population précolombienne haïtienne: Le cas de Île à Rat (série Ostionoide 600–1500 ap. J.-C.). Submitted to *Archaeofauna*.

Guerrero, J. G. 1981. Dos plazas indígenas y el poblado de Cotubanama, Parque Nacional del Este. *Boletín del Museo del Hombre Dominicano* 16: 13–30.

Hage, P. 1998. Was Proto-Oceanic Society Matrilineal? *Journal of the Polynesian Society* 107: 365–379.

———. 1999. Reconstructing Ancestral Oceanic Society. *Asian Perspectives* 38: 200–228.

Hage, P., and F. Harary. 1983. *Structural Models in Anthropology*. Cambridge: Cambridge University Press.

———. 1996. *Island Networks: Communication, Kinship, and Classification Structures in Oceania*. New York: Cambridge University Press.

Hage, P., and J. Marck. 2003. Matrilineality and the Melanesian Origin of Polynesian Y Chromosomes. *Current Anthropology* 44 (supplement): S121–S127.

Harris, M. 1979. *Cultural Materialism*. New York: Random House.

Harris, P. O'B. 1994. Nitaino and Indians: A Preliminary Ethnographic Outline of Contact Hispaniola. Master's paper. University of Florida, Gainesville.

Haviser, J. B. 1997. Settlement Strategies in the Early Ceramic Age. In *The Indigenous People of the Caribbean*, edited by S. M. Wilson, 57–69. Gainesville: University Press of Florida.

Heckenberger, M. J. 2002. Rethinking the Arawakan Diaspora: Hierarchy, Regionality, and the Amazonian "Formative." In *Comparative Arawakan Histories: Rethinking Language Family and Culture Area in Amazonia*, edited by J. D. Hill and F. Santos-Granero, 99–325. Urbana: University of Illinois Press.

Helms, M. W. 2000. *The Curassow's Crest: Myths and Symbols in the Ceramics of Ancient Panama*. Gainesville: University Press of Florida.

Henige, D. 1991. *In Search of Columbus: The Sources for the First Voyage*. Tempe: University of Arizona Press.

Hernández Aquino, L. 1977. *Diccionario de voces indígenas de Puerto Rico*. San Juan, Puerto Rico: Editorial Cultural.

Hesse, R. C., and K. Orr Hesse. 1977. The Conch Industry in the Turks and Caicos Islands. *Underwater Naturalist* 10: 4–9.

Hill, J. N. 1970. *Broken K Pueblo*. Anthropology Papers of the University of Arizona No. 18. Tucson: University of Arizona Press.

Hocart, A. M. 1952. *The Northern States of Fiji*. Royal Anthropological Institute of Great Britain and Ireland, Occasional Publication 11. London: The Institute.

———. 1969. *Kingship*. Oxford: Oxford University Press.

———. 1970. *Kings and Councillors*. Chicago: University of Chicago Press.

Hodder, I. 1979. Social and Economic Stress and Material Culture Patterning. *American Antiquity* 44: 446–454.

———. 1991. Postprocessual Archaeology and the Current Debate. In *Processual and Postprocessual Archaeologies: Multiple Ways of Knowing the Past*, edited by R. W. Preucel, 30–41. Center for Archaeological Investigations, Occasional Paper no. 10. Carbondale: Southern Illinois University.

———. 1999. *The Archaeological Process: An Introduction*. Oxford: Blackwell.

——— (ed.). 2000. *Towards Reflexive Method in Archaeology: The Example at Çatalhöyük*. Oxford: McDonald Institute for Archaeological Research.

Hoffman, C. A., Jr. 1967. Bahama Prehistory: Cultural Adaptation to an Island Environment. Ph.D. dissertation. University of Arizona. Ann Arbor: University Microfilms.

Hofman, C. L. 1993. In Search of the Native Population of Pre-Columbian Saba (400–1450 A.D.), Part One: Pottery Styles and Their Interpretations. Ph.D. dissertation. Leiden University, Leiden.

Hofman, C. L., and M. L. P. Hoogland (eds.). 1995. *Archaeological Investigations on St. Martin 1993: The Sites of Norman Estate, Hope Estate, Anse des Peres*. Basse-Terre, Guadeloupe: Direction Régionale des Affaires Culturelles de Guadeloupe, Service Régional de l'Archéologie.

Hole, F. 1978. Editorial. *American Antiquity* 43: 151–152.

Holling, C. S. 1998. Two Cultures of Ecology. *Conservation Ecology* 2: 4.

Hulme, P. 1986. *Colonial Encounters: Europe and the Native Caribbean, 1492–1797*. London: Methuen.

———. 1988. Chiefdoms of the Caribbean. *Critiques of Anthropology* 8: 105–118.

———. 1993. Making Sense of the Native Caribbean. *New West Indian Guide* 67: 189–220.

Hulme, P., and N. L. Whitehead. 1992. *Wild Majesty: Encounters with Caribs from Columbus to the Present Day—An Anthology*. Oxford: Oxford University Press.

Hutcheson, C. D. 1999. Reweaving the Strands: Continued Exploration into the Basketry Technology of Prehistoric Bahamas. In *Proceedings of the 18th International Congress for Caribbean Archaeology*, 185–198. St. Georges, Grenada: IACA.

Irving, W. 1828. *A History of the Life and Voyages of Christopher Columbus*. 3 volumes. New York: G. & C. Carvill.

Irwin, G. 1992. *The Prehistoric Exploration and Colonization of the Pacific*. Cambridge: Cambridge University Press.

Iverson, J. B. 1979. Behavior and Ecology of the Rock Iguana, *Cyclura carinata*. *Bulletin of the Florida State Museum*, No. 24.

Johnson, A., and T. K. Earle. 1987. *The Evolution of Human Society: From Forager Group to Agrarian State*. Stanford: Stanford University Press.

Jouravleva, I. 2002. Origen de la alfarería de las comunidades protoagroalfareras de la región central de Cuba. *El Caribe Arqueológico* 6: 35–43.

Joyce, R. A., and S. D. Gillespie (eds.). 2000. *Beyond Kinship: Social and Material Reproduction in House Societies*. Philadelphia: University of Pennsylvania Press.

Keegan, W. F. 1981. Artifacts in Archaeology: A Caribbean Case Study. M.A. thesis. Florida Atlantic University. Ann Arbor: University Microfilms.

———. 1982. Lucayan Cave Burials from the Bahamas. *Journal of New World Archaeology* 5: 57–65.

———. 1985. Dynamic Horticulturalists: Population Expansion in the Prehistoric Bahamas. Ph.D. dissertation. Department of Anthropology, UCLA. Ann Arbor: University Microfilms.

———. 1989a. Creating the Guanahatabey (Ciboney): The Modern Genesis of an Extinct Culture. *Antiquity* 63: 373–379.

———. 1989b. Transition from a Terrestrial to a Maritime Economy: A New View of the Crab/Shell Dichotomy. In *Early Ceramic Population Lifeways and Adaptive Strategies in the Caribbean*, edited by P. E. Siegel, 119–128. BAR International Series 506. Oxford: BAR.

———. 1992. *The People Who Discovered Columbus*. Gainesville: University Press of Florida.

———. 1994. West Indian Archaeology. 1: Overview and Foragers. *Journal of Archaeological Research* 2: 255–284.

———. 1995a. Columbus Was a Cannibal: Myths and the First Encounters. In *The Lesser Antilles in the Age of European Expansion*, edited by R. Paquette and S. Engerman, 17–32. Gainesville: University Press of Florida.

———. 1995b. Modeling Dispersal in the Prehistoric West Indies. *World Archaeology* 26: 400–420.

———. 1996. West Indian Archaeology 2: After Columbus. *Journal of Archaeological Research* 2: 265–294.

———. 1997. *Bahamian Archaeology: Life in the Bahamas and Turks and Caicos before Columbus*. Nassau: Media Publishing.

———. 2000a. History and Culture of Food and Drink in the Americas, Section V.D.2: The Caribbean, Including Northern South America and Eastern Central America:

Early History, In *The Cambridge World History of Food*, edited by K. Kipple and K. C. Ornelas, 1260–1277. Cambridge: Cambridge University Press.

———. 2000b. West Indian Archaeology 3: Ceramic Age. *Journal of Archaeological Research* 8: 135–167.

———. 2001. Archaeological Investigations on Île à Rat, Haiti: Avoid the -OID. In *Proceedings of the 18th International Congress for Caribbean Archaeology*, 233–239. St. Georges, Grenada: IACA.

———. 2004. Islands of Chaos. In *The Late Ceramic Age in the Eastern Caribbean*, edited by A. Delpuech and C. L. Hofman, 33–44. BAR International Series. Oxford: BAR.

———. 2006a. All in the Family—Descent and Succession in the Protohistoric Chiefdoms of the Greater Antilles: A Comment on Curet. *Ethnohistory* 53: 383–392.

———. 2006b. Archaic Influences in the Origins and Development of Taíno Societies. *Caribbean Journal of Science* 42: 1–10.

Keegan, W. F., L. A. Carlson, and S. Grouard. n.d. The Culture of Subsistence: Circulating Reference and Taino Alimentation. Submitted to *Latin American Antiquity*.

Keegan, W. F., and M. J. DeNiro. 1988. Stable Carbon- and Nitrogen-Isotope Ratios of Bone Collagen Used to Study Coral-Reef and Terrestrial Components of Prehistoric Bahamian Diet. *American Antiquity* 53: 320–336.

Keegan, W. F., and J. M. Diamond. 1987. Colonization of Islands by Humans: A Biogeographical Perspective. In *Advances in Archaeological Method and Theory*, vol. 10, edited by M. B. Schiffer, 49–92. San Diego: Academic Press.

Keegan, W. F., and M. D. Maclachlan. 1989. The Evolution of Avunculocal Chiefdoms: A Reconstruction of Taino Kinship and Politics. *American Anthropologist* 91: 613–630.

Keegan, W. F., M. D. Maclachlan, and B. Byrne. 1998. Social Foundations of the Taino Caciques. In *Chiefdoms and Chieftaincy in the Americas*, edited by E. Redmond, 217–244. Gainesville: University Press of Florida.

Keegan, W. F., and R. Rodríguez Ramos. 2005. Sin rodeos. *El Caribe Arqueológico* 8: 8–13.

Keen, B. (trans.) 1959. *The Life of Admiral Christopher Columbus by His Son Ferdinand*. New Brunswick: Rutgers University Press.

Kirch, P. V. 2000. *On the Road of the Winds*. Berkeley: University of California Press.

Kroeber, A. L., and C. Kluckhohn. 1952. *Culture: A Critical Review of Concepts and Definitions*. Papers of the Peabody Museum of American Archaeology and Ethnology, Vol. 47. Cambridge, Mass.: Harvard University.

Kuhn, T. S. 1970. *The Structure of Scientific Revolutions* 2nd ed. Chicago: University of Chicago Press.

Las Casas, B. de. 1951. *Historia de las Indias*. 3 vols. Edited by A. Millares Carlo. Mexico City: Fondo de Cultura Económica.

———. 1958. *Apologetica Historia*. Biblioteca de Autores Españoles Desde la Fromacion del Lenguaje hasta Nuestros Dias, Obras Escogidadas de Fray Bartolome de Las Casas, IV. Madrid: Sucs. J. Sánchez de Ocaña y Cia.

Latour, B. 1993. *We Have Never Been Modern*. Cambridge, Mass.: Harvard University Press.

———. 1999. *Pandora's Hope: Essays on the Reality of Science Studies*. Cambridge, Mass.: Harvard University Press.

Leone, M. P., P. B. Potter Jr., and P. A. Shackel. 1987. Toward a Critical Archaeology. *Current Anthropology* 28: 283–302.

Lévi-Strauss, C. 1963. *Structural Anthropology*. New York: Basic Books.

———. 1982. *The Way of the Masks*. Seattle: University of Washington Press.

———. 1987. *Anthropology and Myth: Lectures, 1951–1982*. Oxford: Basil Blackwell.

Longacre, W. A. 1970. *Archaeology as Anthropology: A Case Study*. Anthropology Papers of the University of Arizona No. 17. Tucson: University of Arizona Press.

Lovén, S. 1935. *Origins of the Tainan Culture, West Indies*. Goteborg: Elanders Boktryckeri Aktiebolag.

Maclachlan, M. D., and W. F. Keegan. 1990. Archeology and the Ethno-Tyrannies. *American Anthropologist* 92: 1011–1013.

Malinowski, B. 1978. *Coral Gardens and Their Magic*. New York: Dover.

Mann, C. J. 1986. Composition and Origin of Material in Pre-Columbian Pottery, San Salvador Island, Bahamas. *Geoarchaeology* 1: 183–194.

Marcus, G. E., and M. M. J. Fischer. 1986. *Anthropology as Cultural Critique: An Experimental Moment in the Human Sciences*. Chicago: University of Chicago Press.

Marquardt, W. H. 1992. Dialectical Archaeology. In *Archaeological Method and Theory*, edited by M. B. Schiffer, vol. 4, 101–140. Tucson: University of Arizona Press.

Marquet, S. J. 2002. *Les pétroglyphes des Petites Antilles Meridionales: Contextes physique et culturel*. BAR International Series 1051. Oxford: BAR.

Martínez Arango, F. 1997. *Los Aborígenes de la Cuenca de Santiago de Cuba*. Miami: Ediciones Universal.

Mártir de Anglería, Pedro. 1989. *Décadas del Nuevo Mundo*. 2 vols. Santo Domingo: Sociedad Dominicana de Bibliofilos, Inc.

Martyr D'Anghiera, P. 1970. *De Orbe Novo* [1493–1525]. Translated by F. A. MacNutt. New York: Burt Franklin.

McArthur, N., I. W. Saunders, and R. L. Tweedie. 1976. Small Population Isolates: A Micro-simulation Study. *Journal of the Polynesian Society* 85: 307–326.

McGlade, J., and S. van der Leeuw. 1997. Introduction: Archaeology and Non-linear Dynamics—New Approaches to Long-term Change. In *Time, Process and Structured Transformation in Archaeology*, edited by S. E. van der Leeuw and J. McGlade, 1–31. London: Routledge.

Michener, J. 1988. *Caribbean*. New York: Knopf.

Milbrath, S. 1989. Old World Meets New: Views across the Atlantic. In *First Encounters*, edited by J. T. Milanich and S. Milbrath, 183–210. Gainesville: University Presses of Florida.

Mitchell, S. W. 1984. Late Holocene Tidal Creek-Lake Transitions, Long Island, Bahamas. Addendum to *Proceedings of the Second Symposium on the Geology of the Bahamas*, edited by J. W. Teeter, 1–28. San Salvador, Bahamas: College Center of the Finger Lakes Bahamian Field Station.

Mitchell, S. W., and W. F. Keegan. 1987. Reconstruction of the Coastlines of the Bahama Islands in 1492. *American Archaeology* 6: 88–96.

Montaigne, M. E. de. 1967. *The Essays of Montaigne*. 3 vols. Translated by J. Florio. London, 1892–1893. Reprint. New York: AMS Press.

Moore, C. 1998. Archaeology in Haiti. Unpublished manuscript cited with the permission of the author.

Moore, J. 2001. Evaluating Five Models of Human Colonization. *American Anthropologist* 103: 395–408.

Morison, S. E. 1942. *Admiral of the Ocean Sea*. Boston: Little, Brown.

Moscoso, F. 1981. The Development of Tribal Society in the Caribbean. Ph.D. dissertation. State University of New York at Binghamton, Binghamton. Ann Arbor: University Microfilms.

———. 1986. *Tribu y clase en el Caribe Antiguo*. San Pedro de Macoris, Dominican Republic: Universidad Central del Este.

———. 2003. Chiefdoms in the Islands and Mainland: A Comparison. In *General History of the Caribbean, Volume I: Autochthonous Societies*, edited by J. Sued-Badillo, 292–315. Paris: UNESCO Publishing.

Murdock, G. P. 1949. *Social Structure*. New York: Macmillan.

Murphy, Y., and R. F. Murphy. 1974. *Women of the Forest*. New York: Columbia University Press.

Myers, R. A. 1984. Island Carib Cannibalism, *Nieuwe West-Indische Gids* 158: 147–184.

Nelson, S. M., and A. B. Kehoe (eds.). 1990. *Powers of Observation: Alternate Views of Archaeology*. Archaeological Papers of the American Anthropological Association, No. 2, Washington, D.C.

Newsom, L. A. 1993. Native West Indian Plant Use. Ph.D. dissertation. Department of Anthropology, University of Florida, Gainesville.

Newsom, L. A., and K. A. Deagan. 1994. *Zea mays* in the West Indies: The Archaeological and Early Historic Record. In *Corn and Culture in the Prehistoric New World*, edited by S. Johannessen and C. A. Hastorf, 203–217. Boulder, Colo.: Westview Press.

O'Day, S. J. 2000. Zooarchaeology and Hierarchy in Kahikinui, Maui, Hawai'i: Bringing Together Multiple Lines of Evidence to Interpret the Past. Master's paper. University of Florida, Gainesville.

———. 2002. Late Prehistoric Lucayan Occupation and Subsistence on Middle Caicos Island, Northern West Indies. *Caribbean Journal of Science* 38: 1–10.

O'Day, S. J., and W. F. Keegan. 2001. Expedient Shell Tools from the Northern West Indies. *Latin American Antiquity* 12: 1–17.

Oliver, J. R. 1998. *El Centro Ceremonial Caguana, Puerto Rico*. BAR S727. Oxford: BAR.

Olsen, F. 1974. *On the Trail of the Arawaks*. Norman: University of Oklahoma Press.

Ortíz Aguilú, J. J., J. Rivera Meléndez, A. Príncipe Jácome, M. Mélendez Maiz, and M. Lavergne Colberg. 1991. Intensive Agriculture in Pre-Columbian West Indies: The Case for Terraces. In *Proceedings of the 14th Congress of the International Association for Caribbean Archaeology*, edited by A. Cummins and P. King, 278–285. Barbados: Barbados Museum and Historical Society.

Oviedo y Valdés, Gonzalo Fernández de. 1959. *Historia general y natural de las Indias*. Vols. 1–2. Madrid: Ediciones Atlas.

Pablo Godo, P. 1997. El problema del protoagrícola de Cuba: Discusión y perspectivas. *El Caribe Arqueológico* 2: 19–29.

Pekka Helminen, J. 1988. ¿Eran caníbales los Caribes?: Fray Bartolomé de las Casas y el canibalismo. *Revista de Historia de América* 105: 147–158.

Petersen, G. 1982. Ponapean Matriliny: Production, Exchange, and the Ties That Bind. *American Ethnologist* 9: 129–144.

Peterson, I. 1998. *The Jungles of Randomness: A Mathematical Safari*. New York: John Wiley & Sons.

Petitjean Roget, H. 2001. Contribution à l'étude du Troumassoïde et du Suazoïde (600–1200 AD): Une hypothèse sur les causes de la régression du Saladoïde aux Petites Antilles. In *Proceedings of the 19th Congress of the International Association for Caribbean Archaeology*, edited by L. Alofs and R. A. C. F. Dijkhoff, vol. 2, 227–238. Aruba: Publications of the Archaeological Museum Aruba, No. 9.

Popper, K. R. 1962. *Conjectures and Refutations: The Growth of Scientific Knowledge*. New York: Basic Books.

Price, R. 1966. Caribbean Fishing and Fisherman: A Historical Sketch. *American Anthropologist* 68: 1363–1383.

Rainbird, P. 1999. Islands Out of Time: Toward a Critique of Island Archaeology. *Journal of Mediterranean Archaeology* 12: 216–260.

Rainey, F. G. 1941. *Excavations in the Ft. Liberté Region, Haiti*. Yale University Publications in Anthropology, No. 23. New Haven.

Rainey, F., and J. J. Ortíz Aguilú. 1983. Bois Neuf: The Archaeological View from West Central Haiti. Unpublished manuscript in possession of the author.

Randall, J. E. 1968. *Caribbean Reef Fishes*. Neptune City, N.J.: T. F. H. Publications.

Rathje, W. L. 1971. The Origin and Development of Lowland Classic Maya Civilization. *American Antiquity* 43: 203–222.

Redmond, E. M., and C. S. Spencer. 1994. The Cacicazgo: An Indigenous Design. In *Caciques and Their People: A Volume in Honor of Ronald Spores*, edited by J. Marcus and J. F. Zeitlin, 189–225. Anthropological Papers, No. 89. Ann Arbor: Museum of Anthropology, University of Michigan.

Robiou-Lamarche, S. 1994. *Encuentro con la mitología Taína*. San Juan, Puerto Rico: Editorial Punto y Coma.

———. 2002. Osa Major: La idealización del huracán de Mesoamérica a las Antillas. *El Caribe Arqueológico* 6: 86–93.

Rodríguez, M. 1989. The Zoned Incised Crosshatch (ZIC) Ware of Early Precolumbian Ceramic Age Sites in Puerto Rico and Vieques Island. In *Early Ceramic Population Lifeways and Adaptive Strategies in the Caribbean*, edited by P. E. Siegel, 637–671. BAR International Series 506, Oxford: BAR.

Rodriguez Álvarez, A. 2003. Astronomía en la prehistoria de Puerto Rico: Caguana y Tibes, antiguos observatorios precolombinos. Doctoral dissertation, University of Valladolid.

Rodríguez Ramos, R. 1999. Lithic Reduction Trajectories at La Hueca and Punta Candalero Sites, Puerto Rico: A Preliminary Report. In *Proceedings of the 18th International Congress for Caribbean Archaeology*, 251–261. St. Georges, Grenada: IACA.

Roe, P. G. 1982. *The Cosmic Zygote*. New Brunswick, NJ: Rutgers University Press.

———. 1991. The Best Enemy Is a Drilled, Defunct and Decorative Enemy: Human Corporeal Art (Frontal Bone Pectorals-Belt Ornaments, Carved Humeri and Pierced Teeth) in Precolumbian Puerto Rico. In *Proceedings of the 13th International Congress for Caribbean Archaeology*, 854–873. Reports of the Anthropological-Anthropological Institute of the Netherland Antilles, No. 9. Curaçao: IACA.

———. 1995a. Eternal Companions: Amerindian Dogs from Tierra Firme to the Antilles. In *Proceedings of the 15th International Congress for Caribbean Archaeology*, edited by R. E. Alegría and M. Rodríguez, 155–172. San Juan: Centro de Estudios Avanzados de Puerto Rico y el Caribe.

———. 1995b. Style, Society, Myth, and Structure. In *Style, Society, and Person*, edited by C. Carr and J. E. Neitzel, 27–76. New York: Plenum Press.

———. 1997. Just Wasting Away: Taíno Shamanism and Concepts of Fertility. In *Taíno: Pre-Columbian Art and Culture from the Caribbean*, edited by F. Bercht, E. Brodsky, J. A. Farmer and D. Taylor, 124–157. New York: Monacelli Press.

Rosman, A., and P. Rubel. 1971. *Feasting with My Enemy*. Prospect Heights, Ill.: Waveland Press.

———. 1989. Dual Organization and Its Developmental Potential in Two Contrasting Environments. In *The Attraction of Opposites*, edited by D. Maybury-Lewis and U. Almagor, 209–234. Ann Arbor: University of Michigan Press.

———. n.d. The Material Basis of Dual Organization. Unpublished manuscript in possession of the author.

Roth, L. T. R. 2002. Total Phosphorus Use Area Determination of Lucayan Settlements, Middle Caicos, Turks and Caicos Islands, British West Indies. M.A. thesis. University of Calgary, Calgary.

Rouse, I. 1939. *Prehistory in Haiti: A Study in Method*. Yale University Publications in Anthropology, No. 21. New Haven: Yale University Press.

———. 1941. *Culture of the Ft. Liberté Region, Haiti*. Yale University Publications in Anthropology, No. 24. New Haven: Yale University Press.

———. 1948. The Carib, in Handbook of South American Indians, vol. 4. The Circum-Caribbean Tribes, ed. J. H. Steward. *Bureau of American Ethnology Bulletin* 143: 547–565.

———. 1964. Prehistory of the West Indies. *Science* 144: 499–513.

———. 1972. *Introduction to Prehistory: A Systematic Approach*. New York: McGraw-Hill.

———. 1986. *Migrations in Prehistory*. New Haven: Yale University Press.

———. 1989. Peopling and Repeopling of the West Indies. In *Biogeography of the West Indies, Past, Present and Future*, edited by C. A. Woods. Gainesville: Sandhill Crane Press.

———. 1992. *The Tainos: The People Who Greeted Columbus*. New Haven: Yale University Press.

Rubel, P. and A. Rosman. 1983. The Evolution of Exchange Structures and Ranking: Some Northwest Coast and Athapaskan Examples. *Journal of Anthropological Research* 39: 1–25.

Sahlins, M. 1958. *Social Stratification in Polynesia*. Seattle: University of Washington Press.

———. 1976. *Culture and Practical Reason*. Chicago: University of Chicago Press.

———. 1985. *Islands of History*. Chicago: University of Chicago Press.

Sanders, W. T., J. R. Parsons, and R. S. Santley. 1979. *The Basin of Mexico: Ecological Processes in the Evolution of a Civilization*. New York: Academic Press.

Sauer, C. O. 1966. *The Early Spanish Main*. Berkeley: University of California Press.

Schiffer, M. B. 1988. The Structure of Archaeological Theory. *American Antiquity* 53: 461–485.

Schneider, D. M. 1961. Introduction. In *Matrilineal Kinship*, edited by D. M. Schneider and K. Gough, 1–29. Berkeley: University of California Press.

———. 1984. *A Critique of the Study of Kinship*. Ann Arbor: University of Michigan Press.

Scudder, S. 2001. Evidence of Sea Level Rise at the Early Ostionan Coralie Site (GT-3), c. AD 700, Grand Turk, Turks and Caicos Islands. *Journal of Archaeological Science* 28: 1221–1233.

Sealey, N. E. 1985. *Bahamian Landscapes*. London: Collins Caribbean.

Sears, W. H., and S. D. Sullivan. 1978. Bahamas Archaeology. *American Antiquity* 43: 3–25.

Segerstråle, U. (ed.). 2000. *Beyond the Science Wars*. Albany: State University of New York.

Shanks, M., and C. Tilley. 1987. *Re-constructing Archaeology: Theory and Practice*. Cambridge: Cambridge University Press.

Siegel, P. E. 1991. Migration Research in Saladoid Archaeology: A Review. *Florida Anthropologist* 44: 79–91.

———. 1992. Ideology, Power, and Social Complexity in Prehistoric Puerto Rico. Ph.D. dissertation. Department of Anthropology, State University of New York at Binghamton, Binghamton.

———. 1996. An Interview with Irving Rouse. *Current Anthropology* 37: 671–689.

———. 1997. Ancestor Worship and Cosmology among the Taíno. In *Taíno: Pre-Columbian Art and Culture from the Caribbean*, edited by F. Bercht, E. Brodsky, J. A. Farmer, and D. Taylor, 106–111. New York: Monacelli Press.

Sinelli, P. T. 2001. Archaeological Investigations of Two Prehistoric Sites Representing Hispaniolan Colonization of Middle Caicos, Turks and Caicos Islands. M.A. thesis. University of Florida, Gainesville.

Snow, C. P. 1959. *The Two Cultures and the Scientific Revolution*. New York: Cambridge University Press.

Stevens-Arroyo, A. M. 1986. Warfare among the Tainos: From the Defeat of Caonabo to the Victory of Enriquillo. Paper presented at the First International Conference on the Dominican Republic, Rutgers University, Newark.

———. 1988. *Cave of the Jagua: The Mythological World of the Tainos*. Albuquerque: University of New Mexico Press.

Steward, J. H., and L. C. Faron. 1959. *Native Peoples of South America*. New York: McGraw-Hill.

Stokes, A. V. 1998. A Biogeographic Survey of Prehistoric Human Diet in the West Indies Using Stable Isotopes. Ph.D. dissertation. Department of Anthropology, University of Florida, Gainesville.

Stuiver, M., and P. J. Reimer. 1986. A Computer Program for Radiocarbon Age Calibration, *Radiocarbon* 28: 1022–1030.

Sued-Badillo, J. 1978. *Los Caribes: ¿Realidad o fábula?.* Río Piedras, Puerto Rico: Editorial Antillana.

———. 1979. *La mujer indígena y su sociedad.* 2nd ed. Río Piedras, Puerto Rico: Editorial Antillana.

———. 1985. Las cacicas indoantillanas. *Revista del Instituto de Cultura Puertorriqueña* 87: 17–26.

——— (ed.). 2003. *General History of the Caribbean, Volume I: Autochthonous Societies.* Paris: UNESCO Publishing, Paris.

Sullivan, S. D. 1974. Archaeological Reconnaissance of Eleuthera, Bahamas. M.A. thesis, Florida Atlantic University, Boca Raton.

———. 1976. *Archaeological Reconnaissance of the Turks and Caicos Islands, British West Indies.* Report submitted to the Government of the Turks and Caicos.

———. 1980. An Overview of the 1976 to 1978 Archaeological Investigations in the Caicos Islands. *Florida Anthropologist* 33: 94–98.

———. 1981. The Colonization and Exploitation of the Turks and Caicos Islands. Ph.D. dissertation. University of Illinois at Urbana-Champaign.

Tabio, E., and J. M. Guarch. 1966. *Excavations en Arroyo del Palo, Mayari, Cuba.* Havana: Department of Anthropology, Academy of Science.

Taylor, D., M. Biscione, and P. G. Roe. 1997. Epilogue: The Beaded *Zemi* in the Pigorini Museum. In *Taíno: Pre-Columbian Art and Culture from the Caribbean*, edited by F. Bercht, E. Brodsky, J. A. Farmer, and D. Taylor, 138–169. New York: Monacelli Press.

Taylor, W. W. 1948. *A Study of Archaeology.* American Anthropological Society, Memoir 69.

Terrell, J. 1990. Storytelling in Prehistory. In *Archaeological Method and Theory*, vol. 2, ed. M. B. Schiffer, 1–27. Tucson: University of Arizona Press.

Thomas, D. H. 1979. *Archaeology.* New York: Holt, Rinehart & Winston.

Tromans, M. A. 1986. Temporal and Spatial Analysis of Two Antillean Period Settlements, Middle Caicos, Turks and Caicos Islands, British West Indies. M.A. thesis. Florida Atlantic University, Boca Raton.

Tyler, S. L. 1988. *Two Worlds: The Indian Encounter with the European, 1492–1509.* Salt Lake City: University of Utah Press.

Tylor, E. B. 1871. *Primitive Culture*, 2 vols. New York: Henry Holt.

Ulloa Hung, J., and R. Valcárcel Rojas. 1997. Las comunidades apropiadoras ceramistas del Sureste de Cuba: Un estudio de su cerámica. *El Caribe Arqueológico* 2: 31–40.

———. 2002. *Cerámica temprana en el Centro del Oriente de Cuba.* Santo Domingo: Videograph.

Valdés, J. J. 1994. Paleogeographic Perspectives on the First Landfall of Columbus. *Southeastern Geographer* 34: 73–91.

Varela, C. 1984. *Cristóbal Colón, textos y documentos completos.* 2nd ed. Madrid.

Vega, B. 1980. *Los cacicazgos de la Hispaniola.* Santo Domingo: Ediciones Museo del Hombre Dominicano.

Veloz Maggiolo, M. 1991. *Panorama histórico del Caribe precolombino*. Santo Domingo: Edición del Banco Central de la República Dominicana.

———. 1993. *La Isla de Santo Domingo antes de Colon*. Santo Domingo: Banco Central de la República Dominicana.

———. 1997. The Daily life of the Taíno People. In *Taíno: Pre-Columbian Art and Culture from the Caribbean*, edited by F. Bercht, E. Brodsky, J. A. Farmer, and D. Taylor, 34–45. New York: Monacelli Press.

Veloz Maggiolo, M., and E. Ortega. 1996. Punta Cana y el origen de la agricultura en la isla de Santo Domingo. In *Ponencias del Primer Seminario de Arqueología del Caribe*, edited by M. Veloz Maggiolo and A. Caba Fuentes, 5–11. Altos de Chavón, Dominican Republic: Museo Arqueológico Regional.

Veloz Maggiolo, M., E. Ortega, and A. Caba Fuentes. 1981. *Los modos de vida Meillacoides y sus posibles orígenes*. Santo Domingo, Dominican Republic: Museo del Hombre Dominicano.

Veloz Maggiolo, M., E. Ortega, and F. L. Calderón. 1991. Los ocupantes tempranos de Punta Cana, República Dominicana. In *Proceedings of the 14th Congress of the International Association for Caribbean Archaeology*, edited by A. Cummins and P. King, 262–277. Barbados: Barbados Museum and Historical Society.

Vento Canosa, E., and D. González R. 1996. Paleopatología aborigen de Cuba. *El Caribe Arqueológico* 1: 31–38.

Versteeg, A. H., and K. Schinkel (eds.). 1992. *The Archaeology of St. Eustatius: The Golden Rock Site*. Publication No. 2. St. Eustatius: St. Eustatius Historical Foundation.

Versteeg, A. H., K. Schinkel, and S. M. Wilson. 1993. Large-scale Excavations versus Surveys: Examples from Nevis, St. Eustatius and St. Kitts in the Northern Caribbean. *Analecta Praehistorica Leidensia* 26: 139–161.

Walker, J. B. 1993. Stone Collars, Elbow Stones, and Three Pointers, and the Nature of Taino Ritual and Myth. Ph.D. dissertation. Washington State University, Pullman.

———. 1997. Taíno Stone Collars, Elbow Stones, and Three-Pointers. In *Taíno: Pre-Columbian Art and Culture from the Caribbean*, edited by F. Bercht, E. Brodsky, J. A. Farmer, and D. Taylor, 80–91. New York: Monacelli Press.

Watters, D. R. 1982. Relating Oceanography to Antillean Archaeology: Implications from Oceania. *Journal of New World Archaeology* 5: 3–12.

———. 1997. Maritime Trade in the Prehistoric Eastern Caribbean. In *The Indigenous People of the Caribbean*, edited by S. M. Wilson, 88–99. Gainesville: University Press of Florida.

Watters, D. R., and R. Scaglion. 1994. Beads and Pendants from Trants, Montserrat: Implications for the Prehistoric Lapidary Industry of the Caribbean. *Annals of the Carnegie Museum* 63: 215–237.

Weeks, J. M., P. J. Ferbel, and V. Ramírez Zabala. 1996. Rock Art at Corral de los Indios de Chacuey, Dominican Republic. *Latin American Indian Literatures Journal* 12: 88–97.

West, D. C., and A. Kling. 1991. *The Libro de las Profecias of Christopher Columbus*. Gainesville: University Press of Florida.

Whitehead, N. L. 1984. "Carib Cannibalism": The Historical Evidence. *Société des Américanistes* 70: 69–87.

Wild, K. 2001. Historic and Archaeological Investigations at Cinnamon Bay, St. John, U.S. Virgin Islands. In *Proceedings of the 18th International Congress for Caribbean Archaeology*, vol. 2, 304–310. St. George, Grenada: IACA.

Wilford, J. N. 1991. *The Mysterious History of Columbus*. New York: Alfred A. Knopf.

Williams, M. W. 1986. Sub-surface Patterning at Puerto Real: A 16th Century Town on Haiti's North Coast. *Journal of Field Archaeology* 13: 283–296.

Wilson, S. M. 1990. *Hispaniola: The Chiefdoms of the Caribbean in the Early Years of European Contact*. Tuscaloosa: University of Alabama Press.

Wilson, S. M., H. B. Iceland, and T. R. Hester. 1998. Preceramic Connections between Yucatan and the Caribbean. *Latin American Antiquity* 9: 342–352.

Wing, E. S. 1993. The Realm between Wild and Domesticated. In *Skeletons in Her Cupboard: Festschrift for Juliet Clutton-Brock*, edited by A. Clason, S. Payne, and H-P. Uerpmann, 243–250. Oxbow Monograph 34. Oxford: Oxbow Books.

———. 2001. Native American Use of Animals in the Caribbean. In *Biogeography of the West Indies: Patterns and Perspectives*, edited by C. A. Woods and F. E. Sergile, 481–518. Boca Raton: CRC Press.

Wing, E. S., and E. J. Reitz. 1982. Prehistoric Fishing Communities of the Caribbean. *Journal of New World Archaeology* 5: 13–32.

Wing, E. S., and S. J. Scudder. 1983. Animal Exploitation by Prehistoric People Living on a Tropical Marine Edge. In *Animals and Archaeology: 2. Shell Middens, Fishes and Birds*, edited by C. Grigson and J. Clutton-Brock, 197–210. BAR International Series No. 183. Oxford: BAR.

Winter, J. 1991. A Multiple Lucayan Burial from New Providence, Bahamas. In *Proceedings of the 12th Congress of the International Association for Caribbean Archaeology*, edited by L. S. Robinson, 153–162. Martinique: IACA.

Winter, J., and M. Gilstrap. 1991. Preliminary Results of Ceramic Analysis and the Movements of Populations into the Bahamas. In *Proceedings of the 12th Congress of the International Association for Caribbean Archaeology*, edited by L. S. Robinson, 371–386. Martinique: IACA.

Wittfogel, K. A. 1957. *Oriental Despotism*. New Haven: Yale University Press.

Zohar, I., T. Dayan, E. Galil, and E. Spanier. 2001. Fish Processing during the Early Holocene: A Taphonomic Case Study from Coastal Israel. *Journal of Archaeological Science* 28: 1041–1053.

Index

William F. Keegan is curator of Caribbean Archaeology at the Florida Museum of Natural History and professor of anthropology and Latin American studies at the University of Florida. He is the author or editor of four books, including *The People Who Discovered Columbus: The Prehistory of the Bahamas* (UPF, 1992).

Ripley P. Bullen Series
Florida Museum of Natural History
Edited by Jerald T. Milanich

Tacachale: Essays on the Indians of Florida and Southeastern Georgia during the Historic Period, edited by Jerald T. Milanich and Samuel Proctor (1978); first paperback edition, 1994

Aboriginal Subsistence Technology on the Southeastern Coastal Plain during the Late Prehistoric Period, by Lewis H. Larson (1980)

Cemochechobee: Archaeology of a Mississippian Ceremonial Center on the Chattahoochee River, by Frank T. Schnell, Vernon J. Knight Jr., and Gail S. Schnell (1981)

Fort Center: An Archaeological Site in the Lake Okeechobee Basin, by William H. Sears, with contributions by Elsie O'R. Sears and Karl T. Steinen (1982); first paperback edition, 1994

Perspectives on Gulf Coast Prehistory, edited by Dave D. Davis (1984)

Archaeology of Aboriginal Culture Change in the Interior Southeast: Depopulation during the Early Historic Period, by Marvin T. Smith (1987); first paperback edition, 1992

Apalachee: The Land between the Rivers, by John H. Hann (1988)

Key Marco's Buried Treasure: Archaeology and Adventure in the Nineteenth Century, by Marion Spjut Gilliland (1989)

First Encounters: Spanish Explorations in the Caribbean and the United States, 1492–1570, edited by Jerald T. Milanich and Susan Milbrath (1989)

Missions to the Calusa, edited and translated by John H. Hann, with an introduction by William H. Marquardt (1991)

Excavations on the Franciscan Frontier: Archaeology at the Fig Springs Mission, by Brent Richards Weisman (1992)

The People Who Discovered Columbus: The Prehistory of the Bahamas, by William F. Keegan (1992)

Hernando de Soto and the Indians of Florida, by Jerald T. Milanich and Charles Hudson (1993)

Foraging and Farming in the Eastern Woodlands, edited by C. Margaret Scarry (1993)

Puerto Real: The Archaeology of a Sixteenth-Century Spanish Town in Hispaniola, edited by Kathleen Deagan (1995)

Political Structure and Change in the Prehistoric Southeastern United States, edited by John F. Scarry (1996)

Bioarchaeology of Native American Adaptation in the Spanish Borderlands, edited by Brenda J. Baker and Lisa Kealhofer (1996)

A History of the Timucua Indians and Missions, by John H. Hann (1996)

Archaeology of the Mid-Holocene Southeast, edited by Kenneth E. Sassaman and David G. Anderson (1996)

The Indigenous People of the Caribbean, edited by Samuel M. Wilson (1997); first paperback edition, 1999

Hernando de Soto among the Apalachee: The Archaeology of the First Winter Encampment, by Charles R. Ewen and John H. Hann (1998)

The Timucuan Chiefdoms of Spanish Florida, by John E. Worth: vol. 1, *Assimilation;* vol. 2, *Resistance and Destruction* (1998)

Ancient Earthen Enclosures of the Eastern Woodlands, edited by Robert C. Mainfort Jr., and Lynne P. Sullivan (1998)

An Environmental History of Northeast Florida, by James J. Miller (1998)

Precolumbian Architecture in Eastern North America, by William N. Morgan (1999)